A Jesuit Garden in Beijing and Early Modern Chinese Culture

Comparative Cultural Studies
Steven Tötösy de Zepetnek, Series Editor

The Purdue University Press monograph series of Books in Comparative Cultural Studies publishes single-authored and thematic collected volumes of new scholarship. Manuscripts are invited for publication in the series in fields of the study of culture, literature, the arts, media studies, communication studies, the history of ideas, etc., and related disciplines of the humanities and social sciences to the series editor via email at <clcweb@purdue.edu>. Comparative cultural studies is a contextual approach in the study of culture in a global and intercultural context and work with a plurality of methods and approaches; the theoretical and methodological framework of comparative cultural studies is built on tenets borrowed from the disciplines of cultural studies and comparative literature and from a range of thought including literary and culture theory, (radical) constructivism, communication theories, and systems theories; in comparative cultural studies focus is on theory and method as well as application. For a detailed description of the aims and scope of the series including the style guide of the series link to <http://docs.lib.purdue.edu/clcweblibrary/seriespurdueccs>. Manuscripts submitted to the series are peer reviewed followed by the usual standards of editing, copy editing, marketing, and distribution. The series is affiliated with *CLCWeb: Comparative Literature and Culture* (ISSN 1481-4374), the peer-reviewed, full-text, and open-access quarterly published by Purdue University Press at <http://docs.lib.purdue.edu/clcweb>.

Volumes in the Purdue series of Books in Comparative Cultural Studies <http://www.thepress.purdue.edu/comparativeculturalstudies.html>

Hui Zou, *A Jesuit Garden in Beijing and Early Modern Chinese Culture*
Yi Zheng, *From Burke and Wordsworth to the Modern Sublime in Chinese Literature*
Agata Anna Lisiak, *Urban Cultures in (Post)Colonial Central Europe*
Representing Humanity in an Age of Terror, Ed. Sophia A. McClennen and Henry James Morello
Michael Goddard, *Gombrowicz, Polish Modernism, and the Subversion of Form*
Shakespeare in Hollywood, Asia, and Cyberspace, Ed. Alexander C.Y. Huang and Charles S. Ross
Gustav Shpet's Contribution to Philosophy and Cultural Theory, Ed. Galin Tihanov
Comparative Central European Holocaust Studies, Ed. Louise O. Vasvári and Steven Tötösy de Zepetnek
Marko Juvan, *History and Poetics of Intertextuality*
Thomas O. Beebee, *Nation and Region in Modern American and European Fiction*
Paolo Bartoloni, *On the Cultures of Exile, Translation, and Writing*
Justyna Sempruch, *Fantasies of Gender and the Witch in Feminist Theory and Literature*
Kimberly Chabot Davis, *Postmodern Texts and Emotional Audiences*
Philippe Codde, *The Jewish American Novel*
Deborah Streifford Reisinger, *Crime and Media in Contemporary France*
Imre Kertész and Holocaust Literature, Ed. Louise O. Vasvári and Steven Tötösy de Zepetnek
Camilla Fojas, *Cosmopolitanism in the Americas*
Comparative Cultural Studies and Michael Ondaatje's Writing, Ed. Steven Tötösy de Zepetnek
Jin Feng, *The New Woman in Early Twentieth-Century Chinese Fiction*
Comparative Cultural Studies and Latin America, Ed. Sophia A. McClennen and Earl E. Fitz
Sophia A. McClennen, *The Dialectics of Exile*
Comparative Literature and Comparative Cultural Studies, Ed. Steven Tötösy de Zepetnek
Comparative Central European Culture, Ed. Steven Tötösy de Zepetnek

Hui Zou

A Jesuit Garden in Beijing and Early Modern Chinese Culture

Purdue University Press
West Lafayette, Indiana

Copyright 2011 by Purdue University. All rights reserved.

Printed in the United States of America.

Library of Congress Cataloging-in-Publication Data
Zou, Hui, 1967-
  A Jesuit Garden in Beijing and Early Modern Chinese Culture / Hui Zou.
    p. cm. -- (Comparative cultural studies)
  Includes bibliographical references and index.
  ISBN 978-1-55753-583-2
  1. Yuan Ming Yuan (Beijing, China)--History. 2. Historic gardens--China--Beijing. 3. Gardens, European--China--Beijing--History--18th century. 4. Jesuits--China--Beijing--History--18th century. 5. Kangxi, Emperor of China, 1654-1722. 6. Qianlong, Emperor of China, 1711-1799. 7. Gardens--China--Beijing--Design--History--18th century. 8. Gardens--Social aspects--China--Beijing--History--18th century. 9. Landscape gardening--China--Beijing--History--18th century. 10. China--Civilization--1644-1912. I. Title.
  SB466.C53Y838 2011
  712'.60951156--dc22
                              2010044565

Cover image: Detail, copperplate of the Hill of Line Method, drawn by Lantai Yi, 1786. Yuan Ming Yuan, 1783-1786. Research Library, The Getty Research Institute, Los Angeles, California.

Contents

Acknowledgments	1
Chapter One A Theoretical and Historical Introduction to the Chinese Garden	2
Chapter Two The Chinese Garden and the Concept of the Virtue of Round Brightness	20
Chapter Three The Chinese Garden and the Concept of the Vision of *Jing*	51
Chapter Four The Chinese Garden and Western Linear Perspective	76
Chapter Five The Chinese Garden and the Concept of the Line Method	103
Conclusion	139
Works Cited	145
Appendix	168

1. Kangxi's Record of the Garden of Uninhibited Spring
2. Kangxi's Record of the Mountain Hamlet for Summer Coolness
3. Qianlong's Later Record of the Mountain Hamlet for Summer Coolness
4. Qianlong's Record of the Village of Ten Thousand Springs
5. Qianlong's Record of Kunming Lake by Longevity Hill
6. Qianlong's Record of the Garden of Clear Ripples on Longevity Hill
7. Qianlong's Record of the Best Spring of China on Jade-Spring Hill
8. Qianlong's Record of the Garden of Tranquil Pleasure

Index	185

Acknowledgments

This book is a result of my journey of research over the past ten years. I am indebted to Alberto Pérez-Gómez in architectural history, Michel Conan in garden history, and James Bradford in philosophy, who all influenced my understanding of the built environment through an interdisciplinary perpsective. I also received valuable comments from David Leatherbarrow, Marco Frascari, Louise Pelletier, Gregory Caicco, George Hersey, Stanislaus Fung, Martin Bressani, John Dixon Hunt, Peter Jacobs, Joachim Wolschke-Bulmahn, Steven West, Richard Strassberg, Martin J. Powers, Giorgio Galletti, Xin Wu, Aicha Malek, Jonathan Chaves, Lara Ingeman, John Witek, Duncan Campbell, and John Finlay. This diverse group of scholars came from the various disciplines of architectural history, garden history, and Sinology. During my field and archival research in China, I exchanged views with a number of architecture and garden historians including Xiaowei Luo, Weiquan Zhou, Zhaofen Zeng, Hongxun Yang, and Enyin Zhang, to whom I pay my high respect in the Confucian sense. I am grateful to Barbara R. Martin for reading my manuscript with such patience. My gratitude also goes to John E. Hancock, Jean-Paul Boudier, Wenhong Zhu, and Fangji Wang for their support and friendship. For the research and writing of the book I benefited from assistance from the following libraries and I am grateful for the help I received: McGill University, the Canadian Centre for Architecture, Dumbarton Oaks Researach Library and Collection, Library of Congress, Georgetown University, the Chinese painting collections of Freer Gallery, University of Florida, National Library of China, and The First Historical Archive of China. My translations of the Qing emperors' garden records presented in the appendices were supported by a fellowship of garden history at Dumbarton Oaks of Harvard University in 2001-2002. My research and writing has been wholeheartedly supported by my family and I dedicate this book to them. I thank the editor of the Purdue University Press monograph series of Books in Comparative Cultural Studies, Steven Tötösy de Zepetnek, for his interest in and support of my work. Last but not least, I thank the anonymous reviewers of the book for their valuable comments and the staff of the Purdue University Press for their professional assistance.

Chapter One

A Theoretical and Historical Introduction to the Chinese Garden

In modern-day China, when people hear the term *yuanming* (literally, round brightness), they probably think of two wonders: one is the bright full moon appearing at the middle of each month; another is the Yuanming Yuan, literally, Garden of Round Brightness, which exists only in their minds. On the night of the eighth full moon, when the moonlight is the brightest of the year, each Chinese family celebrates the traditional Mid-Autumn Festival by remembering its family members who live a great distance away. The memory of the dearest under the round brightness somehow echoes the nostalgia for the lost Yuanming Yuan. As an imperial garden of the Qing dynasty, the Yuanming Yuan is unique in the history of gardens because of its grandness as well as its enclosed, small Western garden. For many Chinese, the memory of this lost garden is typically composed of two mental images: the first of a huge fire burning down the garden and the second of white marble stones of Western buildings scattered along the grass. Regarding the name of the garden, Yuanming, there is not a clear and unified understanding of its meaning in scholarship or by the public. What causes confusion is the question of how a poetical Chinese name, which recalls the full moon, can be connected with the exotic images of Western buildings.

The Yuanming Yuan was built by Emperor Yongzheng and named by his father, Emperor Kangxi, in 1709. In his record of the garden, Yongzheng states that he tried to research ancient books for the moral meaning of Yuanming and seek the spring terrace and the happy kingdom for his people (Yongzheng, "Shizong"). He expresses his desires through two historical allusions. The first is the "spring terrace," which, indicating a beautiful touring place, is quoted from the Daoist sage Laozi (Fu and Lu 27); the second is "happy kingdom," which, indicating a fish pool, is quoted from another Daoist sage Zhuangzi (F. Wang 148). Both sages lived during the Warring States period, some two thousand years before Yongzheng's time. He utilized these two historical allusions to express his ideal of a model nation and identified it with his garden residence. Emperor Qianlong, Yongzheng's fourth son, reiterated the same historical allusions in his records and went on to say that an emperor must have his own place for roaming in order to appreciate expansive landscapes. When he made this statement, he had in mind all the imperial gardens throughout history. Such a diachronically comparative perspective was further demonstrated when he stated that the Yuanming Yuan accumulated the blessings of the land and heaven and offered a touring place that nothing could surpass ("Yuanmingyuan"). These two garden records demonstrate a strong historical dimension in interpreting the meanings of the garden. By referring to how other emperors functioned in their gardens throughout history, the Qing emperors tried to build their own meaning for the garden. The historical dimension in their interpretations helped them define the historical horizon, the historicity, for their roaming in the garden. Following the emperors' interpretative approach, I pinpoint here some key aspects of Chinese imperial gardens that helped define the historicity of the Yuanming Yuan.

The terrace in Laozi's spring terrace, as a type of garden building, can be traced back to the earliest imperial gardens in the Western Zhou dynasty, where a square terrace was used for looking into the distance and observing the sky and celestial divinities. A well-known example is King Wen's sacred terrace. According to the *Shijing (Book of Odes)*, King Wen planned the sacred terrace by himself. He was in the sacred enclosure where female deer with colored fur and birds with pure white feathers lived. He walked near the sacred pool where water was full and fish were jumping (S. Li 503). Citing the same story, the Confucian saint Mengzi (Mencious) emphasized the ethical importance of King Wen and his people working together to build the sacred garden they enjoyed together (H. Liu 158). Yongzheng's allusions to the spring terrace and happy kingdom hinted at the ethical importance of King Wen's terrace, that is, his own time in the Yuanming Yuan was spent longing for the happiness of all the people. In the postscript for the emperors' garden records of the Yuanming Yuan, the court editors and annotators alluded specifically to King Wen's terrace and pool as well as to the "happiness" and "brightness" which he received in his garden (E). Yongzheng identified his life in the garden with his moral administration of the nation.

Embodying the belief of a happy kingdom, an imperial garden needed to be large enough for the emperor to roam and appreciate expansive landscapes. During the spring and autumn, the imperial garden Zhanghua Terrace of Chu Kingdom made use of the natural lakes, called Water of Cloudy Dreams, to procure an expansive view. As recorded by the Han scholar Xiangru Sima in his rhapsody, the Cloudy Dreams had nine hundred miles on each side, and there were mountains in it (X. Sima, "Zixu" 49-50). Such an expansive view was characteristic of imperial gardens but impossible in small literati gardens. To understand the close view in a contemporaneous literati garden, we can refer to the romantic poems of Chu Kingdom, such as "Goddess of the Xiang River" by Yuan Qu and "Summon the Soul" by his student Yu Song. The latter poem describes how he leaned on the balustrade to look down on a winding pool (282). Both poems tell of the building of a beautiful place in the water for the arrival of an immortal being. Continuing the tradition of the massive size of imperial gardens, the expansive landscapes in the Yuanming Yuan were unique in that they were entirely man-made, unlike other imperial gardens where the landscapes were primarily natural. The huge scale of such an artificially made imperial garden was unprecedented. The Shanglin Park of the first Chinese emperor Shi Huangdi of Qin was located between the Wei River and Zhongnan Mountain. The garden was expansive, but its largest part was its natural landscapes. The emperor depended upon double-floor passageways to pass through the wilderness in order to move from one palace to another. The covered passageways, according to the history book *Shiji* (*Records of the Grand Historian*), were intended to hide his movement from the public so that he could "act mysteriously to avoid devils and meanwhile embrace virtuous individuals" and his spirit would "remain a secret and panacea would be obtained" (Q. Sima 38).

As stated in the emperors' records, the Yuanming Yuan symbolized the happy kingdom of the whole nation. Such a symbolic relationship between a garden and the world at large can be traced back to the pattern—one pool and three island hills (*yichi sanshan*)—in imperial gardens, which first appeared in the Orchid Pool, east of Shi Huangdi's Xianyang Palace. The pattern symbolized the legendary three islands in the East Sea to which the emperor sent Daoists repeatedly for panaceas. According to the *Shiji*, each previous king was unwilling to give up the fantasy of the three islands. The symbolic relationship between the huge body of water in a garden and the sea was further developed in the imperial Shanglin Park of the West Han dynasty where the huge lake, Kunming, was symbolically taken as a sea for exercising the emperor Wudi of Han's naval fleet. The symbolic relationship between the water in the garden and the sea continued into the Qing imperial gardens, where an expansive lake was typically called a sea. Although the lake symbolized the sea, for the most part Shanglin Park remained as wilderness without symbolization. Xiangru Sima exclaimed in his "Rhapsody of Shanglin" that when one looked at Shanglin Park, it appeared that there was no beginning and no end. In the park, retreat palaces and remote lodges were scattered among the mountains and straddled the valleys. Tall, covered passageways poured out in four directions (X. Sima, "Shanglin" 52-53). Sima, in his descriptions of landscapes, was in awe of mystical nature. Buildings in the enormous park were diminished by the grandness of the landscapes and appeared dwarfed by their surroundings.

Besides the expansive Shanglin Park, Wudi had smaller gardens at his palaces near the capital of Chang'an. In the northwestern corner of the Jianzhang Palace was the Lake of Primary Liquid, where three islands were set up to symbolize the three fairylands: Penglai, Fangzhang, and Yingzhou in the East Sea. According to the *Shiji*, the same names of these three fairylands were given to the three hills in the garden. By giving them the same names, the emperor reinforced the symbolic relationship between his garden and the fairylands. Wudi even built watchtowers on the shore of the East Sea to wait for the arrival of immortal beings, because "immortal beings always prefer a multistoried residence" (Q. Sima 84-85).

Expansive lakes began to formally be called seas in the imperial gardens during the period of the Southern and Northern Dynasties. There was a sea named Pool of Heavenly Deep Water in the imperial Hualin Garden in the capital of Luoyang in Northern Wei. According to the *Luoyang qielan ji* (*Records of the Monasteries in Luoyang*), in the pool there was an island named Penglai on which there was a Celestial Lodge and Fishing Terrace, both of which were connected by a rainbow skywalk, where walking was like flying (X. Yang 57). The *Shuijing zhu* (*Commentaries on the Waterways Classic*) recorded that visitors moved about in this garden like celestial birds, up and down in "a divine residence" (Daoyuan Li 246). Both records create an impression that the imperial Hualin Garden was designed intentionally to imitate a fairyland. The capital of the Southern Dynasties was Jiankang, where there was another imperial Hualin Garden, with the same name as that of Northern Wei. When Emperor Jianwen of Eastern Jin entered this garden, he announced: "To meet my heart, I do not need to go far. The shady woods and cool water have made me feel like being between the Hao and Pu Rivers; birds, beasts, poultry and fish all come to be intimate with me" (Yiqing Liu 31). The Hao and Pu Rivers alluded to the story that the Daoist sage, Zhuangzi, fished by the Pu River and roamed on a bridge of the Hao River. This classic historical tale signified delight in nature (Fu and Lu 272-73). Jianwen's expression was significant in that it demonstrated his longing for remoteness in the garden, which was typical in literati gardens but rare in imperial gardens. It shows that imperial gardens in the Southern Dynasties had been influenced by private gardens.

In later dynasties, such as the Sui and Tang, the capital, Chang'an, was located southeast of the Chang'an of the Han dynasty. Between the Wei River and the capital was an expansive area known as the Forbidden Park. In addition to providing entertainment and hunting for the emperor, the park acted as a buffer zone between the river to the north and the capital to the south. Strategically important for the defense of the capital, the park was also where the imperial troops were based. In consideration of provisions, the Sui and Tang dynasties adopted a two-capital system, with a western capital, Chang'an and an eastern capital, Luoyang. West of Luoyang was another Forbidden Park, which was planned around an artificial lake, called Northern Sea, in which three sacred hills named Penglai, Fangzhang, and Yingzhou were built. In addition, five lakes were created to symbolize, for the first time in history, the geographical feature of China—five lakes and four seas (*wuhu sihai*). Groups of buildings were scattered about on the northern side of the Northern Sea. These building groups were in fact gardens within a garden. The strategic importance for defense and the pattern of gardens within a garden had significant influences upon later imperial gardens. Further, the influence of *fengshui*, the ancient environmental philosophy connected with cosmology, was manifested by the imperial garden, Genyue, of the Northern Song dynasty. The name Genyue means Gen Mount. Owing to the Daoist cosmological graph of eight trigrams, the northeast was called *gen*, signifying mountain, and thus the garden's name. A Daoist *fengshui* master told the emperor Huizong (Ji Zhao) that the northeastern corner of the inner city of the capital was too low and needed to be raised for the prosperity of the imperial family. Huizong was convinced, and took part in the design of a hilly garden in that part of the city. The whole garden was composed of artificial landscapes that included hills, lakes, and some gorges connecting the lakes. No imperial garden throughout history had been constructed with artificial landscapes on such a huge scale. There were over one hundred recorded discrete scenes, most of which were named in two or three Chinese characters in accordance with the views. Huizong's garden record notes that Genyue was to contain all the beauties of the different landscapes in the country (65). The idea that the emperor's garden should be an epitome of the beauties of all other gardens in the country was expressed strongly, and this idea was adopted in creating the Yuanming Yuan.

Following the Song dynasty, the Yuan and Ming imperial gardens continued the pattern of one pool and three island hills. It was during the Yuan dynasty that the capital of China moved to Beijing, and both the Yuan and Ming imperial gardens were located within the city. The gardens were arranged around the Lake of Primary Liquid where water originated from a spring on Jade Spring Hill located in the northwestern suburb of the city. A parallel water source in the same suburb, the Lake of Urn Hill, led into the Lake of Collected Water within the city, just north of the imperial gardens. During the Yuan dynasty, these two watercourses paralleled each other from the northwestern suburb to the west of the inner city, yet they were strictly separated. The water from Jade Spring Hill was used to provide irrigation for the imperial gardens, while the water from the Lake of Urn Hill was used as a method for food transportation. The separation of watercourses showed the importance of water quality in the imperial gardens and it was during the Ming dynasty that these two watercourses were merged. The Lake of Collected Water, initially used for food transportation, was now connected to the Northern Sea, which was part of previous Lake of Primary Liquid, for the purpose of irrigating the imperial gardens. Thus, the water of the imperial gardens now came from both Jade Spring Hill and the West Lake, which was formerly the Lake of Urn Hill. The imperial gardens in both the Yuan and Ming dynasties showed the importance of the water sources in the northwestern suburb. Later, during the Qing dynasty, emperor Kangxi began to perform administrative duties in his residence garden. Owing to the serene environment of the Southern Sea, which was part of the Ming imperial gardens within the city, Kangxi engaged in numerous activities within this portion of the garden, including processing national affairs, receiving officials, and performing agricultural activities. At the midpoint of his reign, following the suppression of internal riots and the stabilization of the country, Kangxi began to shift his attention to the northwestern suburb to make new gardens. The site was selected for a number of reasons, including weather conditions and its proximity to both the beautiful landscape of West Mountain and the wilderness. The Qing emperors' ancestors, the Manchu people, originated from northeast China and were not accustomed to the hot summers in Beijing and thus sought places that provided coolness. The first Qing emperor, Shunzhi, once complained that the environment of Beijing was not clean and its water was salty and that the summer heat of Beijing was unbearable (W. Zhou, "Yuanmingyuan" 149).

The dominant landscape in the northwestern suburb of Beijing is West Mountain, described as the "right arm of the divine capital" (Y. Jiang 52). The mountain range extended from south to north and it had an eastward spur at Fragrant Hill, which surrounded a plain to the south and east where most of Qing imperial gardens were located. Traditionally, the capital of China was located in the north, to look upon the land towards the south; therefore, the imperial throne always faced to the south. Since West Mountain was west of the capital, it looked like the "right arm" of the imperial throne. West Mountain served as a buffer zone between the capital and the northern frontier and thus the northwestern suburb held strategic importance to the city of Beijing. The first imperial garden within the northwestern suburb, known as the Garden of Uninhibited Spring (Changchun Yuan), was built by Kangxi in 1687. In 1684, Kangxi visited the Jiangnan region for the first time and was impressed by its beautiful landscapes and private gardens. Upon his return to Beijing, he built the Garden of Uninhibited Spring on the ruined garden site of a Ming imperial family member. The water source for the garden was spring water from the Village of Ten Thousand Springs (Wanquan Zhuang). At that time, the western water sources from the West Lake and Jade Spring Hill were not yet used for the imperial gardens in this area. Kangxi spent much time in the garden, where he occasionally held audience and performed administrative duties.

In 1703, Kangxi began to build a retreat garden, Mountain Hamlet for Summer Coolness (Bishu Shanzhuang), which was located in Chengde, north of the capital. The location of the garden was related to the emperor's northern patrol where he received Mongolian aristocrats in order to establish a stable state of affairs in the northern territory. Within the garden, he named thirty-six scenes, each with a title of four Chinese characters. Each scene indicated a specific garden view. After naming the thirty-six scenes, Kangxi ordered a court painter to create a painting of each scene, for which he wrote an accompanying poem. The pairing of painting and poetry for the representation of garden scenes was continued by later Qing emperors. In 1709, one year after the Mountain Hamlet for Summer Coolness was built, Kangxi turned his attention to the northwestern suburb of the capital. He granted a piece of land north of his Garden of Uninhibited Spring to his fourth son, Prince Yinzhen. On this site, Yinzhen built the Yuanming Yuan. After Yinzhen took the throne and became emperor Yongzheng, he expanded the garden and used it as his permanent residence and a place for holding audience. This garden served as the permanent residence for five Qing emperors, Yongzheng, Qianlong, Jiaqing, Daoguang, and Xianfeng, before being destroyed by fire in 1860 by the French and British armies.

During the Qianlong reign, the Yuanming Yuan consisted of four gardens: three Chinese—the original Yuanming Yuan, Garden of Eternal Spring (Changchun Yuan), and Garden of Gorgeous Spring (Qichun Yuan) which was later called Garden of Ten Thousand Springs (Wanchun Yuan)—and a small Western garden called Western Multistoried Buildings (Xiyang Lou), which was designed and cobuilt by the European Jesuits, who served as painters and clockmakers in the imperial court. Although the name of Yuanming was originally given to the first garden in this complex, it later was used by the public to signify the whole complex; thus, all four gardens combined came to be known as the Yuanming Yuan (figure 1).

Garden A. Yuanming Yuan
   1. Uprightness and Brightness (Zhengda Guangming)
   2. Diligent Administration and Affection to Virtuous Men (Qinzheng Qinxian)
   3. Peace for All China (Jiuzhou Qingyan)
   4. Carving the Moon and Opening Clouds (Louyue Kaiyun)
   5. Natural Scenery (Tianran Tuhua)
   6. Study Room under Green Phoenix Trees (Bitong Shuyuan)
   7. Mercy Clouds Protecting All (Ciyun Puhu)
   8. Oneness of Sky and Water (Shangxia Tianguang).
   9. Wine Shop in an Apricot Flower Village (Xinghua Cunguan)
   10. Magnanimous and Big Hearted (Tantan Dangdang)
   11. Integrating the Past and the Present (Rugu Hanjin)
   12. Fairy Lodge in Eternal Spring (Changchun Xianguan)
   13. Universal Peace (Wanfang Anhe)
   14. Spring Beauty at Wuling (Wuling Chunse)
   15. High Mountain and Long River (Shangao Shuichang)
   16. Living in Clouds under the Moon (Yuedi Yunju)
   17. Great Kindness and Eternal Blessing (Hongci Yonghu)
   18. An Academy for Great Talents (Huifang Shuyuan)
   19. Jade Temples under Bright Sky (Ritian Linyu)
   20. Simple Life in Peaceful Surroundings (Danbo Ningjing)
   21. Orchid Fragrance over the Water (Yingshui Lanxiang)
   22. Clear Water and Rustling Tress (Shuimu Mingse)
   23. Xi Lian's Wonderful Place for Study (Lianxi Lechu)
   24. Bountiful Crops like Coming Clouds (Duojia Ruyun)
   25. Fish Leaping and Bird Flying (Yuyue Yuanfei)
   26. Far Northern Mountain Village (Beiyuan Shancun)
   27. Elegant View of the Western Peaks (Xifeng Xiuse)
   28. Study Room for Four Seasons (Siyi Shuwu)
   29. Wonderland in a Square Pot (Fanghu Shengjing)
   30. Open Minded and Enlightened (Hanxu Langjian)
   31. Calm Lake under Autumn Moon (Pinghu Qiuyue).
   32. Immortal Abode on a Fairy Island (Pengdao Yaotai)
   33. Cottage with a View of Pretty Mountains (Jiexiu Shanfang)
   34. Another Paradise (Bieyou Dongtian)
   35. Reflection of Two Waters on a Bridge and the Roaring of Waterfall (Jiajing Mingqin)
   36. Bathing Body and Enhancing Virtue (Zaoshen Yude)

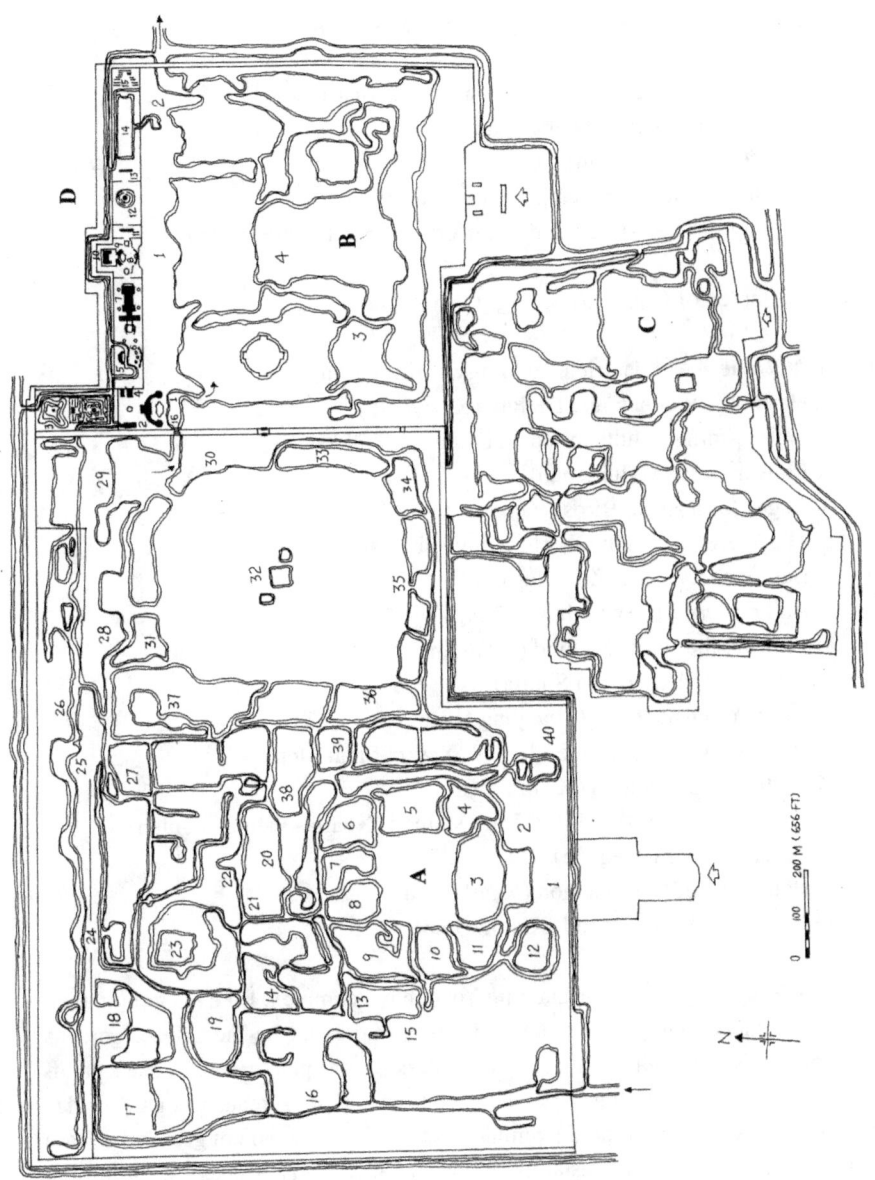

Figure 1. The Yuanming Yuan complex (drawn by Hui Zou)

37. Boundless Openness (Kuoran Dagong)
38. Sitting on a Rock and Taking a Wine Cup from a Winding Stream (Zuoshi Linliu)
39. Waving Lotus in a Winery Court (Quyuan Fenghe)
40. Deep and Remote Dwelling (Dongtian Shenchu)

Garden B. Garden of Eternal Spring (Changchun Yuan):
    1. Hall of Wet Orchids (Zelan Tang)
    2. Lion Grove (Shizi Lin)
    3. Garden of Little Heaven (Xiaoyoutian Yuan)
    4. Gallery of Unsophisticated Transformation (Chunhua Xuan)

Garden C. Garden of Gorgeous Spring (Qichun Yuan)

Garden D. Western Multistoried Buildings (Xiyang Lou):
    1. Harmony, Wonder, and Delight (Xie Qi Qu)
    2. Water Storage Multistoried Building (Xushui Lou)
    3. Flower Garden (Hua Yuan)
    4. Cages for Raising Birds (Yangque Long)
    5. The View beyond the World (Fangwai Guan)
    6. Bamboo Pavilions (Zhu Ting)
    7. Hall of Peaceful Sea (Haiyan Tang)
    8. Viewing the Water Method (Guan Shuifa)
    9. Big Water Method (Da Shuifa)
    10. View of Distant Sea (Yuanying Guan)
    11. Gate of the Hill of Line Method (Xianfa-Shan Men)
    12. Hill of Line Method (Xianfa Shan)
    13. Eastern Gate of the Hill of Line Method (Xianfa-Shan Dongmen)
    14. Square River (Fang He)
    15. Paintings of Line Method (Xianfa Hua)
    16. Bridge of Line Method (Xianfa Qiao)

Qianlong expanded the Yuanming Yuan into a complex. Like his grandfather, Kangxi, he visited Jiangnan six times and was impressed by the private gardens there. For each garden that he liked, he would ask a court painter to produce a painting and bring it back to Beijing for a reference from which to create new gardens. He made his first expansion of the Yuanming Yuan by 1744. He did not greatly increase the land size, but he formally established the so-called Forty Scenes (Sishi jing), at least twenty-eight of which were built by Yongzheng. In 1751, Qianlong built the Garden of Eternal Spring, which was located east of the Yuanming Yuan. Meanwhile, he was building the Western Multistoried Buildings garden on the northern edge of the Garden of Eternal Spring. In 1772, the Garden of Gorgeous Spring was built south of the Garden of Eternal Spring. While expanding the Yuanming Yuan,

Qianlong's garden construction spread westward. He expanded the camping-palace garden on Fragrant Hill, which was founded by Kangxi, and renamed it Garden of Tranquil Pleasure (Jingyi Yuan) in 1747. In 1750, he expanded the Garden of Tranquil Brightness (Jingming Yuan) on Jade Spring Hill. In the same year, he began to build the Garden of Clear Ripples (Qingyi Yuan) based on the newly created landscapes of Kunming Lake and Longevity Hill.

During the Yongzheng reign, the water from the Jade Spring Hill was utilized as a secondary water source because the original water source of the Village of Ten Thousand Springs was no longer sufficient for the needs of the Yuanming Yuan. The combined water sources entered the garden at its southwestern corner, flowed north to the northwestern corner, and from there diffused through the whole garden. The need for water increased as many more gardens were built, necessitating Qianlong to make a thorough reconstruction of the water system in the northwestern suburb. When the spring water from the Village of Ten Thousand Springs no longer sufficiently supplied the gardens, most of the water had to come from the Kunming Lake. Kunming Lake collected water from Jade Spring Hill, but the Jade Spring was the original water source for the river that was used for transporting food to the capital. This created a problem because as water was diverted and used for the gardens, the ferrying of food would be influenced. To solve the problem, Qianlong used Kunming Lake as a reservoir, which collected water from Jade Spring Hill, West Mountain, and Fragrant Hill, which served the needs of the gardens while also providing water for ferrying food.

During the Qianlong reign, the five gardens in the northwestern suburb were Yuanming Yuan, the Garden of Uninhibited Spring, the Garden of Tranquil Pleasure (on Fragrant Hill), the Garden of Tranquil Brightness (on Jade Spring Hill), and the Garden of Clear Ripples (on Longevity Hill). They were usually described as Three Hills and Five Gardens (Sanshan Wuyuan) (W. Zhou, *Yuanlin shi* 338; Hou 120; X. Zhao 110; C. Zhang 52). Because of their bond with West Mountain and their affinity with natural landscapes, these five gardens are categorized by modern scholars as landscape gardens, distinguished from palace gardens and urban gardens, and they are praised as the highest achievement of Qing imperial garden design (W. Zhou *Yuanlin shi* 338; C. Chen, *Zhongguo* 202). There are continuing debates among Chinese scholars on exactly what the title Three Hills and Five Gardens signified during the Qing dynasty. One explanation is that the three hills were, from west to east, Fragrant Hill, Jade Spring Hill, and Longevity Hill, while the five gardens were, from west to east, the Garden of Tranquil Pleasure, the Garden of Tranquil Brightness, the Garden of Clear Ripples, the Garden of Uninhibited Spring, and the Yuanming Yuan (W. Zhou, *Yuanlin shi* 338; X. Zhao 187-89; Beijing difangzhi 15; Ma 87). Because the Garden of Tranquil Pleasure was located on Fragrant Hill, the Garden of Tranquil Brightness on Hill of Jade Spring, and the Garden of Clear Ripples on Longevity Hill, there is a certain overlapping in terms of sites in this explanation, which has created debate. Some scholars have attempted to prove that the five gardens were in fact those of the Yuanming Yuan complex during its most prosperous time (E. Zhang

"Sanshan" 84, "Zaixi" 89; X. Zhao 187). Indeed, the coexistence of the five gardens in the Yuanming Yuan complex lasted only a short period. Moreover, this second explanation excludes the Garden of Uninhibited Spring, the first Qing imperial garden in the northwestern suburb. In my view, the first account sounds more convincing and its seeming redundancy can be understood as an emphasis on the compelling images of the three hills, which were related intrinsically to the five gardens. The debate itself demonstrates that there has been, and continues to be, a historical and physical context important for understanding the history of the Yuanming Yuan.

It was a national loss when the Yuanming Yuan complex was destroyed by fire in 1860. It is said that the year before the arson, the god of the garden visited the emperor in a dream and asked for a leave (Bo 76). There is a pervasive melancholy regarding the ruins that recalls the perfect brightness that the garden once enclosed. Thousands of people have visited the site, attempting to retrieve the lost garden in their minds. A moving prose work of 1991 recalls the unrecoverable scenes: "In front of the ruins, I can only gaze distractedly. Wind whistles in tears in the nearby groves. A voice of 'remain, remain . . .' echoes over the ruins. In the twilight, the white marbles tend to talk to me. Do they want to tell how they experienced the huge fire and how time was measured? . . . Wind, waving over the ruins, is calling" (P. Zong 306-09). With the ambiguity of a garden existing only in the mind, the identity of the Yuanming Yuan keeps splitting apart. Its split identity originates from the fact that both the garden complex and the original garden were called Yuanming. The garden's split identity was exacerbated because the garden was not pure Chinese, but also partly Western, and thus the fire exposed the tension between the Chinese and Western portions. Before the fire, the Western section was hidden within the Chinese garden. After the fire, the Chinese portions were burnt to cinders, while the ruins of the Western portion remained. Currently, the ruins of the Western multistoried buildings are well known and identified as the Yuanming Yuan. Since the garden was an imperial residence, common Chinese people had no chance to view it, but the Jesuits, working as clockmakers, painters, and garden designers for the emperor, had unparalleled and repeated opportunities to see the entire garden (Attiret, "Letter" 47-48). Between the two groups, the Chinese and the Jesuits, the name of the garden did not remain unified and consistent. Although the Chinese called the garden Round Brightness, the Jesuits originally called it "maisons de plaisance." The popular translation in current scholarship, Garden of Perfect Brightness, originates from the Jesuit translation "jardin de la clarté parfaite," which did not include the symbolic vision of "roundness" contained in the original Chinese term.

The Chinese called the Western Multistoried Buildings garden the Palace Halls of Water Method during its construction. The "water method" (*shuifa*) indicated Western mechanical fountains. But the Jesuits referred to this garden in their letters as "un palais européen," "Lust Pallast," or "Europäischer Sommer Palast" (Schulz 21). The use of the term "multistoried building" (*lou*) in the Chinese indicated the exoticism of the buildings to the Chinese eye. Qianlong was said to be amazed by the height and thickness of Western buildings when he saw engravings of them in books (Attiret, "Letter" 34-36). The term "multistoried building" not only indicated the secret exoticism of the Western portion but also hinted at the Chinese portion's contrastive feature of openness and expansiveness. The split and convoluted identity of the Yuanming Yuan maintains a sense of mysterious materiality, which eludes the appropriation of monolithic ideas. In some recent research discussing cultural fusion, abstract concepts such as "hybridity" are frequently used to characterize the Western Multistoried Buildings garden. Such a conceptual interpretation suggests a contemporary horizon of historical understanding, but it fails to account for the sense of the garden at the time of its creation. I argue that we must acknowledge that the sense of the garden came first and that it is the indispensable condition from which any further interpretation can be proposed. The modern Chinese phrase "sense of history" (*lishi gan*) echoes Martin Heidegger's concept of historicity (*Geschichtlichkeit*). According to Maurice Merleau-Ponty, the "sense" is the living relation of the perceiver to his body and to his mind (Heidegger, ch. 5; Merleau-Ponty, *Phenomenology* 208). The Jesuit painter Jean-Denis Attiret (Chinese name, Zhicheng Wang) commented that the only way to understand the Yuanming Yuan was to "see it" ("Letter" 6). In present Western scholarship, this primordial sense of the original vision of the garden, Round Brightness, is hardly given a chance to emerge.

As Yongzheng traced the meaning of Yuanming from ancient books, an etymological analysis is necessary to configure the original vision implied by Yuanming, which literally means "round brightness." In the Southern Dynasties, the full moon was once signified by the term "round *jing*" (*Hanyu da cidian*). The term *jing*, which can be roughly translated as "scene" in English, is a classic concept of Chinese garden design. According to the first Chinese garden treatise, *Yuan ye* (*The Craft of Gardens*), when the spectator's eyesight touches a *jing*, wonder will emerge; when his emotion is contained in viewing a *jing*, the *jing* will become fruitful (Ji 171). A *jing* can integrate a garden scene and the spectator's mind into one unity, where the diffusion of brightness is the very flow of passion. The etymological and theoretical explanations of *jing* lead to the issue of how the diffusing brightness was bounded in the Yuanming Yuan.

The existence of *jing* was deeply rooted in Chinese gardens and well embodied by the Yuanming Yuan. In this book I explore how the diffusion of round brightness was defined, physically and culturally, by its most remote boundary, the Western portion, into the existence of *jing*. The "boundary" here means that from which brightness begins its *presencing*. This term refers to Heidegger's discussions on the ancient Greek conception of horizon, which is "that from which something begins its presencing" (Casey 63). In the Yuanming Yuan, the *jing* can be a broad bird's-eye view in the Chinese portion or an intimate perspective view in the Western portion. My central argument is that it was through the *jing* that Jesuit metaphysics fused into Chinese cosmology rather than the *jing* re-presenting preexisting ideas. It is hard to find a direct causal relationship between the Jesuits' religious norms and their architectural and gardening endeavors in China (*Constitutions* 241). The fact is that garden creation enabled the Jesuits and other European missionaries to accommodate their body and mind within an unfamiliar context. Father Teodorico Pedrini (Chinese name, Lige De) records in a letter that he continually incurred expenses in renovating the Western Hall church, Xi Tang, in Beijing, and cultivating its garden (Devine 74). My approach to *jing* with regard to the history of the Western Multistoried Buildings garden originates from the fact that before any ideas can be imposed on a garden scene, the mind has to be opened to and involved in a certain way with that scene. The a priori opening of the mind towards the materiality of a garden provides the ground for historical interpretation. It is therefore meaningful to study how the *jing* of the Western garden influenced the minds of the emperor and Jesuits in that specific time and space, rather than to claim arbitrarily that the mixed view of the garden represents a posteriori ideas. Being a whole, the *jing* must be approached as a whole. The philosophical approaches of subjectivism and objectivism conflict with the pursuit of *jing*. The theoretical approach of dialectic materialism can provide a nominal synthesis of object and subject without being able to grasp the historical momentum of a *jing*, which can be sensed through analyzing what a scene was and how it was viewed. This is especially true in considering how the beholder's emotion and intention were projected into the garden scene. More precisely, the central question is how the Jesuits projected their intentions into the Round Brightness and how the emperor empathized with Western multistoried buildings. The approach of *jing*, from the very beginning, cannot treat any garden scene as an object external to the sense of the garden. To the contrary, all the visual and linguistic sources are carefully studied and organized in order to preserve and present that sense where the mind dwells.

The book consists of five chapters. In chapter 1, I provide an introduction to theoretical and historical perspectives of the book. In chapter 2, I explore the emperors' intentions concerning Round Brightness and its cosmological and virtuous meanings. This chapter includes my annotated full translations of both Yongzheng's and Qianlong's records of the Yuanming Yuan. In chapter 3, I study the vision of *jing* from the aspects of Chinese garden and landscape literature, Chinese painting theories, and the Forty Scenes of the Yuanming Yuan. In chapter 4, I investigate the translation of Western linear perspective in China, the so-called line method. The analyses start from the traditional perspective in Chinese paintings, then move to the Jesuit perspective, and finally focus on the interweaving of the representations of two cultures. This chapter includes my annotated full translations of the two prefaces of the first Chinese book on linear perspective, *Shixue* (1729, 1735). And in chapter 5, I discuss the application of line method in the design of the Western garden of the Yuanming Yuan. The chapter includes its general plan, buildings, and theatrical settings. My annotated translations of emperor Jiaqing's poems of the Western portion are also presented in this chapter. In the conclusion, I summarize the interpretive meanings of the Western Multistoried Buildings garden, establishing a historical criticism of Chinese contemporary urbanism. In general, the structure of the chapters adopts the procedure of the cultural encounter: the context of Yuanming, the entity of *jing*, the Chinese translation of linear perspective, and finally, the creation of the *jing* of line method.

Since the various gardens in the Yuanming Yuan complex held different names for both the Chinese and the Jesuits, the issue of translation becomes important in my study of the Western Multistoried Buildings garden. Prior to the inception of modern Chinese language at the beginning of the twentieth century, Chinese texts were written in classic Chinese, so-called *wenyan wen*. The translation from classic Chinese to English includes two basic steps: the first step is from classic Chinese to modern Chinese, and the second step is from modern Chinese to English. The translation from classic Chinese to modern Chinese requires research and interpretation and it is at this step that differences of understanding among scholars emerge. As for the literature related to the Yuanming Yuan, little has been translated, which is one of the primary reasons for presenting my own translations in the book. In addition, this provides me with the opportunity to engage in Chinese classic texts without being too far removed from the original texts and allows me to gain understanding from what the author intended, as well as to develop my own interpretation. The third reason for presenting my own translations is based on the situation that in many published translations a clear sense of the Chinese context is absent, especially when the original vision implied by a Chinese work was lost or is overlooked. From the perspective of Sinology, the political context and rhetorical structure might be more important than an implied vision, but for the study of garden history, such a loss is unbearable. In Chinese poetry of gardens and landscapes, a significant aspect consists in the expression of the relationship between the view and the viewer, which is interwoven by an implied vision. The term *yuan*, for example, can be translated as "garden" in English, but it also implies a vision of "enclosure." To preserve implied visions, a strategy that I call literal translation (*zhiyi*) becomes necessary, especially for the research process of comparative studies. The term Yuanming is usually translated as Perfect Brightness, following the Jesuit tradition. For the purpose of this book, I translate it more literally as Round Brightness to draw attention to the original vision of roundness, crucial for retrieving the primary sense of this garden.

Unless stated otherwise, all the translations are mine. Chinese terms relevant for an English-speaking readership to understand the general context or details of the concerned gardens are translated to English; otherwise, they are transliterated to *pinyin*. For special Chinese terms, such as names of places, gardens, scenes, buildings, rivers, trees, and animals, whose meanings are helpful for the English-speaking readership to understand the original context, I translate them to English in order to provide a comprehensive picture. Most of the garden names have to be translated to English, because their meanings are related to the understanding of the gardens, but I keep the garden name Yuanming Yuan untranslated, since it has become familiar to Western scholars. In another example, the town in the northwestern suburb, where most of Qing imperial gardens were located, is called Haidian, which is translated as Shallow Lakes, because this area was well known for plentiful lakes and springs. If it is not translated, the readership will not understand easily the geographical context of the gardens and why water was so important to the creation and evolution of the gardens. The concept *jing* has rich meanings, changed over time, and specific historical contexts. Here, the *jing* is a key concept whose meanings need to be explored. In order for smooth reading, I translate *jing* as "scene" in most cases, except for chapter 3 and other areas in which I attempt to investigate or emphasize the historical meanings of this concept in literature and images. If there is no real advantage for the English-speaking reader to have a specific word or name translated, no translation is made, and a transliteration is given in *pinyin*. For all my translations, the original Chinese texts are not included in order for the English-speaking reader to read smoothly throughout the book and focus on the flow of meanings. For readers who have an interest in translation from classic Chinese to English, they can find the original Chinese texts in the works cited. Regarding key concepts, their English translations and *pinyin* transliterations are copresented in the text, and their Chinese characters are listed in the index. The *pinyin* transliterations of the Chinese names and titles closely related to the Yuanming Yuan are listed in the text. The appendices include my annotated translations of the emperors' eight records of Qing imperial gardens, not including the Yuanming Yuan complex. Except for the Mountain Hamlet for Summer Coolness, all gardens recorded in the appendices were located in the northwestern suburb of Beijing. These garden records provide valuable references for the understanding of the imperial context of the Yuanming Yuan and its enclosed Western garden.

The discourse of *jing* interweaves literature and images. Although the Yuanming Yuan complex no longer exists, the original paintings and drawings of the gardens are preserved. There are forty paintings made by the court painters Dai Tang and Yuan Shen for the Forty Scenes of the Yuanming Yuan in 1744, and twenty copperplates drawn by the Jesuits' Chinese student, Lantai Yi, for the Western garden in 1786. The original set of the Forty Scenes paintings is stored in the Bibliothèque Nationale de France, Paris. A high-quality reprint of these forty paintings was published in Paris in 2000 (Chiu). The original engraving sets of the twenty copperplates can be found at the National Library of China in Beijing and the Imperial Palace Museum in Shenyang. Over one hundred prints in five complete sets were first printed from these copperplates ("Neiwufu" archive 820). Another set of engravings said to be original is housed at the Getty Research Center in Los Angeles. A high-quality reprint of the twenty copperplate engravings in original size was published in Paris in 1977 (L. Yi). There is no noticeable difference between the Getty set and the French reprint. The original construction drawings of the Yuanming Yuan complex were made by the Lei family, so-called Model Lei (Yangshi Lei), the contractor of the Qing court for six generations. The largest part of these ink drawings was purchased by Beiping Library, today's National Library of China, in 1930. Although Model Lei's drawings of the Yuanming Yuan have not been open to the public up to today, ten of these drawings of the Western garden, including site plans, building plans, and building detail drawings, appeared in the journal of Beiping Library in 1932 (Y. Lei). With more copies of the historical representations of the Yuanming Yuan and the digital restorations of this lost garden now available, this book is not intended to repeat what images depict; rather, the objective is to unveil interpretive meanings of these historical representations. Thus, there are only three illustrations included in the book, and readers are encouraged to refer to the published sources for related images. For each image mentioned but not included in this book, a published source is provided. Among the three included illustrations, the first one helps the reader to establish the locational relationship among the four gardens of the Yuanming Yuan complex. The second and third illustrations demonstrate symbolically the *jing* of mountains and waters created with the line method.

This book is a cross-cultural and interdisciplinary study of the history of a Western garden within a Chinese imperial garden and is thus a priori located within the framework of comparative cultural studies. Rather than a historiographical account of the events in the garden, I present historical and philosophical meanings of physical details in the garden and architectural creations. My interpretive approach crosses the traditional borders between physical and metaphysical, architecture and philosophy, literature and architecture, and East and West in order to maintain a critical perspective from either side that we usually take for granted in understanding cultural differences in globalization. This historical study of a Jesuit garden in China will prove beneficial to scholars in several disciplines. From the perspective of architecture and garden history, the book is a case study of hermeneutic interpretation based on empirical evidence concerning the meanings of designed environment. It brings to light the significance of primordial materiality in the transcendence of metaphysics in the area of religious studies. For philosophy, it explores the possibility of extending phenomenology into reflecting on the built environment and further developing such a reflection into philosophical criticism. Overall, with the work presented in the book, I hope to provide advances in the understanding of early modernity in Chinese history and culture.

Since the 1980s, phenomenology has emerged as a major philosophical influence in theories of architecture. Borrowing Friedrich Hölderlin's statement, "poetically man dwells" (249), Heidegger highlighted the significance of a meaningfully built environment in human existence. The understanding from phenomenology compels architecture and related disciplines to explore meanings of design in a much broader and deeper cultural context than the narrowly defined manifesto approach, an ahistorical method adopted by the internationalism of modern architecture. With the shifting of attention to cultural meanings of the built environment, history and theoretical studies act as a motivation towards the production of thoughtful architecture. Correspondingly, regional cultural and comparative cultural studies in architectural history provide the critical historical perspective for international architectural practice in today's era of globalization. Such studies have demonstrated, as I attempt in this book, that the poetical dwelling of human beings is essential for the continuation and development of a regional culture through cross-cultural exchanges. Cases of theatrical architectural encounters in history are crucial in defining the comparability for any comparative cultural study.

There has been an increased concern regarding the problems of an equally universal way of living and the standardization of housing, which Paul Ricoeur describes as mediocre civilization (274, 276). In the movement of globalization, including vulgar architectural internationalism, cultural differences are being flattened. In contrast, a living culture, as argued by Ricoeur, should sustain the encounter of other cultures by being faithful to its origins but at the same time open to creativity (283). Through detailed analysis of historical literature and garden representations, I explore the Chinese poetical context of the Jesuit garden in Beijing and bring to light the drama of the creation of the Jesuit garden. The understanding developed from this comparative cultural studies perspective, I hope, will initiate communication in which traditions and imagination can be sustained within differences. This perspective is proposed by Steven Tötösy de Zepetnek in his framework of comparative cultural studies and is practiced by scholars including those who publish in the Purdue University Press series of books in Comparative Cultural Studies. What I would like to add is a focus on the regional. The Daoist saint Laozi's idea of peaceful dwelling (*anju*) and its implications for today's global world help us to combine the dualities of the regional and the global. In chapter sixty-seven of the scripture *Laozi*, we read that "a nation is proud of its costume, enjoys its own custom, and feels comfortable in its houses. Although neighboring nations can see each other in distance and roosters' crows and dogs' barks of one nation can be heard by another, people remain in their homelands until their death" (S. Zhou 110). In this context, I confirm the tenets of Tötösy de Zepetnek's framework of comparative cultural studies, whereby I focus on the perspective of the regional, a relevant and integral factor where "dialogue is the only solution" (Tötösy de Zepetnek, "From Comparative" 259). Last but not least, my book suggests that the current impact of Western theories of literature and culture in departments of English and US-American literatures in China and hence the almost exclusive reliance on Western thought—even when discussing matters Chinese—needs some rethinking. As I demonstrate throughout the book, Chinese thought in many instances produced similar theoretical frameworks and concepts on a variety of matters, and in comparative Chinese and Western scholarship it would be relevant to involve such thought instead of focusing on Western thought only. The point is to include and to dialogue.

In order to facilitate the understanding and location of historical periods of Chinese culture, I present here a chronology of Chinese dynasties referred to in the book:

Western Zhou (11th century BCE-771 BCE)
Spring and Autumn Period (770 BCE-476 BCE)
Warring States Period (475 BCE-221 BCE)
Western Han (206 BCE-8 CE)
Eastern Han (25-220)
Three Kingdoms (220-265)
Western and Eastern Jin (265-439)
Southern-Northern Dynasties (317-589)
Tang (618-906)
Five Dynasties (907-960)

Northern Song (960-1127)
Southern Song (1127-1279)
Jin (1115-1234)
Yuan (1279-1368)
Ming (1368-1644)
Qing (1644-1911) and emperors:
    Shunzhi (reign 1643-1661)
    Kangxi (reign 1662-1722)
    Yongzheng (reign 1723-1735)
    Qianlong (reign 1736-1795)
    Jiaqing (reign 1796-1820)
    Daoguang (reign 1821-1850)
    Xianfeng (reign 1851-1861)

Chapter Two

The Chinese Garden and the Concept of the Virtue of Round Brightness

If a Qing emperor used an imperial garden as his primary residence, the garden was known as the emperor's garden (*yuyuan*), which was differentiated from other imperial gardens that he visited only occasionally. In this sense, Kangxi's emperor's garden was the Garden of Uninhibited Spring and for Yongzheng to Qianlong, Jiaqing, Daoguang, and Xianfeng, the emperor's garden was the Yuanming Yuan.

Before a prince was assigned his own garden by the emperor, he would be assigned a residence in the emperor's garden, and thus the memory of living in his father's garden was closely related to the meaning of living in his own garden. While living with his father Kangxi in the Garden of Uninhibited Spring, prince Yinzhen, the future emperor Yongzheng, wrote poetry about his feelings for this garden. In his poem, "On the Blooming Peonies in the Garden of Uninhibited Spring," dainty peonies looked so pretty in the breeze that fragrance teased the studio curtain and flowers heaped up like brocades ("Changchunyuan" 5). He was looking through the window of his reading room while appreciating the beauty of the outside peonies. The connection in the prince's mind between peonies and his father's garden was later transformed into the connection between peonies and the memory of his father in his own garden. In the Yuanming Yuan, there was a place called Peony Terrace, which Yongzheng's poem described: "There is no comparison in the world, / This is the best flower in the human world. / Her gorgeous look was appreciated in the Garden of Golden Valley, / Her fame was highly spoken of in Luoyang. / Who can compare with this national beauty? / She wears celestial clothes whose fabric is like rosy clouds" ("Mudan" 87-88). Peonies were called traditionally the king of flowers (L. Wang 7). The Garden of Golden Valley, owned by a powerful official in the Western Jin dynasty, was located in Luoyang, famous for peonies. The Peony Terrace was the place where the three generations of emperors, Kangxi, Yongzheng, and Qianlong appreciated the "national beauty" together. The memory of this place was also recorded by a poem by Qianlong, in which he stated that he still remembered the days when he was a teenager, and that the love and affection he received from his ancestors started at the Peony Terrace ("Louyue" 13).

After Kangxi died, Yongzheng remained in traditional mourning for three years, after which he was eager to return to his garden. Several princes and officials suggested to him that the landscape of the Yuanming Yuan was fresh and clean and that he could reside there as he wished. Yongzheng soon decided to perform administrative duties from his residence garden. An imperial archive recorded that in the eighth moon of the third year of the Yongzheng reign (1725), the emperor arrived in the Yuanming Yuan. He decreed to the Council of State (Junji Chu) that his routine in the garden should not be different from that in the palaces of the Forbidden City and that all the daily administrative affairs in the garden should follow the regular procedure without any delay (*Qing shi lu* 435, 536). Subsequently, he observed that officials did not report to him about national affairs as frequently as before and thought it must be related to his living in the garden. In yet another imperial archive, it was recorded: "I [Yongzheng] sit in the Hall of Diligent Administration in the garden today waiting for officials' reports, but none arrives. They might think that the reason that I live in the Yuanming Yuan is for leisure, thus, they intentionally simplify the reports. The reason I live here is simply because the landscape and air of the suburb are fresher than that of the city. In terms of daily administration, there is no difference between the palaces and the garden. I do not want to relax at any time" (*Qing shi lu* 596). Yongzheng regarded the garden as both his home and his workplace. He wanted to live and work there because of the pretty landscape and fresh air, and the garden made him feel relaxed and at leisure. Leisure to him had nothing to do with laziness and, as he noted in his other writings, it was part of the philosophy of his life.

The garden was located in the northwestern suburb, which was rich with water sources and surrounded by the West Mountain range. In contrast to the south of China, the north traditionally lacked plentiful water sources. Kangxi first selected this site for gardens because he drank the spring water and found it tasted sweet, and he thought that if the residence were located here, the garden would be peaceful and auspicious (Yongzheng, "Shizong" 2, 4). It can be said that the emperor's intention for the garden was formed in accordance with water and by borrowing (in the sense of adopting as one's own) the view of West Mountain. In a poem, Yongzheng described the relationship between the distant view of West Mountain and the garden: "Raindrops strike reed leaves, / I suddenly feel exceptionally fresh and cool. / The misty mountains look high and covered with one thousand layers of greenery, / The light of the lake is brilliant with ten thousand layers of waves. / Swimming fish avoid fishhooks and depend upon cold aquatic plants, / Flying birds dash to hide under green ivy. / Don't be surprised that golden wind hastens to change the order, / Autumn sunlight has a predilection for a quick return to warmth and brightness" ("Yuhou Jiuzhou" 150). The distant West Mountain was a borrowed view for the garden. Through observing the raindrops, reed leaves, misty mountains, the lake's reflection, swimming fish, flying birds, and autumn light, he sensed the order of nature. The perceived brightness in the order of nature was later related to the concept of Round Brightness, which was a reflection of Yongzheng's feelings between his heart and the full moon. As he wrote in another poem on the garden, "inherent character and heaven mix together without differentiation of present and past, / Heart and moon in round brightness brighten through the deep sky. / Get up and shout through the northern window, / Thousands of mountains echo to me smoothly" ("Miaogao" 57). This is the only known poem in which Yongzheng used the phrase "round brightness," meaning that in the unity of Round Brightness, the heart and the moon echo each other. In the Chinese language, the origin of thinking within the body is usually the heart, which is the most remote and most opaque place in the human body. If the heart can be brightened, it means the human being is fully integrated with the surrounding world. The round brightness unifies not only the heart with the moon but also the human being with heaven, the present with the past, and the individual with the landscape.

Yongzheng described in detail how the moonlight slipped into the room and fused with his mind while he was reading on an autumn night: "Thousands of thriving willows, / Shade from willows covers the thatched hall. / Waving silks caress the ink slab and ink stone, / Flying wadding touches the bed for playing music. / Orioles chant and willow's spring branches become warmed up, / Cicadas chirp and autumn leaves get cool. / During the night the moon shadows come to the window, / They mix with the fragrance of books" ("Shenliu" 86). The "silks" indicate slim willow twigs. His eyes kept shifting between the interior and the exterior, where the vision and smell interwove with each other into an atmosphere of reading under moonlight. The deep willows indicated a quiet place where the heart became tranquil, and it was at such a silent moment that the moonlight penetrated through the window and fused with the heart. In another poem of the garden, he demonstrated again how both his view and mind merged under the moonlight: "The brick ground is in the form of the Buddhist swastika, / The pool is filled with water to raise brilliant fish. / Underwater grass looks very green, / Balustrades define the pool on each side. / Fish swim freely after the tide of the brook, / They strike the water under the nascent bright moon. / Their carefree character fits well within the environment, / Watching them closely my mind feels leisurely too" ("Jinyu" 88). The "fish pool" alluded to the Daoist sage Zhuangzi's happy kingdom of fish. Yongzheng first described the physical characteristics of the fish pool, and then depicted the activities of the fish under the moonlight. The final two sentences convey that the carefree characteristics of the fish were also the state of the garden and of his mind. As he gazed at the fish pool under moonlight, both his view and his mind became unified. The heart-moon unity was configured by the roundness of brightness. Yongzheng expressed his notion that the circle of his heart could identify with that of the moon: "The top of the tree disappears into dusk mists, / Clear light chases the water flow. / Laid-back herons stand on shallow sands, / Peaceful gulls float on light waves. / The heart and the moon are two round mirrors, / The lake and the sky are unified into the monochrome of autumn. / It seems like being in heaven, / An illusion of strolling in the Daoist paradise" ("Pinghu" 158).

The symbolic connection between the heart and the full moon was established based on the round form. The term "mirror" meant that the heart and the full moon corresponded to and brightened each other. The interreflection between the sky and the lake enhanced the unity of the heart and the moon.

The concept of Round Brightness was most directly defined in Yongzheng's "Record of the Yuanming Yuan" (1725). My translation of this record is based on both punctuated and unpunctuated Chinese texts (Z. Chen 194-95; Zhongguo Yuanmingyuan xuehui, *Yuanmingyuan xueshu* 4: 102; E 1-19):

> North of the Garden of Uninhibited Spring, the Yuanming Yuan was granted to me as my residence garden. During his leisure time, after a court audience, my father, the majestic emperor Kangxi, strolled along the shore of the Red Hill Lake. After tasting the spring water and finding it sweet, he decided to change a ruined villa from the Ming dynasty, reduce its site and build the Garden of Uninhibited Spring for his residence in high spring and summer. Accompanying him, I was granted an area here with clear elegant forested hills and still, deep, and expansive waters. I built pavilions and houses following the lay of the land, rising with hills and diving with the waters. I chose to delight in nature and spare myself the vexations of construction. Flowers by the balustrades and trees on the dike flourished without watering. Flocks of birds enjoyed soaring; schools of fish dove freely. The place was bright, high, and dry; fertile soil and abundant springs promised prosperity. How peaceful and auspicious it was to reside here! When the garden was built, thanks to my father's benevolence, it was granted the name Round Brightness. [Note: The Red Hill is also the name of the birthplace of the legendary emperor Yao. The name therefore implies a blessed imperial land. The Garden of Uninhibited Spring was located on the site of the former Garden of Delicate Brilliance (Qinghua Yuan) of the Ming dynasty. In addition to springs on the site, the water of the Yuanming Yuan came from the Jade Spring Hill in the west and the River of Ten Thousand Springs in the south. During the construction of the garden, earthworks from digging watercourses were used for creating many hillocks. In the garden, birds and fish enjoyed their own nature. Such a world where everything enjoys itself alludes to Zhuangzi's idea of "obtaining oneself" (*zide*) (Q. Guo 24-26).]
>
> I waited respectfully for my father's arrival, enjoyed his kindness, celebrated with him the heavenly joy, and expressed how sincerely I cherished this moment. Flowers and trees, forests and springs, all bathed in his glory and philanthropy. After inheriting the throne, I mourned day and night and fasted to pay respect to my departed father. Although the summer was hot and muggy, I did not mind it. Three years passed and the rite of mourning was over. Because of all the administrative affairs now waiting for me, I should calm down to be blessed with good fortunes and keep away from disturbances. For a clear and beautiful atmosphere, a garden residence is the best. I therefore ordered the Bureau of the Imperial Households to restore the garden with great care. All the pavilions, terraces, hills, and gullies were returned to their original appearances. A wing was added for various administrative departments, so all the retinues and on-duty officials could have

workplaces. A hall was built in the south of the garden for audiences. [Note: In the third month of 1722, prince Yinzhen invited his father Kangxi to the garden twice. They met at the Peony Terrace where hundreds of peonies were planted. The three generations of the Qing emperors, Kangxi, Yongzheng, and Qianlong, liked to appreciate peonies together in the spring. Such an activity was taken as a symbol of peace and prosperity of the country. The "garden residence" (*yuanju*) is a significant concept developed in Qing imperial gardens, implying a multiple function of imperial residence, entertainment, and administration. According to the Qing imperial system, all national projects were administrated by the Ministry of Public Works (Gong Bu) and had to abide by the unified building codes. But the construction of imperial gardens was under the charge of the Bureau of Imperial Households (Neiwu Fu), especially, the later Yuanming Yuan had its own specific building regulations without being subject to any others.]

When the first rays of the morning sun appear and the shadow of the sundial is still long, I call officials for consultation. I frequently change my diurnal schedule in order to spend more time with my officials. Plots were planted for crops and vegetables. The flat farmland is fertile and crops are abundant. With a casual glance into the distance, my reverie extends to the whole country, as well as wishes for a good harvest. When I lean on a balustrade inspecting the crops or stand beside the field watching the clouds, I wish for a good rain to come during the right time and hope for a climate responsive to sturdy seedlings. Images of assiduous and tired peasants and of the toil of tilling the land suddenly seem to appear in the garden. When the forest light shines bright and clear, the pools are crystal clear and tranquil; the distant peaks break into this mirror. The morning sun and the evening moon; greenery is reflected and the sky is contained by the water. Hence, the magic effects of Dao emerge unconsciously and the bosom of heaven suddenly becomes bright. [Note: The agricultural field in the emperor's garden alluded to Confucius's thought that a country must have sufficient provisions (D. Zhang 280). The emperor's intention towards the mirror-like water surface alluded to Zhuangzi's idea of "still water" (*zhishui*), which meant that only when water was still was the world most clearly reflected and collected (Q. Guo 193-94).]

During short breaks from my administration, I study the classics to shape my character. I explore rhythm for poems, practice calligraphy, and dedicate myself to the study of the classics. My life follows a strict routine, enlightened by my father's holy model, which I respectfully observe all the time and dare not surpass. The ceilings, columns, walls, and doors of the buildings are in a simple form without superfluous ornament, following the lead of my father's simple life. I communicate with vassals during the day, review their reports and propositions at night, collate texts while standing on a front step, and watch archers in a practice field. At leisure or on duty, I follow the same rule of conduct, following the lead of my father's diligence. In the fine days of spring and autumn, when the scenery is fresh and fragrant, and birds sing a harmonious chord and limpid dew congeals on flower petals, I sometimes invite princes and ministers to appreciate the scenes at their own pace, to boat and enjoy fruits. We give a free rein to our feelings, displaying accordingly our sense of well being, looking up and gazing down and roaming at leisure. Nature discloses itself to the fullest; heart and mind exult with joy, following the lead of my father's openness to worthy and virtuous people and his consideration for his courtiers and ability to avail himself of circumstances. [Note: Studying classics was based on Confucius's thought that a virtuous man should have extensive knowledge of classics and that diligent study could enhance virtue (D. Zhang 259-61). The phrase "looking up and gazing down" alludes to the historical sentence, "Look up at the bigness of the cosmos, gaze down at the flourishing of categories of things" from the prose work, "Recount of the Orchard Pavilion," by Xizhi Wang, a calligraphy artist of the Eastern Jin dynasty. The phrase "roam at leisure," originating from Zhuangzi, meant that when the heart was not burdened by things and expectations, it could move to infinity (Q. Guo 1).]

Round Brightness, the name granted by my father, has a deep and far-ranging meaning, not easily perceived. I have tried to research ancient books for the moral meaning of Round Brightness. Round means the perfection and concentration of the mind, implying the timeliness and moderation of the behavior of a virtuous man. Brightness means to illuminate all things to reach human perspicacity and wisdom. Round Brightness is used to highlight the meaning of the residence, stimulate the body and mind, piously experience the idea of heaven, cherish forever my father's holy instruction, propagate all creatures, and maintain harmony and peace. I do not ask for peace for myself but rather wish it for the whole country. I do not seek leisure for myself but rather long for happiness for all the people, so that generation after generation can step on the spring terrace and wander in the happy kingdom. I stabilize the mighty foundation of the country to make people's good fortune and well being last into the future. If what I have done can show my gratitude to the blessing my father bestowed upon me, my heart at this moment might feel a little relieved. I therefore write this record to express my deep feelings. [Note: In the ancient cosmological book *Yizhuan* (*The Great Commentary of the Book of Changes*), which is Confucius's annotations of *Yijing* (*Book of Changes*), it says: "Therefore, the virtue of *shi* becomes round and divine; the virtue of *gua* becomes square and intelligent. . . . Thus, the Dao of heaven is brightened" (M. Tang 216). This quote is probably the oldest extant source about the original meaning of round brightness. The "concentration of the mind" alluded to Zhuangzi's idea, "condensation of the mind" (*ningshen*). When the mind is condensed, one can accomplish anything without being conscious of it; once the mind is condensed, all other things will be obtained without effort (Q. Guo 28). In such condensation of the mind, the world is fully occupied by an individual's spirit (F. Wang 7). Zhuangzi's condensation of the mind does not simply mean to draw attention. At the precise moment when the mind is condensed, there is nothing in the mind on which to focus and true freedom is thus released. Such a seemingly paradoxical Daoist idea is close to Jean-Paul Sartre's concept of nothingness. According to Sartre, man is free because he is not himself, but present to himself. Freedom coincides with the nothingness that is at the heart of man (568). The phrase "timeliness and moderation," literally "timely middle" (*shizhong*) was a central idea of Confucius. The "middle" echoed with the "round" form. The connection between the timeliness and moderation and a virtuous man was established by Confucius, who said in the *Zhongyong* (*Doctrine of the Mean*): A virtuous man acts timely and moderately (X. Zheng 1). Yongzheng alluded to two Daoist terms to compare his garden to a model of the ideal nation where happiness was shared by all people. The first term, "spring terrace," was from Laozi's saying, "Lustily, the people seem enjoying a feast or ascending a terrace in springtime," and signified in general the beautiful place for touring (Fu and Lu 27). The second term, "happy kingdom," was from Zhuangzi, who used it to describe the freedom of fish. He said: "To wander leisurely is fish's happiness" (F. Wang 148).]

In 1744, Qianlong expanded the Yuanming Yuan into Forty Scenes. Three years later, the construction of the Garden of Eternal Spring and the Western Multistoried Buildings garden began. Although his garden expansion moved eastward, he maintained the view towards the distant West Mountain, which his father so enjoyed. In the poem of the twenty-seventh scene, "Elegant View of West Mountain Peaks," Qianlong stated: "On the terrace a high wood pavilion was built, / In summer the wind is invigorating as if in autumn. / The western windows face right towards the West Mountain, / The distant peaks were connected to feel like they were several feet away" ("Xifeng" 59). The pavilion on the high terrace was intended to view the West Mountain. This distant view was framed by the western window of the building. In this way, the distant mountain range appeared as a part of the garden. The view towards the wilderness in the west, in contrast to the view towards the Forbidden City in the east, expressed the emperor's desire for remote depth of the mind. Compared with his father, Qianlong held a larger picture in his vision of Round Brightness. His intention was made clear by his ordering the court painters to paint a huge panorama of the Yuanming Yuan in 1737. For the painting, he penned the title Grand View, which was poetized later by a Qing scholar as "incorporate the sky and earth into the imperial bosom" (K. Wang 1125). The cosmos was integrated with the emperor's mind into the diffusing perfect brightness, which was best experienced as a whole. The most direct source for understanding Qianlong's concept of Round Brightness is his "Later Record of the Yuanming Yuan" (1770). My translation of this record is based on both punctuated and unpunctuated Chinese texts (Z. Chen 200-01; Zhongguo Yuanmingyuan xuehui, *Yuanmingyuan xueshu* 4: 185; E):

> In the past, my father Yongzheng repaired and improved a garden that my grandfather Kangxi granted him. Basic administration space was added so that he could issue decrees at will, establish new policies, and keep close to his worthy officials. For the administration buildings, garden buildings, the jutting hillocks, and receding pools arranged behind them, plainness rather than magnificence, seclusion rather than conspicuous display were valued. When planting is enjoyed, shrubbery and flowerbeds excitedly burst open into bloom. When agricultural activity is conducted by experienced people, fields and vegetable gardens are managed as if weather were under control. The wind through the pines and the moon deep in the water penetrated his bosom and magic Dao surges by itself. He carefully protected the country, communicated frequently with learned officials, and studied classics to shape his character. Here he could thoroughly enjoy himself, sing or recite

poems, have all his senses in full alert or at ease. [Note: The "plainness" (*pu*) is a key concept of Laozi's thought, which indicates the primordial materiality that was raw, opaque, and unnamable. When it dispersed, useful tools were born (D. Liu, *Laozi* 10). In Chinese, the term "seclusion" (*you*) means in general deep and concealed. Laozi first used this word to describe Dao that was obscure and active (Yin 331). The same concept was used in the Daoist book *Huainanzi* (*Masters of Huainan*) to describe Dao as "concealed, deep and dark" (D. Liu, *Huainanzi* 1).]

The concerns for the welfare of the country that both my father and grandfather placed ahead of their own pleasure surrounded all things and thus came to form the Round Brightness. The meaning of Round Brightness indicates the timeliness and moderation of the behavior of a virtuous man. My grandfather gave this name to the garden he granted to my father, who accepted it respectfully as an uplifting of his own person and spirit, and as an ever-present memory of his father in the garden. Rather than expecting peace for himself, he wished it for the whole country. Rather than seeking leisure for himself, he longed for all the people to live a merry life. It was my father's intention to make the people's well being and wealth last forever. I, as his son, revere the ancestors' palaces and gardens and am often afraid of demeaning them. How could I dare add to or modify them? Therefore, after inheriting the imperial throne, when the construction department submitted a proposal to build a new garden, I refused. Since then, out of mourning, I have resided in the old garden of my father. During leisure hours between court audiences, an emperor must have his own place for roaming around and appreciating expansive landscapes. If a balance of work and leisure is obtained, the garden will foster good personality and shape the character. If balance is not achieved, he will indulge in futility and confuse his sense of purpose. If he pays too much attention to palace buildings, riding and archery, rare skills and curiosities, his attention to worthy officials and their propositions, his diligent administration and his love of the people will grow thin. The damage is really beyond description. [Note: The phrase, "surrounded all things and thus came to form the round brightness" is a key sentence for understanding Qianlong's interpretation of the meaning of Round Brightness. The Fairy Lodge in Eternal Spring, the twelfth scene in the garden, was where Qianlong as a prince used to live. To commemorate this place, he created a new garden in the east with the same name, Eternal Spring. The phrase, "a balance of work and leisure" is translated from the Chinese term *yi*, which means in general calm and appropriate. Zhuangzi thought that each thing had its own appropriate place in the world; only when everything became appropriate was infinity reached (Q. Guo 232).]

My father did not reside in the Garden of Uninhibited Spring of his father, because he already had the Yuanming Yuan. By turning down carvings and decorations, he was of one mind with the pure and simple inclinations of his father. However, the spacious and open scale, deep gullies and quiet hills, bright and beautiful landscapes, and high and remote buildings of this garden are beyond imagination. Such a place, accumulating the blessings of the land and heaven, offers a touring place that nothing can surpass. For the same reason, my offspring should certainly not give this garden away and waste people's wealth to build another one. This matches deeply with my desire of following my father's diligent and frugal inclinations. Although ancient books say an emperor should not live in his parents' houses, this imperial taboo cannot be compared with the smart praise made by Lao Zhang of the Jin Kingdom. It is worth meditating on this. [Note: Lao Zhang, named Meng Zhang, was a court official in the Jin kingdom of the Spring Autumn period. The prince of the Jin kingdom, Wenzi, named Wu Zhao, built a new residence, and the grand officials went to visit it. Lao Zhang praised the residence: "How sublime and beautifully ornamented it is! Here, you can sing for rites, cry for mourning and celebrate with friends and relatives." Wenzi then realized that Lao Zhang pretended to praise the building but rather in fact criticized its extravagance in order to prevent him from doing this again. Virtuous men therefore acclaimed Lao Zhang for his "smart praise" (Xidan Sun 1: 299). Qianlong used this story to allude to the fact that he preferred living in his father's garden to building a new one.]

My father has accounted in his record the history of building the garden and his intention to avail himself of circumstances, increase his scholarly wisdom and military courage, multiply all life under the sun, protect the harmonic and peaceful world, and let the people step on the spring terrace and wander about the happy kingdom. How dare his son restate them here! [Note: The phrase, "protect the harmonic and peaceful world" alludes to the historical phrase, "protect peace for universal harmony" in the ancient cosmological book *Yizhuan* (H. Gao 55).]

A major expansion made by Qianlong to the Yuanming Yuan was the creation of the Garden of Eternal Spring, about which he wrote many poems. My full translation of his "Poem of the Garden of Eternal Spring with a Preface" is based on a punctuated Chinese text ("Qianlong" 1379-80):

Preface: Mountains and waters symbolize joy and longevity, and a pleasant mood follows that which is encountered. The sun and the moon bring out scenes from fairylands. Springtime thus becomes eternal. I opened up an unused field in the imperial garden (i.e., Yuanming Yuan) and named it after the good title of my former residence in the Yuanming Yuan, Eternal Spring. Reflecting on this title, given by my father Yongzheng in the past, I happen from time to time to get close to the principle of the whole. Wishing for a peaceful residence in the future, I begin to arrange it beforehand. [Note: During Qianlong's teenage years, his residence in the Yuanming Yuan was called Fairy Lodge in Eternal Spring. The name Eternal Spring itself thus became the connection between the two gardens as well as between the two generations of Qing emperors. The "principle of the whole" indicated the unity of history, which integrated past and present.]

The water is connected to the Fortunate Sea in the Yuanming Yuan, and an unused field to the east is covered with magnificent sacred mulberry trees. The wall winds along the banks of the Clear River, and sweet smells of corn float over the northern fields. Glancing at ancient books entertains my spirit; a hall is used for storing them. I wield the brush in writing poems to enjoy myself; a gallery named Unsophisticated Transformation in the Garden of Eternal Spring is used for storing stone tablets. The longing for diligence is everlasting and it is modeled after a chapel. With my bosom opened to spectacular views, I climb this tower. Views of any hill and any valley are pretty enough to delight my heart. Pavilions along the water or on top of a hill offer views that attract my eyes. [Note: The water of the Garden of Eternal Spring came from the Fortunate Sea in the Yuanming Yuan through a five-arch floodgate in the northwest, which was near the entrance to the Western garden. Mentioning that the water source of the Garden of Eternal Spring was from the Yuanming Yuan was intended to demonstrate the close relationship between these two gardens. The sacred mulberry tree, *fusang*, is well known in Chinese mythology. According to the *Huainanzi*, the sun rises from the foot of the *fusang* tree (Major 158-61). The Gallery of Unsophisticated Transformation, located at the middle of the Garden of Eternal Spring, was built for storing stone tablets from the Tower of Unsophisticated Transformation of the Song dynasty. Seeking "spectacular views" demonstrated his major intention for the garden expansion.]

Strolling and resting here during moments snatched away from public affairs, I think of staying forever in good health and in peace into my eighties and nineties. If a reign should last for sixty years (before retirement as my grandfather did), I am afraid my long hoped-for wish will turn out to be extravagant. Up to now I still have twenty-five years to fulfill, how could I dare feel tired already? I compose a poem to go along with the above preface: The Garden of Eternal Spring dares not compare to the Garden of Uninhibited Spring, / I imitate the scenes of the famous gardens in Jiangnan for a certain reason. / My past residence in the Yuanming Yuan was named Fairy Lodge in Eternal Spring, / When getting too old to work I will seek a residence for retirement. / Plant pine tree saplings and observe their growth, / Collect precious rocks and wait peacefully for a future reward. / The remaining twenty-five years still requires prudence, / In my late eighties and nineties I shall stroll about leisurely and joyously. Note: The Garden of Uninhibited Spring is south of the Yuanming Yuan. It was built by my grandfather. Now it is the residence of my mother. The Fairy Lodge in Eternal Spring is one of the Forty Scenes of the Yuanming Yuan. It was named by my father emperor Yongzheng. I use the same name for the new garden. I have a long cherished wish that in the sixtieth year of my reign, namely at the age of eight-five years old, I should retire. I therefore prepare a garden east of the Yuanming Yuan for my future residence. Although this might be an extravagant hope, if the garden is really built, it could also be seen as a good fortune for my country and as a celebration of my people. I am sixty years old now and still need another twenty-five years to retire. Nevertheless, I dare not relax at all and my will is for diligence in public affairs. Only after retirement can I enjoy myself. [Note: Although Qianlong says he imitated the views of the famous gardens in Jiangnan "for a certain reason," he does not explicate what that reason was. Referring to his record of the Yuanming Yuan, it can be argued that the primary reason for his garden imitation was to encircle all the beautiful gardens into the Round Brightness. He also claims that his Garden of Eternal Spring dared not to compete with his grandfather's Garden of Uninhibited Spring. In fact, in the Garden of Uninhibited Spring, Kangxi had already asked craftsmen from Jiangnan to imitate the scenes of literati gardens. Qianlong certainly learned this from his grandfather.]

Qianlong's major strategy for constructing this garden was to imitate the famous gardens in Jiangnan, one of which was the Lion Grove garden in Suzhou, which was well known for its eccentric rocks. The Lion Grove had been replicated at least twice in Qing imperial gardens. One example was the Lion Grove located in the retreat garden, Mountain Hamlet for Summer Coolness; another example was the Lion Grove located in the northeastern corner of the Garden of Eternal Spring, which bordered the eastern end of the Western Multistoried Buildings garden. The Lion Grove in the Garden of Eternal Spring not only imitated the model in Suzhou but also replicated some of the well-known landscape buildings of Zan Ni's villa in his hometown, such as the Hall of Cloudy Forest and the Pavilion of Aloof Remoteness. Qianlong originally thought that Ni was the designer of the Lion Grove garden in Suzhou.

The entrance of the Lion Grove garden was a water gate. To the east of the Lion Grove was the seven-arch exit floodgate of the watercourse of the Garden of Eternal Spring. In the poem "Water Gate," which implied both water gates, Qianlong wrote: "The water flows through a gate beyond the garden wall, / Paddling here tastes like being at the water source of Wulin. / Though the Wuling was recorded by [famous] Yuanming Tao, / It cannot match the old pedant's [Zan Ni's] painting scroll" ("Shui Men" 66). Both water gates implied the traditional painting concept "water mouth" (*shuikou*), a term indicating the entrance or exit of a watercourse, which evoked a mystical feeling to the emperor. By alluding to Yuanming Tao's paradise beyond the peach blossom spring at Wuling of the Eastern Jin dynasty, Qianlong retrieved the mystical image of the water mouth. He further compared the mystical water flow to the unfolding of a painted garden scroll. Qianlong was impressed by the Lion Grove in Suzhou during his multiple visits to the Jiangnan region. A Qing record of this garden states: "The Lion Grove belonged to the Huang family in Suzhou. In the *renwu* year (1762), Qianlong revisited this garden. He committed painting the scene of the garden and inscribed a poem within the painting. He then compared his painting with Zan Ni's, which he specifically brought with him from Beijing. Upon returning to his home, he decided to build a Lion Grove in the Garden of Eternal Spring. When the garden was built, he asked a court painter to paint a scroll of the garden in Ni's style. He wrote a poem on the scroll and stored it in the Pavilion of Aloof Remoteness in the new Lion Grove. Meanwhile, he hung Qiong Du's painting of Lion Grove of Suzhou on the wall" (Zhenyu Wu 880). The record demonstrates the cohesive relationship between paintings and the new and old Lion Grove gardens. Qianlong documented the old garden with a painting based on which the new garden was built for another painting. In the colophon of his Lion Grove scroll created in 1373, the Yuan painter Zan Ni wrote: "I and Mr. Shanchang Zhao discussed creating a painting of the Lion Grove garden with intentions [*yi*], which would inherit the intentions of Masters Hao Jing and Tong Guan" (Zhu and Cao 1: 415). This statement shows that the painting was not a mere representation of the garden, but rather an expression of the painter's intention towards the garden. Following Ni's intention, Qianlong shifted among the old garden, the new garden, and their pictorial representations. Qianlong wrote poetry about his Lion Grove at least six times. In the preface of a poem in 1772, he wrote that the fame of the Lion Grove evolved from Pedant Ni's painting scroll. The bamboo, rocks, hillocks and gullies in his new Lion Grove all imitated the scenes in Ni's painting ("Shizi Lin [1]" 65). In the preface of another poem, he recalled that when he visited the Lion Grove in Suzhou, he ordered the painting masters from Suzhou to make some small paintings for his replicating the original garden ("Jiashan [1]" 65). These descriptions demonstrate the cohesive relationship between the old and new Lion Groves in Qianlong's mind. In the preface for a group of poems, he wrote in more detail:

> In the colophon of his painting, Zan Ni wrote that he discussed creating a painting of the Lion Grove with Shanchang Zhao: "The painting did come from Ni's hand, but whether the laid rocks and buildings also came from him is not certain. Furthermore, it has been over four hundred years since the building of the garden and the owner has changed several times, with the current owner being the Wang family. Although today's pavilions, terraces, peaks and pools of my own Lion Grove can be similar to the Lion Grove of Suzhou, it cannot be completely similar to what Ni's painting depicts. Although I chant poems to express my admiration, my intention goes to Ni rather than the Huang family. People like to keep talking about what is worth talking about, therefore I continue to carry on what can be chanted in the other eight scenes for the Lion Grove" ("Xuti" 65).

Qianlong admired not only the garden of Lion Grove in Suzhou but also the painting of the garden created by Zan Ni. His intention of replicating the Lion Grove and building a new one in his Garden of Eternal Spring was to imitate Ni's intention. As his poem in 1773 confirmed, "The painting of the Lion Grove was created by Yunlin Ni [that is, Zan Ni], / The spirit of the whole scroll flows through to today. / I, however, replicate it by building a garden, / It is like painting a copy of the original painting" ("Shizi Lin [2]" 67). For Qianlong, making the Lion Grove garden was like recreating the painting. It can even be inferred that the garden was built only because of that famous garden painting.

The activity of replicating a famous garden from Jiangnan within an imperial garden in Beijing raises the question of truth. In a poem on his own Lion Grove, Qianlong wrote, "I want to ask about the bounded environment of the Lion Grove, / Which one is fictional and which one is real? / The She Garden [that is, the Lion Grove in Suzhou] is in fact a representation of Ni's painting, / But the original painting is actually in my Treasure Box of the Stone Ditch" ("Tanzhen" 68). The Treasure Box of the Stone Ditch (Shiqu Baoji) indicated the imperial gallery specifically for storing ancient paintings. Among the Lion Grove in Suzhou, the Lion Grove in the Garden of Eternal Spring, and Ni's painting of the Lion Grove, which one was more truthful? For Qianlong, the answer was the last one. This does not mean the painting was more valuable than the actual gardens; rather it demonstrates that the intention (*yi*) expressed by the pictorial representation of the garden was as important, if not more important, as the garden itself. As long as the pictorial intention was preserved, it did not matter if the garden was a replica, as that was a secondary consideration. A famous feature of both the old and new Lion Grove gardens was their eccentric rocks. The hill made of rocks was called an artificial hill (*jiashan*) in Chinese gardens. In the poem "Artificial Hill," Qianlong wrote: "The Lion Grove of Suzhou, / Is structured by Yunlin Ni. / Today, my resembling imperial garden, / Is not much different from the original model. / Think about that in the Stone Ditch collection, / There are many works by this old pedant. / Unscroll and look at them, they look so real, / Why should we say this one of the Lion Grove does not? / The painting is so vivid that it even lets you walk around, / It certainly is better than his other paintings. / But in a long or short time, / The reason cannot be understood by many" ("Jiashan [2]" 75-76). With the topic of the rock hill, Qianlong was thinking about the issue of truthfulness and the relationship between the original garden and the garden replica. For him, it did not matter whether it was a garden replica or the pictorial representation of the original garden. If they looked real and vivid in the mind, they all would be perfect. The "real" (*zhen*) here does not necessarily mean exactly how much the garden replica physically resembled the original garden but rather how much the garden replica caught the true intention of the original garden, which was most truthfully expressed by a painting masterpiece.

Thus, through reviewing the various pictorial representations of the Lion Grove in Suzhou, Qianlong attempted to verify the true designer of this garden. In 1786, the same year that the twenty copperplates of the Western Multistoried Buildings garden were engraved, he wrote a preface for a grouping of poems:

> I originally thought the Lion Grove was created by Ni, / But who knows that the monk Weize had taken the title of the designer. / It was appreciated that he did not forget his Buddhist master, / Whom he put in his heart. Notes: The Lion Grove in Suzhou was always said to be Zan Ni's design. During my visit to the south in the *jiachen* year (1784), I obtained twelve paintings of the Lion Grove by Ben Xu. Guangxiao Yao's colophon for those paintings says that Xu painted for Ruhai, the third-generation disciple of the monk Weize. I thus know that the hearsay that the Lion Grove was Ni's design is wrong. Furthermore, Shen Lu's colophon for those paintings says that Weize obtained his Buddhist principles from the master Ben-zhong-feng who lived then by the Lion Crag on Tianmu Mountain. It is most likely that by building the garden Weize intended to recognize where he received Buddhism without forgetting his master." ("Ti Shizilin" 84)

Further, during the Ming dynasty, two painters created paintings of the Lion Grove in Suzhou: the first one was Ben Xu and the second, Qiong Du. In the colophon of Du's painting, the painter wrote: "Youwen Xu [namely, Ben Xu] once created the paintings of the Lion Grove for the Buddhist master Ruhai. There are twelve sections each of which was paired with a poem" (Guoli, figures 19, 30). In his preface, Qianlong expressed his high appreciation of the moving friendship between the monk Weize and his master Ben-zhong-feng. By emphasizing this historic friendship that evolved around the Lion Grove garden, Qianlong tried to express the memory of his father and grandfather "whom he put in his heart." Through expanding the garden from his father and replicating the gardens in Jiangnan, he engaged in his memories while seeking the truth of the world.

Unity of ultimate sincerity

The emperor's intentions concerning Round Brightness can be further related to the cosmological orders of the typical symbolism of cosmos in Chinese imperial gardens. The connection between heaven, the round form, and brightness was first mentioned in the ancient book of rituals, *Da Dai li* (*The Ritual Texts of the Elder Dai*), which says: "The Dao of heaven is called round; the Dao of earth, square. The square is called remote; and the round, bright" (*Pei wen*). This ancient theory established the direct symbolic connection among Dao, roundness, and brightness. In the Daoist book, *Huainanzi* (*Masters of Huainan*), the round form of the human head was compared to the round form of heaven. Through the similarity of forms, the author attempted to establish the essential connection between the human being and the natural world. He wrote: "Tranquility and indifference is the house of spiritual brightness; void and nothingness is the dwelling of Dao. . . . The head is round and like the heaven; the feet are square and like the earth. . . . The gallbladder is clouds; the lung is *qi*; the liver is wind; the kidney is rain; the spleen is thunder; so that the human body corresponds to heaven and earth, and the heart is the master [of the world]. Therefore, the ear and eye are the sun and moon; the blood and *qi* are wind and rain" (K. Xu 367). In both quotes, "round brightness" is clearly related to heaven, the Dao of the world. The connection between tranquility and brightness and between the round head and the round heaven is established. Because the heart was traditionally seen as the origin of thinking, a tranquil heart was therefore related with the round brightness, which embodied the cosmos. Yongzheng discussed the ancient philosophical thought that the heart was the master of the world in his essay, "The Discourse on Inherent Character and Reason" ("Xing li lun" 228-29):

> The relationship of inherent character (*xing*) to reason (*li*) is like, at the high level, nonpolarity (*wuji*) to ultimate polarity (*taiji*), or at the low level, *yin* to *yang* within ultimate polarity. Inherent character is established in accordance with reason; reason emerges from inherent character. . . . Reason means the appropriateness of things. All things in the world have their own appropriateness in nature, which is not imposed by human beings. [Note: Nature has its reason in which all things appear appropriate. Human existence depends upon reason for its internal appropriateness.] The inherent Dao and the discourse on merciful character cannot be reached without ultimate sincerity (*zhicheng*). So-called sincerity means that one individual is always sincere without being fake. If there are two parts in the individual, then that sincerity can only be fake. The Dao of sincerity means, for the relationship between an emperor and officials and between father and son, loyalty and filiality. In other words, all things have their own appropriateness. Is there any other loyalty and filiality besides that of the emperor-of-

ficial and father-son? For the same reason, all things and all reasons can be brightened within the same unity and become autonomously clear. [Note: Yongzheng described the situation in which all things had their own appropriateness as ultimate sincerity, which defined the sincere relationship between the emperor and officials and between father and son. These two relationships were emphasized in his record of the Yuanming Yuan in which he stated how he followed the lead of his father's openness to worthy and virtuous people just as nature disclosed itself to the fullest.] Can the human heart be the heart of Dao? It is worse that somebody adamantly takes his arbitrary view as the heart of Dao. By selecting and giving away, one by one, from thousands of clues (about the relationship between the heart of Dao and the human heart), he takes mediocre and hackneyed expressions as rules. Following such a way of seeking boughs and leaves without seeing trunks is as difficult as counting sand grains in the sea to reach upwards to the Dao of unified *yin*, *yang*, and ultimate polarity, namely the origin of inherent character and reason. [Note: Yongzheng differentiated the heart of Dao from the human heart. The inherent character and reason of the human being can only be established through the heart of Dao, which presents as the cosmic unity. The human heart tends to produce arbitrary views and can never reach the cosmic level by itself. This is why in his poems of the Yuanming Yuan, Yongzheng always emphasized the connection between the heart and the moon in order to "stroll in the Daoist paradise."] Chengzi wrote that once a thorough understanding was obtained, the outer and inner and the essence and appearance of things were easily reached and the entirety of the heart was completely enlightened. His discourse really reaches the inherent character of ultimate polarity, *yin* and *yang,* and the reason of deliberating things to gain knowledge. Later scholars should understand why ancient sages left those words, eliminated their own lusts, always maintained the heavenly reason and followed it devoutly. [Note: Chengzi, namely, Hao Cheng, and his younger brother, Yi Cheng, were two leading neo-Confucian philosophers in the Northern Song dynasty. Neo-Confucianism advanced the idea that the thorough understanding, the bright unity, could only be reached through deliberating things to gain knowledge. The idea of "deliberating things to gain knowledge" (*ge wu zhi zhi*) was developed from Confucius's classic *Da xue* (*The Great Learning*) and analyzed by the neo-Confucian philosopher Xi Zhu in his book *Sishu jizhu* (*Collected Commentaries on the Four Books*). It has been established that there is a relationship between neo-Confucian pedagogy and the neo-Confucianist concept of landscape (X. Wu 160-64).]

Following the idea of deliberating things to gain knowledge, Yongzheng emphasized the importance of engaging in the physical world with heavenly reason in order to obtain metaphysical brightness. The idea of engaging the physical world while maintaining the cosmic connection was best manifested by his life in the Yuanming Yuan. There are many philosophical concepts in Yongzheng's discourse. How he defined each concept is less important than his seriousness about understanding what a human being was. He found that all things in the world had their own appropriateness in nature and that all things could be "brightened within the same unity" and become autonomously clear; a human being living in such a bright unity could reach ultimate sincerity where the entirety of the heart was completely enlightened. Within the same bright unity, the human heart identified with the heart of Dao and it was unnecessary to differentiate them. Yongzheng did not isolate the inside of a human being in order to understand the human being; rather, he looked for that bright unity that could unify the human being with the cosmos.

According to ancient thought, the cosmos could be integrated with craftsmanship. In the earliest Chinese treatise on crafts, "Kao gong ji" ("Records of Examination of Craftsman"), of the late Warring States period, any masterwork of human beings was considered to be connected with divinity: "works made by craftsmen are all committed by saints. Wrought metal to make a knife; congeal clay to make a household utensil; make a cart to travel on land; make a boat to travel on water. All these utensils are committed by saints. Heaven has its timeliness; earth has its *qi*; each material has its beauty; and craftsmanship has its ingeniousness. When these four aspects come together, a masterwork can be produced" (Qian 387-88). Work by human beings was the integration of heaven, earth, material, and craftsmanship. The traditional Chinese term for "cosmos" literally meant "heaven and earth" (*tiandi*). China was traditionally called Nine States, founded by emperor Ku (Q. Wang 458) and the term "nine states" appeared in the ancient book *Shangshu* (*The Book of History*). During the Zhou dynasty the world was divided into nine states according to constellations in the sky (M. Yu 1: 1) and the concept of "nation" (*guo*) was not differentiated from the concept of "world" (*tianxia*). In Yongzheng's Yuanming Yuan, the front portion was composed of nine islands surrounding a circular lake, which echoed the full moon that enveloped the peaceful world into its universal brightness. The layout of nine islands surrounding a circular lake was intended to symbolize that the full moon unified the whole nation. The emperor sat in the hall of Peace for All China at the third scene, the southernmost island, and looked north across the Back Lake, viewing the other eight islands with the clear and tranquil water surface as the central round brightness.

The relationship between the round form of the full moon and perfect brightness had been established as a Chinese mindset long before the Qing dynasty. We find in a poem of the Song dynasty, "The Moon at the Mid-Autumn Day," that the moon is so full that everyone cherishes this perfect brightness (Q. Han "Zhongqiu" 107). The "perfect brightness" suggests the brightness from the circle of the full moon and in this respect, the Round Brightness as the meaning of perfect brightness can be understood. Yongzheng once poetized the moonlight of a mid-autumn day as one vast sheet of enclosing light in which all things looked the same ("Zhongqiu" 85). The existence of Round Brightness was related not only to the full moon but also to the desire for perfect brightness in the garden. In order for buildings to receive the perfect brightness, they had to face towards the south for full sunlight to emanate throughout the building. The orientation to the south was also connected to the bright mindset and management needed by the emperor. In his *Lunyu* (*Analects*), Confucius stated, "The master of the nation should face south during his administration" (B. Liu 111). This means that the emperor should physically face southward in order to receive brightness in his mind for the management of the country. This symbolism was clearly embodied by the audience hall at the first one of the Forty Scenes, Uprightness and Brightness. One way a person perceived the diffusing brightness was to stand high while looking into the distance. It was already observed in the Western Han dynasty that standing high made a person desire to look into the distance; being close to the deep distance made the person desire to peer at it. It was the place itself that made a person act like this (K. Xu 971). By standing high, the spectator borrowed the view of distant landscapes into the garden. Prior to the Qing emperors, scholars in the Ming dynasty had written extensively about the unique view of West Mountain. In the poem "Watch West Mountain from Town of Shallow Lakes," a poet proclaimed the West Mountain as "my old friend" (Jiamo Wang 322). The Ming dynasty garden, Dipper Garden, located in the northwestern suburb and well known for its water views, was owned by the painter Wanzhong Mi. In a poem on the garden, Mi's friend described that standing in the high tower under the night of bright moon, he smiled at West Mountain as if communicating with a friend (Ye 325). The Ming poems demonstrate how the view of West Mountain was a characteristic that was frequently borrowed in the gardens in the northwestern suburb. The borrowed view of West Mountain expanded the spectator's bosom.

The borrowed view of West Mountain was maintained through multiple high places in the Yuanming Yuan. In the preface of a poem of the fifteenth scene, High Mountain and Long River, Qianlong wrote that in the southwestern corner of the garden, the topography was flat. Therefore, a multistoried building with several bays was built. Whenever he looked over from the building, the distant West Mountain looked like a woman's hairdo and the near suburbs appeared as interwoven embroideries. In the poem, he confirmed that with the multistoried building resting upon the flat land, "the ten thousand scenes of lakes and mountains become complete" ("Shan'gao" 35). The high place in the garden brought about a complete view of the world while the borrowed view of West Mountain extended the emperor's vision of Round Brightness to the cosmic scale. It was at the same high place that fireworks were periodically viewed as they brightened the whole garden at night. From the thirteenth to nineteenth days of the first moon, there would be splendid firework displays at this scene. The emperor would often invite many guests to view the fireworks, including tribal leaders and foreign ambassadors; thus, the artificial brightness from fireworks and lanterns became a means for the emperor to unify the loyalty of foreign tribes (M. Yu 3: 1349). In describing the fireworks in the garden, the Jesuit painter Attiret praised them in his letter: "I have never seen anything of that kind, either in France or Italy" ("Letter" 21). The garden brightened through magic fireworks held, in the emperor's mind, the political symbolism of unifying the world.

Height was often symbolized through an artificial hill of rocks in Chinese gardens. An example of an artificial hill, which "lured people to stroll spiritually," in the Yuanming Yuan was the Longevity Hill, located behind the audience hall at the first scene, Uprightness and Brightness. In his poem of this scene, Qianlong wrote that the spacious caves in the rocks often made his heart open, and the cool environment composed by the rocks blocked the dusty world ("Zhengda" 7). The openings of the rocks resonated with the open heart; the cool field defined by the rocks implied the remote spiritual world. The symbolism of the rockery art had been well established by the Song dynasty. In the Ming pattern book of garden rocks, *Suyuan shipu* (*Pattern Manual of Rocks in the Plain Garden*), we find descriptions noting that the wonderfulness of a rock lies in its elegance and transparency and that a rock has its own form and spirit. If a rock is merely a block of mass without any singularity, although it is very old, it is not worth recording. A drawing can only record the form of a rock, but when the rock is in its wonderful place there are varied postures of dancing and changing, which lure people to stroll spiritually there and let the fascinated viewers thus obtain the wonderfulness of their own accord (Lin 42).

The cosmological dimension of height was also embodied in the topography of the garden. A Buddhist temple, containing the portraits of previous emperors, was built on the northwestern hill in the garden. The purpose of placing the temple at the highest point within the garden was to provide protection by ancestors that would permeate throughout the entire garden along the course of *qi*. In the preamble of his poem on the seventeenth scene, Great Kindness and Eternal Blessing, Qianlong explained that because the northwestern corner of the garden was the brightest and highest place, he built the temple there for worshiping his grandfather and father in order to extend their endless solicitude ("Hongci" 39). In Qianlong's mind, the brightness of the ancestors' blessing flowed down in accordance with the topography. The combination of the ancestors' portraits and the Buddhist temple in the garden manifested the fusion of Confucianism and Buddhism, which was a typical phenomenon in Chinese religions. Like the gesture of an extensive bosom, the border of the garden was identified with the West Mountain range and the blessing of the ancestors was spread over the entire garden. In addition to the West Mountain, another environmental characteristic of the northwestern suburb was its rich water sources, which constituted a significant part of the Yuanming Yuan. According to *Mengzi*, the symbolism of water in Chinese cosmology can be traced to certain religious thought on nature, and Confucius regarded it as important. The origin of the world was like a spring (H. Liu 271). Guanzi, a political philosopher during the early Spring and Autumn period, proposed that a virtuous man, such as an emperor, must have knowledge about the natural movement of water in order to cultivate his virtues. He described water as the blood of earth flowing through the veins. A virtuous man can cultivate his virtues by roaming in the suburb to stimulate the *qi* of earth (H. Xie 529, 556). The brilliance created by reflecting water was considered a visual demonstration of the omnipresent, formless Dao. The *Huainanzi* describes water as the grandson of the origin of things. Water can be followed but cannot be destroyed. Among images, then, water is most respectable, and what is clear and tranquil is the ultimate virtue (K. Xu 30). The northwestern suburb was famous for its rich water sources as far back as the previous Ming dynasty. According to a book on the landscapes of Beijing, the northwestern suburb was where the Town of Shallow Lakes was located. The "shallow lakes" meant the gathering of water. Ten miles northwest of the Sorghum Bridge, springs gushed out onto the level ground. They gurgled in all directions and watered grass and trees. In that area, there was an extensive water surface available for paddling. It was the location of a garden belonging to a Ming imperial relative, Wei Li. A high tower rose up in the garden, and from the deck of the tower one could see, at eye level, the Fragrant Hill and Jade Spring Hill in the distance. East of Li's garden was the Dipper Garden of Wanzhong Mi. Although this garden was small, it looked deep and remote because of the full presence of water (Liu and Yu 320). Both the Ming gardens were well known for water. The depth of view was intentionally enhanced so that the mind could transcend the physical scale of the garden and move into the unknown world.

The cosmological association with water was not only related to the regional environment surrounding the Yuanming Yuan but also to the topography within the garden. In 1724, a local government official in Shandong Province was invited by Yongzheng to survey the site for appropriate *fengshui* features. According to this *fengshui* master, the northwest portion of the garden was the head of the dragon, and the water flowed towards the tail in the southeast corner of the garden, thus simulating the topographical characteristics of the country where the major mountains and rivers began in the northwest, and undulated and meandered toward the southeast ("Shandong" 6-7). The application of *fengshui* for site selection and physical planning is a tradition in Chinese imperial gardens, such as Huizong's Genyue of the Northern Song dynasty and Yongle's Jing Hill of the Ming dynasty. The role of *fengshui* was crucial in planning an imperial garden, yet it was not elevated to the same level of importance in garden theories of literati gardens. This is attested to in ancient garden records and the first garden treatise, *Yuan ye*. As early as the time of the Southern Dynasties, the landscape poet Lingyun Xie proposed not to use the *fengshui* system of traditional astrology for site selection, but, rather, to count on the wonderful and unique views of the landscape itself ("Shanju" 13). Thus, to match the *fengshui* concept, the water source of the Yuanming Yuan was redirected. The water in the southwest corner of the garden was first led to the northwest corner to form a new water entrance, so that all water could flow eastward into the Fortunate Sea and flow out of the garden from the southeast corner. Following this watercourse, *qi* was supposed to diffuse throughout the garden: because the water surface reflects light, the diffusion of *qi* can be understood as the diffusion of brightness.

A water entrance was traditionally called a "water mouth" (*shuikou*). According to one landscape-painting theory, the water mouth is the most difficult to paint (Huang, "Lun" 165), because it is the most sacred and secret part of a natural watercourse. It is also a key concept for the understanding of watercourses in gardens and human dwellings. When Qianlong added the Garden of Eternal Spring to the Yuanming Yuan, the original water exit of Yongzheng's Yuanming Yuan was relocated to the northeast corner and became the water entrance of the Garden of Eternal Spring. The entrance of the Western Multistoried Buildings garden was close to the water entrance of the Garden of Eternal Spring, and from here the *qi* of perfect brightness flowed into both gardens. Often, small watercourses would finally flow into a large body of water, such as a lake, which provided the illusion of a sea in the garden. The largest lake in the Yuanming Yuan was Fortunate Sea (Fu Hai). The Chinese term for "lake" in this case was "sea," which hinted at the legendary story of the fairylands in the East Sea. Qing emperors devoted much of their poetry to this huge lake that appeared like a round mirror. On the fifth day of the fifth moon, at the Duanwu Festival, the emperor and the imperial family would watch a show of dragon boats from the western bank of the lake. Only Qianlong's mother had the privilege of watching the show from the central island, which was known as Immortal Abode on Fairy Penglai Island, located at the thirty-second scene. The name of the island alluded to the legendary fairylands. In the poem, "Chant on Antiquity on the Penglai Island," Yongzheng wrote: "The ancient kings wasted energy to build Towers for Watching the Fairyland, / In the Qin and Han dynasties, nobody ever reached the tenth state. / Outside the dusty world I chant and sing at the evening red trees, / Within the pot I sit and recline under the autumn blue sky. / Temples and halls wait for the accompaniment of mists and rosy clouds, / Springs and stones look at the wandering cranes and deer. / The water could not be crossed by three thousand persons in the past, / The present imperial family has its boat for crossing it" ("Penglaizhou" 173). China was traditionally called Nine States and the "tenth state" was known as the fairyland. The "pot," originating from a Daoist legend, indicated the garden enclosure where the emperor would "sit and recline under the autumn blue sky" and Yongzheng wrote that his garden was like the legendary Daoist pot that contained all the beautiful landscapes. As in all the previous imperial gardens, the legendary story of the fairyland in the East Sea was frequently introduced to establish the cosmological dimension of the huge body of water.

The last one of the Forty Scenes was named Deep and Remote Dwelling, which was related to the Daoist tradition of seeking remoteness in the presence of nature. According to Daoist thoughts, Dao is connected to remote darkness, which the *Huainanzi* describes vividly: "The physical soul asks the spiritual soul: What kind of body does Dao have? The latter answers: Its body is nothingness. The former asks: Does the nothingness have a physical form? The latter answers: None. How do you know? I have encountered it. I looked at it and it had no form; I listened to it and it had no sound. This is the so-called remote darkness. The remote darkness can demonstrate Dao but is not Dao itself. The physical soul then responds: Listening to you, I begin to understand that Dao is to look inward and reflect on myself" (K. Xu 939). In the preface of the poem on the fortieth scene, Qianlong said that the winding path meandered like an ant nest and that the scene should be deep and remote ("Dongtian" 85). The poetical journey along the meandering pathway of the Forty Scenes, which ended at the last scene, the deep and remote dwelling, can be understood as a journey of searching for Dao and reflecting on oneself. The Dao of Round Brightness lies in the remote depth of the mind towards which the diffusing brightness moves. The paradoxical relationship of diffusing brightness through seeking remoteness draws attention to the Jesuit-designed Western Multistoried Buildings garden, which was the remotest corner of the Yuanming Yuan complex. One can question if the issue of *fengshui* existed in this exotic portion. Although the imperial archives regarding the *fengshui* arrangement of the Western garden have not been located, we can guess that the emperor and the Chinese planners exhibited great apprehension about the influence of this exotic garden on the *fengshui* of the Yuanming Yuan. One can look at other examples where Jesuits in other cities built their Baroque style of architecture within the *fengshui* of local customs. Residents of Hangzhou, where the famous West Lake was located, were upset over the height of the façade of a Jesuit church because they thought the vertical height projecting in straight lines was inauspicious as it unbalanced the harmony of nature by plunging into the earth's flesh. As a compromise, the church had a courtyard in front to allow the *qi* to penetrate the building (Mungello 38). Even after missionaries were allowed to buy properties freely in China, in an agreement signed with a French minister in 1865, the Chinese authorities added that the local officials should, previous to any acquisition by the church, decide if it were acceptable to the neighborhood and if it would not take away the *fengshui* (Devine 155). According to the *fengshui* survey by Yongzheng, multistoried pavilions should be built in the northeast corner to correspond to Saturn ("Shandong" 6-7). It was in the northeastern corner of the Yuanming Yuan complex where the Western garden was built. Hidden near this corner with a separate watercourse, the shadows of the Western multistoried buildings were cautiously considered so as not to affect the diffusion of brightness yet correspond with the *fengshui* arrangement.

When Qianlong expanded the garden, he developed the idea that the emperor's garden should include the views of other beautiful gardens in the country. This idea was best expressed by his creation of the Garden of Eternal Spring, which contained many replicas of the literati gardens in Jiangnan. The form of the new garden differed from the original one, but the subject remained unchanged and the re-creation was in accordance with the local context (H. Yang 192-93). The same phenomenon seldom happened in literati gardens, where an owner always strived to establish his own ideal subject while avoiding duplication. One of the Jiangnan gardens replicated by Qianlong was the Garden of Little Heaven in Hangzhou. Qianlong wrote in the "Record of the Garden of Little Heaven within the Garden of Eternal Spring" ("Yuzhi Xiaoyoutian" 1384):

> With the Temple of Pure Benevolence to the left, facing the West Lake and comprising pretty landscapes, the best garden near the Mountain of Southern Screen is no other than the Wang family's Garden of Little Heaven, which was named in the year of *xinwei* (1751) when I toured in the south. In the last year *dingchou* (1757), I revisited the garden, lingering and praising its beauty in poems" [Note: The Temple of Pure Benevolence was a famous scenic spot near West Lake, southwest of Hangzhou. The name Little Heaven expressed the desire of being close to the cosmos through the existence of the garden. The garden was physically small, but its symbolic existence was as extensive as the universe.] Contemplating on how a painter could possibly include a vast landscape into a small painting, I fortunately found a site with woods and a building east of the Chapel of Longing for

Eternity. The room is ten *hu* big and the window half the size. The uncultivated field outside the window is ten *hu* too. I ordered craftsmen to overlay rocks to make artificial peaks, which, to my surprise, looked like the Peak of Illuminating Wisdom. The models of buildings were made of tin, but still looked like the Thatched House in Gully. Water is agitated to make a waterfall. With sweet sounds and cool feeling, the setting is not different from the grotto of secluded residence that I heard about. However, the saplings of the Yellow Mountain pine are only one foot high, but suddenly give a sense that they are reaching for the clouds. Exquisite and twined, high and low, they stick out in a disorderly fashion among stalagmites and trailing plants on cliffs. Coming back to the scene of the Music Terrace with its slim and elegant old trees and green cliffs, there is no possible comparison. [Note: The Chapel of Longing for Eternity was located in the southwestern corner of the Garden of Eternal Spring. The Garden of Little Heaven belonged to the eastern part of the Chapel of Longing for Eternity. In ancient times, the *hu* was a hand-board held by an official in the reception by the emperor. People used such phrases as "ten *hu*" or "five *hu*" to describe the size of a very small place. The Peak of Illuminating Wisdom, the Thatched House in Gully, the "grotto of secluded residence" and the Music Terrace all were well known scenic spots related to the Garden of Little Heaven in Hangzhou.] How can I say they are different? I thus realize that scenes in the world are infinite and that the human heart is also infinite. Landscapes, however, display variety, but to the human heart they can be understood in the same way. These galleries, pavilions, stone steps, pools, woods and springs, cliffs and valleys (in my Garden of Little Heaven) cannot be climbed with my hands and tramped upon with my feet, but when experienced by eyesight the Dao appears immediately and meets the heart's understanding, cannot all of them become vividly accessible? New fledging chickens and dogs can identify their respective homes. This would be an extravagance for us human beings. [Note: The phrase, "meet the heart's understanding" alludes to the poetical phrase. "The place of meeting the heart should not be far away," which was said by emperor Jianwen of East Jin when he strolled in his Hualin Garden in the capital Jiankang (Yiqing Liu 31). This phrase was frequently cited in history to express appreciation of the natural view in a garden.] The scenes in Deyu Li's garden of Mountain Hamlet with Open Springs resemble the Gorges of Ba Kingdom and the Dongting Lake. But one needs not attempt to emulate his ways and means for achieving infinite distance, rich forms, and utmost prettiness. Only his intention can be imitated. However, my intention in my Garden of Little Heaven is not to draw near the remote beautiful landscapes, but rather to remind myself of the administration of officials and the compliance of the common people in Jiangnan. I therefore write this record. [Note: The Mountain Hamlet with Open Springs was in the suburb of Luoyang of the Tang dynasty. The original term, "open springs" literally means "flat springs," which indicate springs welling up on a flat and open field. This feature was similar to the springs of the Village of Ten Thousand Springs where the Qing imperial gardens were nearby. Compared with Li's garden that replicated the famous landscapes in China, Qianlong's Garden of Little Heaven was quite small. For Qianlong, the small size of the garden was not a problem, because "scenes in the world are infinite and the human heart is also infinite." If a scene in the garden were met with the heart, the truth, Dao, would emerge.]

Qianlong's Garden of Little Heaven was actually a small-scale garden model, which was viewed through a house window. The symbolic window view evolved from his contemplation on "how a painter could possibly include a vast landscape into a small painting." This micro-macro relationship was further expressed in another of his poems on the Garden of Little Heaven: "Rapids throw out a snow-like waterfall, / Overlaid peaks tower aloft out of cloud roots. / There is no dusty place in the pot, / But there is a garden of little heaven in the window" ("Lin wu" 69). Indicating the window-framed view of the garden, a "dusty place in the pot" continued the Daoist idea that the whole world, including mountains and rivers, could be contained in a magic pot. Both the pot and the window provided a clear border, which framed the magic view of the garden scene and enabled the micro-scale view to symbolize the macro-scale cosmos. Such a framed view is physically small and finite but symbolically big and infinite, where Dao meets the heart's understanding.

Light of a virtuous man

In both their records of the Yuanming Yuan, Yongzheng and Qianlong expressed respect for their ancestors, and this tradition was continued by later generations. In the poem "State My Will in the Garden Residence," emperor Jiaqing, the fifteenth son of Qianlong, expressed his feelings when he first moved into the garden after mourning his deceased father: "Live in mourning for twenty-seven months, / The ceremony is over and I face the garden. / Recollect my father's remote words and face, / I look blank at the extant buildings. / To govern the country I need to first administrate diligently, / To console the people I must put virtuous men in important positions. / Reside in the garden and follow the old principles, / My heart is not in forests and springs" ("Yuanju"). He first expressed how sad he was when he faced the garden where his father had resided for such a long time. He decided that residing in the same garden and following the old principles would enable him to maintain a good administration and perform his duties well. It is important to note that Jiaqing, by living in the same garden, was attempting to maintain the same virtues as his ancestors in his administration. The relationship between living in a garden and enhancing virtues can be traced back to Confucius's famous sentence: "An intelligent man delights in water; a humane man delights in mountains" (Liu and Qiao 51). The Confucian analogy between nature and virtue was theorized as the concept of comparative virtue (*bide*). In the *Lunyu*, Confucius said: "Water is the comparative virtue of a virtuous man" (B. Liu, 127). In the *Shuijing zhu* (*Commentary on the Waterways Classic*) of the Northern Dynasties period, the author wrote that the bosom of bamboo and cypress competed with the divine heart for remoteness; the nature of humane intelligence competed with mountains and rivers for depth (Daoyuan Li 133). The idea that the remoteness of the human heart was linked to the depth of the view of natural landscapes was well developed through Chinese gardens, where brightening the view was meant to reveal the heart. During the Han dynasty, the connection between moonlight and human virtues was already established. A rhapsody,

"Yue fu," asserts that the moon that comes out in such brightness is the light of a virtuous man (S. Gong 40).

Yongzheng wrote many poems about the moonlight in his garden. In the poem "Face toward the Moon at the Mountain Cottage of Circling Prettiness," at the thirty-seventh scene of the Forty Scenes, he wrote: "The summer heat has withdrawn and the garden is fresh, / In the new autumn the scenes look pretty. . . . / Lay down the brush and comment on the distant mountain colors, / Grip a wine cup and face toward the moon brilliance" ("Huanxiu" 166). The "fresh garden," "pretty scenes," and "mountain colors" revealed that his sight was gradually brightened and finally his heart was opened to the moonlight. The gesture of inviting the moon for appreciating wine alluded to the Tang poet Bai Li's poem "Drink Solitarily under the Moonlight." While Li paid attention to moon shadows with a pessimistic sentiment, Yongzheng expressed his joy with the moon brightness. In the poem "Leisurely Stroll under the Moon," he wrote: "Leisurely walk along the meandering shore, / The western peaks look deep green at the sunset. / Move, rest and look at the woods top, / In the clouds the shadow of the moon shifts" ("Yuexia" 10). The movement of his body through the garden synchronized with that of the moon. Accompanied by moon shadows, the joy of Yongzheng's leisurely stroll is very different from the pathos of Bai Li's solitary drinking. Li focused on the relationship between the moon, moon shadows, and "myself," but Yongzheng perceived the whole world brightened by the moon. For Yongzheng, the leisurely situation in the garden was his conscious way to approach Dao of the world. In the poem "Beside the Pool," he wrote: "The colors of the mountain come from the west, / The sounds of the spring flow daily to the east. / Quietly observe why things in nature are so leisurely, / In a detached situation I get a brilliant enlightenment" ("Chi bian" 65). The season of spring started from West Mountain, passed through the garden, and moved towards the east, where the Forbidden City was located. The enlightenment that he received was the leisurely situation in which all things had their appropriate positions. The "detached situation" further defined such a leisurely situation in the garden where he could "observe quietly" with his mind enlightened.

Yongzheng's leisure in the garden was not a demonstration of his avoiding administrative duties. To the contrary, it enhanced the efficiency of his work. In the poem, "Write at the Place Where My Heart Is Met," he stated that in the garden his spirit met the magic delight, and his heart became diligent for processing daily thousands of affairs ("Huixinchu" 146). The desire to meet his heart already meant that the heart could not be met easily. As advanced by emperor Jianwen of Eastern Jin, the place where the heart was met was the garden. When the spirit was delighted in the scenes, the mind became diligent. Yongzheng usually processed administrative affairs at the Hall of Diligent Administration, a part of the second scene of the Forty Scenes. In the poem, "Observe the New Moon at the Hall of Diligent Administration in the Summer," he stated that the half circle of the crescent reminded him to be vigilant against a satisfied heart ("Xiari" 149). He was using the circle of the full moon and the half circle of the crescent as metaphors. He cautioned himself that he should be a modest man like the crescent. In a different situation, the circle of the full moon was related to the eternity of the cosmos. In the poem, "Face toward the Moon after a Rain," he chanted, "In the dark-blue sky a circle is undulating, / It is so bright that spreads ten thousand miles of clear brilliance. / The night clock echoes among the soundless courts and buildings, / Silently, I attempt to understand the ceaselessly circulating principle" ("Yuhou duiyue" 178). "Ceaselessly circulating" hints at the circle of the full moon and indicates the eternity of the cosmos. Under either the full moon or the crescent, the moonlight evoked his contemplation of the world and his sharp observation of duties. The relationship between Yongzheng's leisure in the garden and his enhancement of virtue was closely related to his religious contemplation. He greatly enhanced the status of Confucianism during the Qing dynasty while writing many articles to interpret Confucian classics. After taking the throne, he granted Confucius's fifth-generation descendent the title of King. He also believed in and studied Buddhism and Daoism. Before taking the throne, he had been in close contact with monks. He named himself the Buddhist Resident of Round Brightness (Yuanming Jushi) and took part in the debates among various Buddhist schools.

To understand Yongzheng's garden concept of "leisure" (*xian*) in relation to his religious thoughts, it is necessary to refer to his preface to his poem anthology, *Yongdi shiji* (*Poem Anthology of the Palace of Prince Yong*) ("Yongdi" 235-36):

> In the past, when I lived in the Palace of Prince Yong, I regarded myself as the greatest leisure man in the world. But so-called "leisure" is not a repetition of the ancient story of Ji Mountain and Ying River or the kind of flaunting of wills and ambitions in bamboo groves. I was born in the prosperous age of this country when the three rebels were suppressed and peace was everywhere. I was affected by my respected father Kangxi and spoiled myself under his knees. I was granted a prince's palace. After closing the door and resting in the palace, I have nothing to do. The territory of my residence is so leisurely. Furthermore, my personality does not like ostentation. I am not keen on wealth and nobility, nor do I worry about being poor and lowly. I only expect to spend time and thus feel joyful anywhere. Where my emotion projects itself is so leisurely. Although I have lightheartedly strolled and been a leisurely man for over forty years, if there had not been my father's great kindness of teaching me, I would have no achievements. [Note: The famous hermits You Xu and Fu Chao in the time of the legendary emperor Yao were said to live at the foot of Ji Mountain. It was said Xu once lived by Ying River. The later generations used the Ji Mountain and Ying River to signify hermitage. The "bamboo groves" signify the seven virtuous men in bamboo groves (Zhulin Qixian) of Three Kingdoms. They liked to speak on mystical things in bamboo groves. It is interesting to note that Yongzheng repeatedly emphasized that he was a leisurely man and enjoyed the joy of being leisurely. He linked his leisure with his filiality to his father and indifference to ostentation.] I am often not good at poems. When I accompanied my father to the northern territories or the Jiangnan, my father sometimes ordered me to write a poem under the title given by him. I reluctantly responded in order to make him happy. In the beginning, I did not pay attention to the rhythm of words and sentences. As for the occasions when I attended a banquet or climbed high to look into the distance, or when

things evoked my emotion, I would write poems based on my feelings or record events with poems so as to mold my temperament. How could it be said that my poems intended to compete with the literati's? With the passing of time, poems get larger and larger. [Note: Yongzheng expressed here the close relationship between his emotions and his poetry.] In the winter of the *renyin* year (1722), I inherited my father's will and took on the administration of the country. Reviewing documents one after another, my work is busy and onerous. Eating late and dressing up early, I care about everything to do with the country. Getting up early and sleeping late, I dare not seek a rest. The past lightheartedly strolling has changed into the present vigilance, diligence, and caring. The poetizing on morning flowers and evening moon has changed into the present contemplation in bleak winters and summer rains. [Note: Yongzheng expressed in this passage that he missed "lightheartedly strolling" in the garden when he was young. He did not oppose the leisurely situation in the garden to his busy administration, rather, he attempted to express that his current diligence evolved from his long-time self-cultivation of leisure.] Reviewing these old poems, how much I feel lost. Recalling past leisurely emotion within a leisurely territory, it seems too far away from me now. I write this preface for my *Poem Anthology of the Palace of Prince Yong* to express my intentions. [Note: The search for leisurely emotion within a leisurely territory continued throughout Yongzheng's life, especially through the residence in the Yuanming Yuan.]

Yongzheng expressed a central idea of his life philosophy—leisure (*xian*). He regarded himself as the "greatest leisurely man in the world" and connected his leisurely emotion with his modest personality and his indifference to both "wealth and nobility" and being "poor and lowly." Importantly, such a leisurely situation was not nihilism but rather a kind of emotion evoked by beautiful garden scenes. His poems, mostly on morning flowers and the evening moon over the garden, were completely based on his leisurely feelings and were not written to compete with literati. He pointed out the close relationship between his leisurely emotion and being within a leisurely territory and established the connection between this leisurely situation and the virtues of integrity and sincerity. The Palace of Prince Yong (today's Lama temple Yonghe Gong) was his residence within the city prior to residing in the Yuanming Yuan. The palace had its garden. His life experience in this palace compound was described in his preface of the prose anthology, *Yue xin ji* (*Anthology of Delightful Heart*) ("Yuexin ji" 258-59):

> My life always takes simple elegance as its principle. My personality is quiet, self-appreciative, satisfied with my own fate, peaceful in accordance with circumstances. When I lived in the Palace of Prince Yong, although it was located in a bustling area, in my sleep I felt tranquil, remote, at leisure, and open and seemed to transcend the dusty world. However, I did not let my body and heart idle, and browsed many anthologies edited by others in my spare time of studying classics and historical books. If I found those wonderful articles and sentences that can provoke my interest, expel my leisure or express my desire of transcending, I collected them and simply compiled them. These texts, as the bright moon hangs in the clear sky, or as cool wind expels summer heat, or as seasonal flowers brighten eyes, or

as birds sing in woods, or as springs flow melodiously in deep mountains, or as clocks strike at midnight, can eliminate stagnancy and wash away uneasiness and noises. They make me feel open-minded, spiritually delightful, and extremely free and comfortable. I therefore selected some of these texts at will and put them on my table for casual reading. [Note: Yongzheng described his life principle as seeking "simple elegance" and differentiated his leisurely attitude from idling. It is interesting to note that he used a series of metaphors from garden scenes to express the enlightenment that he obtained from his readings, for example, the phrase "the bright moon hangs in the clear sky" indicated the enlightenment of his mind.]

Since being in charge of national affairs, I have been working day and night and cannot help missing past delightful things, which are not available anymore. However, the control of tranquility is not influenced by the motion of things; and the extreme of simple elegance cannot be changed with the change of environments. This is certain and I believe it. I therefore compile what I collect into a book and name it *Anthology of Delightful Heart*. The heart is the human being's divinity. It is the origin of all transformations and things. If the heart is burdened, it will feel bitter; if bothered, uneasy; if hidden, opaque; and if suffocated, stagnant. Hence, ancient sages teach us clearly to pacify and clean our hearts. Buddha has talked about the bright heart and the tranquil heart. The principle is no more than the void and subtlety of the self-restrained heart. If such a heart is not burdened and completely fused with the primary *qi* of the harmonic heaven and earth, any place can be reached and anything can be obtained. It is the same as Confucians' sitting in spring breeze and bathing in Qi River, or as Daoists' inhaling dews and eating rosy clouds, or as Buddhists' wisdom rains and fragrant flowers, or as ancient sages' talk of rain, moon, light, wind, the root of heaven and the cave on the moon. Since their principles are the same, aren't their purposes and interests the same? Therefore, in this anthology there are words of Zhuangzi, words for leisure, words for freshening up, words for delight, words that are easy to understand, and they don't signify the same rhetoric style. An author can be an official or a hermit, a Confucian or a Buddhist, of high fame or no fame, and he does not fall into a single identity. [Note: The "bright and tranquil heart" echoed the brightness and tranquility of Round Brightness. If a heart was completely fused with the primary *qi* of the harmonic heaven and earth, the ultimate perfection could be reached. Such a situation implied the fullness of Round Brightness. The Qi River flowed through Qufu, the hometown of Confucius. For Yongzheng, no matter what religious connection could be made, this "bright and tranquil heart" was the fundamental existence.]

Generally speaking, we need to be vigilant against greed and arrogance, avoid worrying and open up contemplation, inhabit the clear and tranquil heart, wander the happy land, talk freely about the far and near, and use simple expression while meaning deep significance. By doing so, between looking down and up we meet our hearts all the time. Although the environment can be bustling and noisy, what is not bustling and noisy can only be at the heart. Somebody seeks to live in remote and quiet landscapes but still cannot avoid the disturbance of anxiety; somebody lives in a noisy environment but feels peaceful and carefree. This is the difference of observing and not observing the Dao. In the past, a Chan master, Mr. Lang, wrote to another Chan master, Yongjia, to invite him to live in the mountain. But Yongjia answered: "If one does not observe Dao before dwelling in a mountain, he sees only the mountain rather than Dao. If one observes Dao before dwelling in the mountain, he sees Dao but certainly forgets he is in the mountain. For the one who sees Dao but forgets the mountain, he feels peaceful even in the dusty world; for the one who sees only the mountain but forgets Dao, he feels restless even in the mountain." These words are exactly what I intend to say. Only those who understand this meaning can begin to read my *Anthology of Delightful Heart*. [Note: The situation of "see Dao but forget the mountain" did not mean that the mountain was not important, but rather that the heart was completely fused with the view of the mountain and they became one. In order to reach the fusion of one, the emperor had to "inhabit the clear and tranquil heart, wander the happy land," and "look down and up," just as he did in the garden. Such activities, as he said, improved his "vigilance against greed and arrogance".]

Yongzheng also interpreted the ultimate unity of the primary one from the Confucian perspective. In the essay "A Teaching Text for the Court Lectures on Classics" ("Jingyan" 267-68), he explained his understanding of the Confucian idea "timely middle" (*shizhong*), which appeared in the definition of Round Brightness in his garden record:

Confucius said,"What is called middle is the ultimate principle of the world. What is called harmony is the ultimate Dao of the world." The middle and the harmony belong to the same principle. They cannot be regarded as a distinctive two, nor can they be taken as an ambiguous one. The principle of the middle already contains the harmony. If the middle has reached the ultimate, but the harmony still remains separate, this middle must not be ultimate. The Dao of the middle already contains the middle. If the harmony has reached the ultimate but the middle remains separate, the harmony must not be the ultimate. Only if each of them has its function reach the ultimate can they converge into the essential one. If so, heaven and earth will be positioned and all things will be raised; the profitable function can be ready. Confucius said, "When the ultimate middle and harmony is reached, heaven and earth will be positioned and all things will be raised." The inherent character is called the heavenly fate, which heaven, earth, and all things share together. The middle is the essential oneness, and the harmony dissolves differences. When the ultimate middle harmony is reached, everything is positioned and raised. This is so-called nature, but sages do not claim it as their credit. It is therefore said: "Heaven and earth have no intention but can create nature; sages have intentions but do nothing purposefully." [Note: The idea that if "the ultimate middle and harmony is reached, the heaven and earth will be positioned and all things will be raised" is similar to the idea that if a heart is "completely fused with the primary *qi* of the harmonic heaven and earth, any place could be reached and anything could be obtained," stated in the preface of the anthology.]

Confucius said, "A virtuous man's middle way is his being timely and on the middle." As for the word "middle" in the term "timely middle," many teaching texts interpret its tone of pronunciation as the fourth one, but this does not exhaust the essence of its meanings. The middle of a virtuous man is to respectfully unify all his behaviors towards the middle. The behavior of a virtuous man is to sincerely implement the middle in his behaving. Otherwise, the "timely middle" cannot be realized. This is my interpretation. [Note: There are basically four tones in the Chinese language. The Chinese character of "middle," *zhong*, has in fact two tones: the first and the fourth, each of which indicates different meanings. The first-tone character means "middle;" the fourth-tone, "appropriate or exactly." Yongzheng preferred the first-tone meaning, namely "middle," in his interpretation of the concept "timely middle." This detail is significant, because it shows that for him the Confucian concept "timely middle" should first be understood based on the vision of middle rather than its metaphorical meanings. As he explicated, "the middle of a virtuous man is to respectfully unify all his behaviors towards the middle." This virtue of "unifying all behaviors towards the middle" was vividly expressed by his vision of Round Brightness.]

The classic *Zhongyong* states, "Only the ultimate sincerity shared by the whole country can let us establish the highest principle for administrating and stabilizing the country and knowing the transformation of nature." The usual interpretation thinks that establishing the principle and knowing the transformation are applications of ultimate sincerity. I rather think that they are the very body of ultimate sincerity. Ultimate sincerity is the universal heavenly truth that is true without absurdity. The highest principle and essence of the world and the transformation of nature all are contained in inherent character. Beyond the highest principle, essence and transformation, there is no ultimate sincerity, or vice versa. The whole body of ultimate sincerity contains everything, and this is so natural and simple as such. If we take these sentences from classics literally and understand them as the applications of ultimate sincerity, I am afraid such an understanding is not thorough yet. [Note: The connection between virtues and the ultimate oneness was further developed into the idea that "the whole body of the ultimate sincerity contains everything." The model of interpreting classics in the court started with the emperor Wudi of Han. In the Qing, there was a seminar on classics at the Wenhua Palace each spring and summer. After the lecturer's instruction, Yongzheng would give his own interpretation. It is clear from the above text that Yongzheng extended the definition of the Confucian concept "middle" into the Daoist concept "harmony." For him, the ultimate integration of middle and harmony meant nature; the transformation of nature, for example, like the creation of a garden, was not an application of ultimate sincerity; rather, it was the "whole body (embodiment) of ultimate sincerity."]

It can be argued that the Yuanming Yuan was the very embodiment of ultimate sincerity. Yongzheng's interpretation of Confucius's idea of "timely middle" demonstrated how he attempted to research ancient books for the moral meaning of Round Brightness. It also helps us understand the definition of Round Brightness in his garden record, where the "round" meant the perfection and concentration of the mind, implying the timeliness and moderation of the behavior of a virtuous man, and the "brightness" meant to illuminate all things in order to reach human perspicacity and wisdom. Compared with his father's philosophical exploration of the virtue of Round Brightness, Qianlong's reflection on this issue was frequently expressed in his poems of the Forty Scenes in the garden. On the first scene, he stated that a blue-green grass reminded him of showing frugality, and a still mountain made his body close to humaneness ("Zhengda" 7). The title of the scene itself, Uprightness and Brightness, expressed the cohesion of the virtuous heart and the humane appearance intended by the emperor. In the poem of the twenty-first scene, "Orchid Fragrance over the Water," Qianlong stated that his garden residence was meant not only to serve the purpose of touring and gazing, but also to think beyond, for example, watching the agricultural activities from his window ("Yinshui" 47). The poem expressed his concern in regards to agriculture and the life of common people. With such symbolism, an agricultural field was a typical setting in the Qing emperors' gardens. Besides the symbolism of an agricultural field, plants in the garden usually held ethical meanings. In the poem of the twenty-third scene, "Xi Lian's Wonderful Place for Study," Qianlong stated that the lotus flowers in the garden, which signified virtuous men, were his mentors. These humble flowers were as meaningful as those huge lotus flowers in heaven that symbolized immortality ("Lian Xi" 51). The metaphor of lotus flowers alluded to Dunyi Zhou, a neo-Confucian philosopher of Northern Song, whose essay "Write on the Love of Lotus" defined lotus flowers as virtuous men of flowers. Although Qianlong claimed the lotus flowers in the garden had already satisfied his need for virtues, he in fact implied that the lotus flowers in his garden had no difference from the legendary lotus flower in heaven. His poems demonstrated in detail how his understanding of virtue was closely related to the symbolism of the garden scenes, which followed Confucius's idea that virtue was comparable with nature (*bide*).

For Qianlong, living in the garden was an effectual way for enhancing virtues. In the poem of the thirty-sixth scene, "Bath Body and Enhance Virtue," he wrote, "The autumn water is in harmony with the skylight, / It is neither exhausted nor overfilled, / Only such a situation is the virtue of a virtuous man. / I look upon the empty brightness of the water, / In this mirror I recognize myself silently" ("Zaoshen" 65). The water in the poem indicated the huge lake, Fortunate Sea, whose mirroring surface produced a round brightness. As the title of the scene expressed, bathing the body in the brightness of the round lake could enhance virtues. Reflecting the brilliant moonlight, the brightness of the round lake enlightened his consciousness—"I recognize myself silently."

Some titles of the Forty Scenes indicate both the view and virtue. In the poem of the thirty-seventh scene, "Boundless Openness," Qianlong writes: "The northern window is widely open in the long summer. The fragrance of water keeps on wafting to me. The view really opens up my bosom. / A mountain won't let earth slip away, / Therefore, it becomes so high. / A river won't be picky of any small streams, / Therefore, it becomes so wide. / This is so-called boundless openness, / I therefore use it to name this scene. / Whenever I feel fresh, peaceful and leisurely, / I lean on the windowsill and look over the lake honestly, delightfully and respectfully" ("Kuoran"

79). The concept of "boundless openness" came from Hao Cheng, a neo-Confucian philosopher of Northern Song, who stated that "The knowledge of a virtuous man is no other than the boundless openness" (qtd. in Qianlong, "Kuoran" 79). Another issue that integrated the view and the virtue was depth. In the poem of the fortieth scene, "Deep and Remote Dwelling," Qianlong stated: "Rattling bamboos in the autumn, / Standing pine trees under a moon night. / If I seldom stay here to study, / How can I sense the passing of time? / I am willing to be a Confucian virtuous man, / Rather than do a leisurely stroll as a Daoist" ("Dongtian" 85). Because the fortieth scene was the place where teenage princes, including Qianlong, studied, it is at this place that Qianlong attempted to emphasize the traditional connection between scholarly diligence and Confucian thoughts. The title of the scene and the last sentence of the poem expressed the connection between a deep view and a deep heart, as this scene was the last stop of his journey in seeking Round Brightness. The poem also implied that the virtue of Round Brightness was the combination of both Confucian and Daoist virtues, as expressed by Laozi's concept of "deep and distant virtue" (*xuande*) (S. Zhou 108).

Chapter Three

The Chinese Garden and the Concept of the Vision of *Jing*

Jing in landscape literature

The vision of Round Brightness, with its cosmological and ethical meanings, was embodied by the multiple scenes of the Yuanming Yuan. The brightness not only diffused along the route of the Forty Scenes (Sishi jing) but also was composed by each scene. One of the principal questions is this: Is the transcendental Round Brightness essentially related to the physical scenes in this garden? To answer the question, a historical analysis of the concept of *jing* is necessary. Through focusing on multiple scenes in this garden, we can retrieve the vision of Round Brightness. The meaning of *jing* as the unity of both mind and scene has gone through a historical change. The earliest known discussion of *jing* was in the Moist canon, *Mozi* (5th century BCE), which defined *jing* as "what is static; when sunlight comes, it will disappear" (Liang 112). Here, the *jing* hints at a shadow. The similar meaning of *jing* can be found in the treatise of craftsmen, "Kao gong ji" (3rd century BCE), which states, "Observe the sun and the *jing* to know directions" ("Kao" 193). The *jing* here means the shadow emanating from a sundial with sunlight projecting down. It is clear that around the Warring States period the two characters: *jing* and *ying* (shadow) were not differentiated, and the understanding of shadow was closely related to sunlight.

During the Han dynasty, the *jing* as a bright existence was emphasized and its connection with cosmology was established. The *Huainanzi* states: "The Dao of heaven is called the round; the Dao of earth, the square. The square is in charge of the deep and remote; the round, the bright. That which is bright is something that breathes out *qi*. Therefore, fire is called the external *jing*. What is the deep and remote is something that contains *qi*. Therefore, water is called the internal *jing*" (K. Xu 107). The *jing* was defined as the flowing brightness, *qi*. There was a cosmological connection between Dao, the round form, brightness, and *jing*. The "Rhapsody of the Western Capital," which includes observations of buildings, describes: "The curving-up roof; the flying eaves. The flowing *jing* brightens the interior; draws the light of sun and moon" (H. Zhang 12). The *jing* here indicates a moving bright view, which could be brightened by either the sun or the moon. Since the *jing* could brighten an interior, the concept of *jing* was now differentiated from shadows and emerged as an independent phenomenon. Another Han rhapsody of buildings, entitled "Rhapsody of Lingguang Palace of Lu," states: "A high terrace is at the center of a pool; it circulates up to nine levels. . . . On the top of the terrace, I sit at the center under the falling *jing*; looking over the shooting stars" (Wenkao Wang 645). The "falling *jing*" is a vivid description of moonlight. Because the author was looking over the shooting stars, the *jing* must be related to the moon. Further, landscape literature was greatly developed in the Western and Eastern Jin dynasties. In the poem, "Movement of Time," the pastoral poet Yuanming Tao of Western Jin stated: "Foreword: This poem is about touring in the late spring. Spring clothes have been worn, and the *jing* and things are in harmony. I wander solitarily in an occasional *jing*, and happiness and emotion interweave with my heart. Poem: The distant *jing*, carries my happiness and my gaze" (Tao, "Shi yun" 1-2). The first *jing* indicates sunlight; the second, a place under sunlight; the third, a distant view in sunlight. It is important to note that the *jing* began to be related with an individual's emotion and held multiple meanings. In the "Rhapsody of Leisurely Emotion," Tao wrote: "I wish to be a shadow in daytime; Follow tangible forms here and there. . . . I feel sad for the shining sacred mulberry tree; When a *jing* is over, the tree's brightness is hidden. . . . The sun carries its shadow all the time; The moon flatters the *jing* at the end of clouds" ("Xianqing" 31). Since the sacred mulberry tree stands at the place where the sun rises, the first *jing* means sunlight; and the second, a distant bright view. The Chinese term, "shadow" here is *ying* instead of *jing*. It is clear that the term "shadow," *ying*, was differentiated from the term *jing*, which was purely related to brightness at that time.

After Yuanming Tao, an important figure in landscape literature, Lingyun Xie of the Southern Dynasties period, chanted in the poem "Watch the Late Guest from the Southern Tower": "The round *jing* has been full for a long time, / My friend has not arrived" ("Nanlou" 101). In this case, the "round *jing*" signifies the full moon. His concern for his friend, his desire for a reunion, and his despair over waiting were fused with the round brightness of the full moon. In the preamble of another poem, Xie wrote: "In the world, a good time, a beautiful *jing*, an appreciative heart and a happy event are hard to be together in the meantime" ("Ni Weitaizi" 105). The *jing* here indicates the view of a beautiful landscape. It can be argued that the concept of *jing* in the Southern-Northern Dynasties period began to indicate a view of a landscape, which was brightened by the projection of sunshine or moonlight. Furthermore, the *jing* surprised the spectator and was beyond the control of his intention. The meaning of *jing* as a specific garden or landscape view began to emerge in the Tang dynasty. A poem entitled "Enjoy Coolness in a Buddhist Temple" depicts this: "The mountain *jing* is quiet and obscure, / The temple in wilderness becomes vast and hazy" (Y. Wei 6: 1980). The *jing* here indicated a view of mountain landscapes. Although there was no emphasis on the brightness of the *jing*, it can be imagined that the *jing* should have been bright in order to be a view. In the poem, "Present to the

Official Wei for His Promotion," the landscape painter and poet Wei Wang stated: "The cold pool reflects feeble grass, / Phoenix-tree leaves scatter on a high lodge. / At such a late time of the year, / I look at the *jing* and sadly chant for the old man. / My old friend can no longer be met, / Solitude falls on the eastern woods" ("Fengji" 6). The *jing* indicated the view of the eastern woods, which was distant from the domestic dwelling consisting of a cold pool, feeble grass, phoenix-tree leaves, and a high lodge. The *jing* over there bore the projection of solitude from here. The distance between the landscape *jing* and the garden-like home embodied the pathetic distance between the author and his friend. The tension between the viewer and the view was enhanced in his consciousness of the depth of the *jing*. In the "Deer and Firewood," a poem on one of the twenty named scenes of his Wangchuan Villa, Wang wrote: "There is nobody in the empty mountain. / But I seem to hear echoes of human voices. / The returning *jing* penetrates into the dense forests, / Brightens up again the green mosses" ("Lu chai" 70). The first two sentences seem paradoxical but bring out the tranquility of the author's heart. In such an extreme silence, the view became prominent and heart related. The *jing* here means sunlight, which brightened the view of landscapes. Ultimately, the concept of *jing* as a view of a beautiful landscape was fully developed through Tang poetry. In the poem "Living Overnight at the Cuiwei Temple on the Zhongnan Mountain," the landscape poet Haoran Meng wrote: "Although Confucianism and Daoism are different religious schools, / As for clouds and forests they are the same. / Two hearts delight in meeting with each other, / We exhaust the *jing* in an enjoyable talk and laugh" ("Su" 154). The "clouds and forests" indicated beautiful landscapes. The terms "delight," "enjoyable," and "laugh" portrayed the *jing* as the appreciable view of landscapes. It is also interesting to note that the *jing* could act as a common ground for different religions. In yet another poem, "Move About in the Morning at Yupu Lake," he wrote: "Paddling expels my depression, / At this moment a clear *jing* opens up" ("Zaofa" 158). The *jing* here means a bright view of landscapes. The phrase "opens up" demonstrates that a *jing* did not always exist and was different from a mere view of nature. The opening up of the *jing* mirrored the enlightenment of the heart and it could be big or small. In the poem "Watch in Spring at Linling," the landscape essayist Zongyuan Liu chanted, "Gathering my emotion, I look admiringly at the expansive *jing*; / The ten thousand-mile shady Cangwu Mountain" ("Lingling" 623). The author expressed clearly that he had to gather his emotion to perceive this expansive *jing*, namely the continuous mountain range. A similarly expansive *jing* was phrased in another Tang poem: "Ten thousand *jing* gather toward me" (Yuxi Liu 29). In this example, the larger *jing* was composed of multiple individual *jing*, each of which designated a specific scene of a landscape. For both the authors, the gathering of *jing* was a moment in time for the evocation of emotion. From Wei Wang's solitary *jing*, to Haoran Meng's opened-up *jing* and Zongyuan Liu's admired *jing*, the *jing* was appearing as a *jing* phenomenon where it emerged in the stream of consciousness. The concept of *jing* phenomenon is proposed here to echo Edmund Husserl's concept of house phenomenon. He differentiated the house phenomenon from the objective view of a house. According to him, the house phenomenon is the perception of a house in which the house is thus and so in the seeing consciousness (57).

Once the *jing* could be formulated on a small scale, attention was shifted from landscape views to garden scenes. The meaning of *jing* as a specific view of a landscape, which emerged in the Tang dynasty, was solidified and transformed into a specific view of a garden scene during the Five Dynasties. A poem entitled "Wandering of Aristocrats," described "Playboys in embroidery clothes are having a banquet by the pool, / The pretty *jing* fuses with fragrances of ten thousand flowers" (J. Liu 333). The *jing* here means garden scenes. Once the *jing* began to indicate a specific view, which appeared near the spectator, the term was frequently used for what the viewer observed in a garden. In addition, the *jing* of a garden was connected to the development of virtues. In the poem "Courtyard Reeds," the author connected the *jing* with the aesthetic and poetic feelings of human beings: "The moral character is clear in bamboo, / The *jing* in a poet's eyes is the remotest" (Z. Li 709). In this case, the *jing* was a remote garden scene, which echoed with a deep bosom. With the clarification of the individual *jing*, attention began to be paid to the depth of a *jing*, which was related to the remoteness of the heart. On such an intimate scale of a garden scene, the *jing* became a poetical approach for ethical improvement.

During the Five Dynasties, a clear idea that a *jing* was typically beautiful was established. The poem "Reside in the Chishui Temple on Qingming Day" stated: "Turbid wine cannot bear the *jing* beyond clouds, / Green peaks cool off springtime in front of the temple" (Luo 16). The *jing* here indicates the view of a distant landscape. In Chinese culture, wine was a poet's friend, but a *jing* could be more attractive than wine. In the poem entitled "Reside at the Qixian Temple in Autumn and Miss a Friend," a different author wrote: "Only after chanting poems again and again do I see the *jing*, / It is pitiful that I cannot share it with my friend" (Du 45). In this case, the *jing* is an example of a pretty view of landscape in the mind. It is interesting to note that the *jing* could be obtained only through a poetical perspective. Another poem, "The West Garden in Early Spring," states: "How to take this *jing*? / Adjust and bring it into a painting" (Z. Wang 164). The *jing* here means a view of garden scene. The exchangeability between a *jing* and a painting was a crucial development regarding the concept of *jing*. Like a painting, the *jing* was adjustable in accordance with the viewer's perspective. It can be said that the concept of *jing* as a poetical view of landscapes or garden scenes was well established during the Five Dynasties, a politically unstable period in Chinese history, immediately following the Tang dynasty. It was because of the poetization of the *jing* that the representation of a *jing*, such as the landscape painting, was highly developed after the Tang dynasty.

In the Song dynasty, the definition of *jing* was more connected with its objective existence. In "A Spring for Common People," the author asserted: "Delight in things is like being created by heaven, / The *jing* of things has no end" (Yuanzhi Wang, "Shuzi" 21). The *jing* points to a meaning of the view of things. The "thing" or "thingness" was a key philosophical concept of neo-Confucianism throughout the Song dynasty. The attention to the physical things that composed a *jing* demonstrated the analytical trend of observing the world. In "Chant at the Tower of Waves-under-Moon," the same author wrote: "If a good *jing* is not encountered by people, / How can its fame last?" (Yuanzhi Wang, "Yuebolou" 28). The differentiation between the *jing* and what the spectator implied was intended more as an objective existence than before. However, the interactive relationship between the *jing* and the spectator remained emphasized. That is, it was because of the recognition of the distance between the view and the viewer that the interactive relationship between the two was stressed. Once the *jing* was kept as an objective existence, the spectator's subjective influence over the *jing* was more controlled. In the poem "Write at the West Pavilion to Respond to the Official You-sheng-pu-she" we read that a *jing* follows what a viewer likes and that it is a thing that seeks its own appropriateness (X. Xu 95). The poem emphasized that a *jing* was perceived by the spectator from a particular position. People in the Song dynasty realized that a *jing* could be selected and began to build structures within a garden to include an intended *jing*. In the "Record of a Tower for the Distant *jing* in Meizhou," the poet Shi Su wrote, "The official [my friend] thus expanded his residence based on the northern wall of the original residence, and the Tower for a Distant Jing was built. He strolled with his guests and other officials on the tower everyday. . . . In order for such a delight of standing on the tower gazing broadly and the beauty of landscapes, I shall retire back to my hometown Meizhou, dressed in plain clothes, and serve my friend on this tower. Drinking to the full and feeling joyful to write, I lift the pen brush to write this record to praise the official Li's kind heart" ("Meizhou" 140). A tower was built in the garden for the purpose of viewing a distant *jing*. It is interesting to note that the tower was not located within the garden, but rather on the garden wall, on the border between the inside and the outside. The location on the border demonstrated a strong desire to bring the distant *jing* that was outside the garden into the garden's boundary. The borrowed view demonstrated the observer's attempt to control the depth of the *jing*, which was a cultural characteristic of the Song dynasty.

Once the control over the view was strengthened, more attention began to be paid to details of the *jing*. In his "Record of the Pavilion of a Drunk Old Man," the historian Xiu Ouyang wrote, "I go there in the morning and return in the evening. The *jing* of four seasons are different, and my delight has no end" (116). The *jing* here represents a seasonal view of the landscape. The *jing* changed in accordance with the different seasons and these changes brought pleasure to him. About a screen-like rock, Ouyang's poem says, "In the empty woods there is nothing except happily singing birds, / Ancient trees block the sky and boughs bend and stretch. / There is a strange rock standing among the trees, / It is buried by smoke and hidden by grass and is full of moss. / Could I ask who painted this *jing*? / It is the stone screen of the Wu family" (qtd. in Lin 109). The author compared the *jing*, a strange rock standing among the trees, to a painting. The phenomenon that a unique rock could become a *jing* demonstrated that the perceptual distance between the view and viewer was being shortened, and the scale of the *jing* was being reduced to the human scale. The scholar Gefei Li wrote an essay, "Records of the Famous Gardens in

Luoyang" where he wrote: "A visitor walks out of the house, turns to the east, passes through the Pavilion of Exploring Spring and climbs up to the Hall of Four Jing, then the whole *jing* and beauty of the garden can be viewed and obtained" (39). The first *jing* means a garden scene during a particular season. The second *jing* indicates a panoramic view of the garden. On another garden in the same city, Li wrote: "South of the water pavilion is the Tower of Multiple Jing" (41). The *jing* here was a specific view of a landscape; each *jing* was different from the other and all the *jing*, one after another, were appreciated from a tower. It is clear that in the Northern Song dynasty, each *jing* became a singular entity and one *jing* was distinctively different from another. An important criterion for judging the singularity of a *jing* was its propensity (*shi*), that is, its inclination or tendency. The force of propensity links its various elements as a whole, which can be understood as the landscape's full face physiognomy (Jullien 98-101). According to a study, at the end of the Northern Song dynasty, the tendency of a view became impressionistic and expansive, and only after that did the symbolic approach of seeing the big in the small (*xiao zhong jian da*) in later gardens become possible (J. Feng 66-67). One of the methods of creating an expansive *jing* was to extend the view from the inside of the garden into the outside distance. According to Guang Sima's garden record, he specifically made a terraced house in his garden to see the three distant mountains outside the garden (25). At the same time, emperor Huizong erected a hill pavilion which he named Nest in the Clouds within his magnificent garden Genyue. The purpose of the hill pavilion was to provide a place for viewing the distant peaks that were outside the garden. He wrote: "It seems the mountains are on my hand" (63). By equating the size of the mountains with his hand, he appeared to delete the distance by integrating the distant landscape into a unified *jing*.

In the Southern Song dynasty, the concept of *jing* began to emphasize the interactive relationship between the view and the viewer. Greater efforts were invested in analyzing and controlling a *jing*. In the "Record of the Panzhou Villa," one scholar stated: "When the window curtain is rolled up, all the things of the *jing* come up to me together and it is impossible to appreciate them one by one" (Hong 66). The *jing* here means a view framed by a window. The author wanted to emphasize that the *jing* was composed of various components, which were arranged, one by one, for appreciation and analysis. He paid attention to each compositional element of the *jing*. In the "Record of the Yanshan Garden," another scholar stated: "Drink my fill and feel well. Meditate the present and miss the past. I pick up the surrounding things and imbed them into a *jing*. Rivers, mountains, grass and woods thus all fit my chanting" (D. Feng 79). This time the *jing* means an inclusive view of natural phenomena. Again, the viewer's attention was drawn to the components of the *jing*. In both garden records, the *jing* was described as moving toward the spectator for his appreciation and chanting. The spectator thus became an elevated subject in his relationship with the *jing*. In the literature from the Ming dynasty, the *jing* was more frequently connected to paintings after landscape painting was highly developed in the Song dynasty. The poet Sheng Zhu wrote that "the *jing*, when perceived at that moment, looks like a painting" (63). The *jing* here indicates a picturesque view of the landscape. Like a landscape painting, the *jing* began to be completely composed by the viewer and became the full expression of his emotion. The scholar Mian Wang wrote in a poem: "Ten thousand *jing* return to my two eyes" ("Deng Zhufeng" 88). Thus *jing*, in this case, indicates multiple views of landscapes. Without a deep bosom, the author would not be so certain that thousands of *jing* could be included into his eyes. In another poem, he said, "Facing the *jing*, I wrote poems lightheartedly" ("Ci Shentuzi" 119). In a similar poem, entitled "Facing the Jing," he wrote that "If a *jing* is beautiful, the poet's bosom will be vast" ("Dui jing" 132). Both poems present the interactive relationship between a *jing* and a poet, specifically that a beautiful *jing* could enhance a viewer's virtue or, metaphorically speaking, could expand his bosom. Wang's poems demonstrate that the concept of facing the *jing*, *duijing*, was widely used in the Ming dynasty. The term *duijing* can be understood as facing a *jing* or as a type of *jing*, called head-on *jing*, in which the viewer has a face-to-face relationship with a *jing*. In the poem "On a Boat," Wang touched again on the concept of facing a *jing*. He wrote, "Facing the *jing*, I seem to be drunk by my emotions" ("Chuan shang" 140). The *jing* and the viewer's emotion were inherently connected. The concept of head-on *jing* later became fused with the *jing* created with linear perspective by the Jesuits in the Yuanming Yuan.

In the "Record of the View of Snow and Moon," the painter Zhou Shen stated, "On this night, the moon came out and competed with the snow for prettiness. I sat by a window covered by paper, feeling extremely clear and tranquil. I thus added a cloth and climbed to a small tower west of a brook. . . . Considering that such a *jing* cannot be encountered frequently in my life and it is easy to forget something day by day; furthermore, my mind wanders for several days but I cannot remember what I thought, I therefore write thoughts down" ("Ji xueyue" 228). The *jing* here indicates a particular view of a landscape observed from a particular place at a particular time. It is interesting to note that even a great painter like Zhou Shen was attempting to record the *jing* through writing. Shen's student, Zhengming Wen, also used writings to record a *jing*. In the "Record of the Wang Family's Garden of an Unsuccessful Politician," he wrote: "I pick up the things of the *jing* in the garden and write poems on all of them. Meanwhile, I also write this record" ("Wangshi" 101). The *jing* here means beautiful views of the garden scenes. A total of thirty-one *jing* was described from this garden, about which he wrote poems and created paintings. Such a format of pairing painting and poetry of the *jing* into a couplet influenced recordings of *jing* in the Qing imperial gardens. In sum, during the Ming dynasty, the *jing* became a central concept of Chinese gardens. The "Record of the Garden of Harmonic Appreciation" states: "When being looked upon, the *jing* of the garden can be obtained eighty to ninety percent. . . . A door faces a square pool. . . . At the center of the pool, a pavilion with three bays was built. The windows of the pavilion are open in order to receive *jing* from the four sides. . . . When my heart meets the *jing*, fish and birds appear intimate" (D. Gu 108-09). The first *jing* means a panoramic view of the garden; the second *jing*, a specific view of a garden scene from a particular direction;

and the third, a beautiful garden scene. From these three concepts of *jing*, it can be observed that a *jing* can be big or small, general or specific, but the key for a beautiful *jing* is that it touches the viewer's heart.

The view of a distant landscape could be borrowed and integrated into a *jing* within a garden. This is the so-called borrowed *jing* (*jiejing*). In the "Record of the Yugong Valley," a painter wrote: "As for the relationship between a garden and its surroundings, if a mountain is too distant from the garden, it will look aloof; if it is too close, it will lack the distant rhythm. Only for that which is neither far nor close, or seems to come while it seems to leave, its *jing* is easy to be included and its beauty can be composed and accessed" (D. Zou 189). The *jing* in this case is a view of a distant mountain observed from the inside of a garden. For the author, a *jing* could be created just as a painting was fashioned and the key for this control was the expression of distance. The "borrowed *jing*" as a meaningful method of garden design was analyzed in detail in the garden treatise *Yuan ye* (*The Craft of Gardens*), written by Cheng Ji. He devoted the last chapter to the discussion of borrowed *jing*, but he had already pointed out the importance of borrowed *jing* in the first chapter, which said: "The ingeniousness of garden design lies in borrowing, and the quintessence lies in appropriating. . . . The so-called borrowing means: Although there is a difference between the inside and outside of a garden, obtaining a *jing* is not limited to such a distance. . . . Extend the eyesight as far as you can. If the view is vulgar, block it; if it is good, include it [into a *jing*]" (47-48). In the final chapter, he wrote that "constructing a garden has no fixed pattern, but borrowing a *jing* has its principle. . . . Borrowing a *jing* has no other principle than this: when a *jing* is perceived, emotion will emerge" (243-44). In the preface of the treatise, Ji discussed the Garden of Solitary Joy owned by Guang Sima of the Song dynasty. According to Sima's "Record of the Garden of Solitary Joy," he built up a terraced pavilion in the garden in order to look over the mountains in the distance (26). The concept of borrowed *jing* was already typical in Song gardens and frequently appeared in garden records prior to the time of *Yuan ye*. Ji's theorization of the borrowed *jing* as a key pattern of garden design demonstrated the designer's increasing control in the creation of a *jing*. Buildings play a crucial role in composing a *jing*. For example, the scholar Biaojia Qi wrote "the pavilion does not take itself as a scenic beauty but rather gathers multiple *jing* as scenic beauties. It is not necessary to put all scenic beauties onto the pavilion, but rather let the pavilion show why they can be scenic beauties" (Qi 272). The author emphasized the active role of the pavilion in "gathering" and "selecting" the *jing*. Although being a receptor of *jing*, the pavilion itself was not the focus, but rather worked as an agent for stimulating the *jing*. The unity between a landscape or garden building and the *jing* became an aesthetic intention in the Ming dynasty. When visiting a Buddhist Chan temple in a mountain, the landscape traveler Xiake Xu observed that although this temple looked very clear and tidy, it held no extraordinary *jing* (H. Xu 8). In other words, any Chan temple should provide the visitor a beautiful *jing*; otherwise it was a pity.

In the Ming opera, *Mudan ting* (*Pavilion of Peonies*) by Xianzu Tang, the heroine sang from the backyard garden, "I occasionally come to the backyard garden where various flowers are blooming. Looking at the *jing*, I feel sad" (56). The *jing* in a garden was usually connected with the feeling of appreciation and happiness. With the paradoxical sentence, "looking at the *jing*, I feel sad," the author expressed the young lady's deep melancholy regarding love. When her mother vigilantly asked her, "Why did you go to the garden?" the heroine answered cleverly, "Because there are good *jing* in the garden" (62). The *jing* here—the beautiful garden scenes—played a different role in semantics. By stating that she went to the garden for the beautiful *jing*, which was easily understandable and acceptable to her mother, she hid her real emotion, which was that she longed for her lover from the garden. The use of the concept of *jing* in the two distinctive semantic contexts demonstrates the role of the *jing* of a garden in the domestic relationship of mother and daughter, the affectionate relationship of lovers, and the individual's sentiment in the Ming dynasty. Further, the novel *Honglou meng* (*Dream of the Red Chambers*) was written by Xueqin Cao in the Qianlong reign. He wrote this book while living at the foot of Fragrant Hill in the northwestern suburb of Beijing. It has been debated whether the aristocratic Garden of Grand View in the book was actually based on the imperial Yuanming Yuan. A main reason for this debate is that a panoramic painting of the Yuanming Yuan was named Grand View by Qianlong (E. Zhang, *Yuanmingyuan daguan* 138-39). In chapter seventeen, when the Garden of Grand View was just built, the father of the hero of the story was leading a group of people to tour the garden. During the tour, the group tried to name each *jing* that impressed them. In front of others, the father first pretended to show his humbleness and said: "The garden scenes should be named by the Noble Imperial Concubine [who is his older daughter]. If she does not personally see the *jing* of the garden, how could I dare to name them for her?" (104). However, he decided to attempt naming the garden scenes for her future reference. After entering the gate, he encountered an artificial hill, which blocked the visitor's view to the inside. He commented, "If without this hill, all the *jing* of the garden will appear to us and there will be no curiosity anymore" (105). What is interesting here is that the *jing* was blocked intentionally in order to provoke the viewer's curiosity as it enhanced the viewer's projection of his intention towards the *jing*. While the group was discussing how to name this hill, his son, the hero of the story, interrupted, saying, "Because the hill is not a frontal *jing* facing towards the main hall, it is actually not necessary to name it. However, the hill can be named for leading to exploring the further *jing*" (105). These two uses of *jing* demonstrate that a garden *jing* was carefully positioned, even temporarily hidden, for appreciation by the viewer's mind.

Once a garden disappeared, its *jing* could be preserved in literature or paintings. The scholar Mei Yuan of the Qianlong reign owned a garden. After his death, the garden was destroyed during war. People tried to appreciate the *jing* of this garden through a painting but found the depiction was not detailed enough. Yuan's descendant thus wrote "On the Painting of the Shui Garden" to present more detail: "Climb up to the Tower of Green Dawn. The sunrise, waking greenery, and the white pagoda of Tender Green all gather into the *jing* in front of the window. . . . The Southern Terrace . . . stands at the middle of the garden. Look over the various territories from the terrace, extend the view and receive multiple *jing*. . . . If you reach the end of the passageway and walk up on the slope, the *jing* of the garden will completely appear" (Q. Yuan 363-65). The first *jing* is a window-framed view of distant scenes, the second *jing* is the unframed view of distant scenes, and the third *jing* has yet another meaning, which is a panoramic view of the garden. From these definitions, it is apparent that the *jing* changed with the shift of the viewer's position among different buildings. In Mei Yuan's own "Record of the Shui Garden," he described how the viewer's body strolled in accordance with the topography of the ground in order to obtain a *jing* on each specific position (M. Yuan 361). Once the subjective control of a *jing* became complete, all the objects in the garden had to be perceived through the structure of the *jing*. In the Qing imperial gardens, even flowers and trees were called the ground *jing* (*Yuanmingyuan damuzuo* vol. 3, ch. 10. This implies that flowers and trees in a garden were observed from the perspective of a *jing* rather than taken as objective items. This also demonstrates that flowers and trees were planted on the ground to be appreciated as a *jing*. In another sense, if something could be connected to a *jing*, it must exist for appreciation. Such a concept clarifies why the Western-like scenes created in the imperial gardens were called the Western *jing* (*xiyang jing*). At the very least, they were for appreciation in some context. An imperial archive recorded that on the ninth day of the fifth moon of the twelfth year of the Qianlong reign (1747), the Jesuit painter, Shining Lang (that is, Giuseppe Castiglione), was ordered to paint the Western *jing* on the windows of a Western multistoried building in the Yuanming Yuan (*Zaobanchu* archive 3415).

Jing is a view that appears bright, bounded, emotionally connected, and poetical to the mind. Before the Southern-Northern Dynasties, the brightness of *jing* and its cosmic connection had been observed. During the Tang dynasty, the *jing* became the projection of emotion. A breakthrough took place during the short Five Dynasties when the poetical dimension of the *jing* was developed and the *jing* began to be compared to the view of a landscape painting. It was at the intimate and poetical scale that the *jing* became an expression of a garden. The equivalence of *jing* with painting was further developed in the Song dynasty into the composition of a *jing*, which led to the theoretical concept of the Ming dynasty that the creation of a *jing* could be fully controlled by human emotion. In the Qing dynasty, the interaction between the garden *jing* and the painting *jing* enabled the Western garden scenes to be depicted as an exotic *jing* within a Chinese garden.

Jing in theories of painting

With the high development of landscape painting in the Song dynasty, the *jing* became an important concept in Chinese painting literature. In the history of Chinese painting, painting on a fan was a traditional type of painting, originating from various paintings on the surfaces of round fans. In her poem "Chant on a Fan," the Han dynasty courtier Jieyu Ban wrote, "The gossamer fan is like the round moon, / It is made of silk on machine" (249). This is an early record where the ancient Chinese compared the round fan with the round moon. Probably made by the author herself, the fan was most likely an intimate belonging of hers, while her comparison to the full moon suggests its emotional pull for her as well. The fan had the same round form as the moon, and the light reflected from the gossamer, which was made of silk, was similar to the glow of moonlight. During the Han dynasty, other authors made similar comparisons between the round fan and the full moon. For example, in the poem, "Rhapsody of the Round Fan," we find "Look up at the bright moon to obtain an image, / Formulate the obtained form of the circular body into a fan" (G. Xu 628). In this passage, the author expressed how the round form of the fan was borrowed from the moon, and noted that the moon was bright; this brightness of light in nature was an important quality in Chinese painting.

Observations about shades of light, or brightness, within nature were recorded quite early in Chinese painting theories. The painter and painting theorist, Kaizhi Gu of Southern and Northern Dynasties, observed that a mountain had its face and flank, and its back had a shadow (581). The observation of shades of light was the beginning of painters exploring the concept of truth, that is, how painting could truthfully represent nature. A story from the same period portrayed a prince who was skilled at painting portraits. He painted his guests so well that "all the children could recognize which figure was who" (Yan 15). Notably, the original Chinese term for "portrait" is *xiezhen*, which literally means "write truth." In this example, the term meant inscribing and recording intentionally a real face. Early Chinese painting theories were concerned with the relationship between representation and truth. During the Tang dynasty, the understanding of truth in painting was further developed. In his "Record of Painting," the poet Juyi Bai wrote that a "painting needs no other skill than resemblance. To learn how to paint has no other teacher than truth [*zhen*] itself" ("Hua ji" 25). Bai emphasized the importance of depicting truth in painting by having an object in a painting appear real. Truth in painting was not simply the imitation of an existing object; rather, the higher the level of concentration from the artist, the greater level of truth would be reached. Jingxuan Zhu commented on this, saying that "in painting, portraits rank the highest, then animals, then landscapes, and buildings are the lowest. Why? . . . It is because people and animals have mutable qualities and endless changes of complexion. A painter has to highly concentrate his mind to fix their images. Therefore, they are quite difficult" (22). This ranking, then, was determined by how much concentration of mind was needed to grasp the resemblance of truth. It is interesting to note that Zhuangzi's concept of "condensation of the mind," *ningshen*, was more connected with portrait painting than landscape painting: "as for terraces, pavilions, trees, carts and utensils, no liveliness can be imitated and no *qi* or rhythm can be equated. What is required for painting them is simply to find their locations and positions" (Y. Zhang 32). It is clear that what was highly valued in resemblance was the imitation of liveliness. In the Tang dynasty, paintings of landscapes and buildings were not yet supposed to contain such liveliness.

Although landscape painting did not rank high in the Tang dynasty, the landscape concept of *jing* began to appear in theories of painting. In his discourse on landscape paintings, the poet and painter Wei Wang wrote, "a small painting in a few square feet can depict a *jing* one thousand miles deep. In the painting, the east, west, south, and north all seem to be in front of my eyes.... The distant *jing* appears misty and vague, and remote crags are always blocked by clouds" ("Huaxue" 149). This is one of the earliest records where the concept of *jing* appeared and where the *jing* was connected to the depth of view. A distant *jing* was appreciated for its misty and vague look. Wang continued to depict detail in the time-related change of *jing*: "In the spring *jing*, fogs and mists block the view.... In the summer *jing*, old trees hide the sky.... In the autumn *jing*, the sky and water are the same color.... In the winter *jing*, the ground is covered with snow" ("Huaxue" 150). It is important to note that these *jing* were observed for the purpose of painting. The emergence of the concept of *jing* in Wang's theory of painting demonstrates the elevation in importance of landscape painting. Hao Jing of Five Dynasties advanced the famous "six essentials" of landscape painting, one of which was *jing*. He defined the *jing* as seeking wonderfulness and creating truthfulness in accordance with time. According to him, a truthful *jing* in a painting must contain *qi* as well as other qualities. If a painter works hard on painting and reaches the level of forgetting the brush and ink, a truthful *jing* will be obtained (605-06). In another article on landscape painting, he wrote that landscape painting stood on the top of all the thirteen categories of painting (614). Di Song, of the Northern Song dynasty, created eight paintings of varied-distance landscapes of Xiaoxiang (in today's Hunan Province) and named them the Eight Jing of Xiaoxiang. Through these eight paintings, a new custom emerged in using a certain number of *jing* to characterize regional landscapes. A painting project that followed the model of Song's work was the Eight Jing of Yanjing (Yanjing is an old name of Beijing) in the Jin dynasty (Beijing daxue lishixi 99). In Song's case, each *jing* was a painting, and vice versa. The regional *jing* of an area became famous because of the paintings of the specific *jing* in that region. The Xiaoxiang area, for example, became well known for the Eight Jing that were established by Song's paintings.

In his essay, "The Sublimity and Elegance of Landscapes," the painter Xi Guo suggested that "when composing a painting, it must correspond to heaven and earth. What are heaven and earth? It means that within a painting surface, with one and half feet on each side, the upper part should be left for the sky and the lower part for the earth. The middle part is for establishing the intention to build up the *jing*" (642). In this case, Guo described *jing* as an intended view of a landscape. The division of the three parts, the bottom for earth, the middle for the *jing*, and the top for heaven, expressed the depth of a painting, especially in a vertical scroll. Moving from the bottom up within the painting was a method to perceive from near to far. The control of distance in a painting was crucial. He continued, "The painting of a landscape has its own appropriateness: spreading the landscape into a big painting without wasting space; condensing it into a small *jing* without sacrificing anything.... Rivers and mountains are big objects and need to be observed from a distance so that their topographies and propensity in general can be obtained" (632). The author brought out the important concept of "propensity" (*shi*) of landscapes, as in each *jing* there was its specific propensity. Keeping the distance in a painting helped the expression of momentum, where the propensity of the landscape could be inherently fused with the projection of the viewer's intention.

In the Southern Song dynasty, the concept of attention to specific details within a *jing* was advanced and the size of a *jing* became miniaturized. It was the concentration of details that forced the size to be smaller. The scholar Chengshou Li commented that detailed *jing* composed by cohesive brush strokes were worth being appreciated (622). At the same time, the framed *jing* in paintings became very popular. The etymological origin of *jing* hints at the existence of bounded brightness. Such a vision could be experienced in a fan painting, for example, the painting "Plum Blossom by Moonlight" by Yuan Ma, in which the moon circle and the frame of the round fan corresponded to each other (Barnhart figure 4). As the fan symbolically enclosed mountains and waters, the full moon unified the whole world. The traditional connection between the round fan and the full moon within the Han dynasty was now developed into the round *jing* of a fan painting. Of note is here that in landscape paintings of the Yuan dynasty, the symbolic round form was related not only to the full moon and the round fan but also to the painter's bosom. The painter Gongwang Huang wrote that "when an ancient painter made a painting, his bosom was very broad and his composed *jing* was very natural. If we follow the ancient intentions, the principles of painting will be complete" ("Xie shanshui" 702). Huang suggested that a landscape painting be a composed *jing*, which should be composed with a broad bosom. His comments also demonstrate the subtle resonance between the hidden heart and the visible *jing*. The boundary of the heart needs to be intentionally expanded in order to receive an expansive *jing*. Only when both match each other did the composition of a painting become perfect.

In the Yuan dynasty, the building-dominated *jing* began to emerge in paintings, such as Yong Xia's work, *Yellow Crane Tower*, where distance was expressed through the idea of hiding, such as peaks hiding behind clouds and objects in the distance being hidden behind objects nearby. In this way, the depth of the *jing* was gained through atmospheric perspective. On the category of building painting, a scholar commented, "Building paintings ranks the lowest in painting categories. However, among measures of multistoried buildings and overlaid pavilions there is the differentiation of face and back. Although roof corners are connected to complicated brackets, the view should not appear mixed and disorderly and should be in accordance with regularity. This is the most difficult" (Rao 697). The original Chinese term for "building painting," *jiehua*, literally means "border painting," indicating the use of a ruler in drawing borderlines of building elements. According to Ziran Rao, building paintings still ranked the lowest in the Yuan dynasty, but the increased depiction of complicated building details was valued and appreciated. In a building-dominated *jing*, the depth of the *jing* still depended upon traditional atmospheric perspective. In the painting theories of the Ming dynasty, paintings from previous dynasties were critiqued in greater detail. A painter commented, "Wei Wang [of the Tang dynasty] could evoke interest outside the *jing* but seemed not to exhaust it yet. Tong Guan, Yuan Dong and Ran Ju [Song dynasty] could produce real interest with sublime and distant qualities" (S. Wang 116). The "sublime and distant qualities" indicates the depth of the *jing*. These comments confirmed that the depth of the *jing* was much more explored through painting in the Song dynasty than in the Tang dynasty. As stated in another source, "vivid magic is obtained by looking into the distance, and this is a heavenly interest. Morphological resemblance results from perceiving the landscape closely, and this is of human interest" (L. Gao 121). For the author, the depth of *jing* was more important than morphological resemblance and was related to the magical force of heaven. In theories of painting in the Ming dynasty, increasing emphasis was placed on the painter's intention, which was projected into a *jing*. As a scholar wrote, "Painting has three ordered aspects: first, the position of the painter's body . . . from which multiple *jing* can be included; second, the scenes on which the eyesight is projected; . . . third, the places where the intention can stroll about. At such a place, though the force of eye becomes exhausted, the vein of emotion continues. . . . When a distant *jing* is depicted, it usually happens that the intention comes out but the brush cannot correspond to it. The brush is swallowed by spiritual *qi*. It is not that attention is not paid to the brush, rather that the brush has to be so" (R. Li 131). The place where "the intention can stroll about" and "the vein of emotion continues" indicates the depth of *jing*. In a distant *jing*, where the depth of *jing* was deep, the intention even overwhelmed the brush skills of the artist. The painter Zhou Shen vividly confirmed the overwhelming intention towards the *jing*: "The beauty of landscape is obtained by the eye but resides in the heart. Between the physical form of landscape and the painting, there is no other thing than enthusiasm. This painting was created under artificial light in a room. Because it resulted from my enthusiasm, I did not have time to seek for precision" ("Shitian" 711). Here, the artist consciously let his enthusiasm overwhelm the form of a *jing*.

Once a *jing* could be controlled on a small scale, the expression of depth became more symbolic of the macro-world and more garden related. As Shilong Mo—a Ming painter—recorded, he painted a small *jing* in level distance on a fan whose meaning was endless, with one significance after another. The round boundary of the fan framed the small *jing* whose meaning was deep. Although the fan painting was not a new creation in the Ming dynasty, the *jing* in landscape painting on a small scale became the norm. This trend was confirmed by the emergence of garden painting, where small details were exemplified in a *jing*, which was differentiated from traditional landscape painting. In his theories, the same painter clearly differentiated a distant and misty view from a close *jing* in a garden. He thought that if trees in "a *jing* of a garden" were transplanted into a *jing* of a mountain dwelling, it would be unsuitable (Mo 716-17). It is worth noting that the author advanced the concept "garden *jing*" (*yuanjing*) and defined it as a close *jing*. The visibility of details in a garden *jing* expressed, in another sense, the controllability and regularization of the *jing*. The control of the visibility of the *jing* became a conscious activity in paintings during the Ming dynasty. As another painter commented, the more a *jing* was hidden, the bigger its intentional field (*jingjie*); the more obvious a *jing* was, the smaller its intentional field (Z. Tang 745). In this way, a small *jing*, especially a garden *jing*, could appear big and deep through being partially hidden.

Chinese woodcut artistry, used for reproducing multiple paper prints, became highly developed during the late Ming dynasty, with many of the artists originating from Huizhou (in today's southern Anhui Province). A famous work was the *Drawing of the Garden Jing of the Hall Encircled by Jades*, drawn by Gong Qian and carved by Yingzu Huang. The Hall Encircled by Jades was also the name of a publishing workshop owned by the official Tingne Wang in Jinlin (today's Nanjing), who originally came from Huizhou (P. Feng 37-41). The *jing* in this piece of artwork describes multiple garden scenes, which was composed of various and separate *jing* with the entire scroll measuring almost fifty feet. The scroll appears to unfold as if a flow of consciousness within a dream, so there is doubt as to whether such a garden called Hall Encircled by Jades truly existed. One *jing* flows into a completely different *jing* with a smoothness, creating an inability to discern one *jing* from the next, so that the viewer might forget he is viewing separate, very different *jing*. The connection of the various *jing* was made by a continuous path that the observer's eyes traveled along throughout the whole scroll. The fact that the multiple garden *jing* were composed as a flow of consciousness within a dream demonstrates that the *jing* was completely driven by the painter's intention and emotion. It has been asserted that once the *jing* was created with emotion, no matter the difficulty, any painting could be easily completed as long as the intention and emotion flowed (Kong 272).

In the garden treatise, *Yuan ye*, the painting concept of composing a *jing* was applied to garden design. It states, "The cliff-like rocks are arranged against a wall, to rely on the white wall as the painting paper and take the rocks as what is painted. Lay the rocks according to their textures. Imitating the method of ancient paintings, plant Yellow Mountain pines, cypresses, old plum trees and elegant bamboo. Arrange them into a round window and it seems you are rambling within a mirror" (Ji 213). This "rambling within a mirror" (*jingyou*) vividly described the state of mind that was concentrated into the round bounded window *jing* where the effect was similar to that of viewing a fan painting. At this point, the symbolic connection between the full moon, the round fan painting, and the round window view in a garden was finally established and integrated into the existence of *jing*. Although *jing* had been a typical concept in garden records and landscape painting theories, the actual representation of the *jing* from within a garden did not appear until the Ming dynasty. In the Jiangnan region, where many scholar gardens were concentrated, garden representation became popular, and *jing* began to be composed from a ground point of view instead of a bird's-eye or aerial view. The *jing* therefore began to appear more humanized and artificially controlled; viewing a *jing* was like looking at a painting, and vice versa. Zhengming Wen, a representative of the Ming garden painters, painted all thirty-one *jing* of the Garden of an Unsuccessful Politician in Suzhou (Kerby). In these paintings, the rocks, plants, buildings and human figures were carefully arranged, yet the building remained opaque, half-hidden, and lacking in detail (Barnhart figure 22).

During the Qing dynasty, it became a cliché that "when people see a beautiful landscape, they will always say it is like a painting" (Jian Wang 295). An example from the early Qing dynasty was Yu Li's concept "mountains and waters of a fan face" (*bianmian shanshui*), where the window-framed landscape was equated to a fan painting. In yet another of his concepts, "window of painting" (*chifu chuang*), he created a painting on a wall that merged with a small round opening where the distant scenery, such as a mountain in the distance, allowed the onlooker to see the wall painting and the distant landscape as a bounded unity—a *jing* (170, 178). On his concept, "mountains and waters of a fan face," Li elaborated: "the knack of making a *jing* lies in borrowing. . . . The wonderfulness of the opening of a window is to borrow a *jing*. . . . Make a wood window frame, with arched top and bottom and vertical flanks. This is the so-called fan face. When a boat is moving, each paddling will bring a new image and each poling will bring a new *jing*. Even when the boat is tied, because of the wind, waves, and water fluctuating, the *jing* changes at any moment. Within a day, there are created thousands of pretty landscape paintings and all of them are gathered by the fan-face window. . . . Not only the external endless *jing* is taken into the boat, but also all the people, furniture, and decorative wares are projected out of the window for a passerby's appreciation. . . . Looking inside out, there will be a fan-face landscape painting; looking outside in, there will be a fan-face portrait" (170). The mountains and waters of a fan face established the connection between the fan painting and the window-framed *jing* based on their commonality of the bounded view.

As for the framed *jing*, he continued: "Before a window is set up, the view is just of things; once there is the window, no need to say, everybody will look at the view as a painting. . . . A real mountain can be a painting, which in turn can be a window. . . . I once made a window for watching a mountain and named it 'window of painting' or 'unintentional painting' (*wuxin hua*). . . . The room with such a window needs to have a big depth so that the viewer can look at the mountain far from the window. The outer part of the window is the painting and the inner part is the real distant mountain. The mountain is connected with the painting without any separation. If the viewer does not ask, he might think it is a natural painting" (178). The "window of painting" best demonstrates the fusion between painting and *jing* in the early Qing painting theories.

In the Qing dynasty, the *jing* was oriented fully and sometimes even overpowered by the painter's internal feelings. The painter Yuanqi Wang wrote, "When painting a landscape, attention should be paid to its momentum of *qi* and contour. It is not necessary to seek out a pretty *jing* or be limited by an old composition" (170). The expression of emotion through painting required an accent on the visibility of the landscape on a large scale rather than that of a small one. Attention to details seemed to stagnate the synchronic movement of the heart and view. The painter's preference of the momentous contour to pretty details demonstrated the strong projection of his impression over the view of landscapes. In Qing theories of painting, there was a paradox between the expression of emotion and the typified *jing*. On the one hand, the individual's emotion became dominant; on the other hand, the means of expressing emotion became typified and dull. It became a cliché that a figure in a landscape should fit into the particular scene. A figure should seem to be contemplating the mountain; the mountain, in turn, should seem to be bending over and watching the figure (Sze 234). In this mutual correspondence between the viewer and landscapes, the propensity of the whole was expressed. Because people tended to view the relationship between figure and landscape in a painting as a pattern of unity, even if the *jing* was not present in the painting, it could be implied by the posture of the figure. Once the depiction of the relationship was patternized, the expression of propensity and passion became superficial. In Qing painting theories, many scholars tended toward detailed discussion of varied patterns of painting skills without in-depth exploration of fundamental issues.

Another interesting phenomenon in Qing theories of painting was the comparison between *jing* and the human face. For example, Gao Ding suggested that "when painting a *jing* on the margin or at the center, their colors are certainly different. When the sun revolves slightly, the complexion of the *jing* of face will be different. . . . If the figure is in front of a multistoried pavilion, floating light will easily sweep in. If it is in a round pavilion with open sides, it will be hard to find a starting point. If a boat pavilion has three open sides, where can the spirit of the figure be grasped?" (559). The *jing* here are features of a human face. This demonstrates the metaphorical relationship between landscapes and the human figure in a *jing*. Ding observed that the face *jing* changed with the position of the human body in a building setting. If a figure was positioned right in front of a multistoried building, the light effects would be perfect for grasping the spirit of the face *jing*. And later in the Ming dynasty, the features of the physiognomy were actually signified by landscape and constellation terms (Q. Wang 1485) and the face was compared to cosmic landscapes. The connection between the *jing*, face, and multistoried building are helpful in defining the relationship between the emperor's face and the Western multistoried buildings in the exotic *jing* in the Yuanming Yuan.

In Qing theories of painting, the relationship between a human figure and its surrounding *jing* was also discussed. In regard to portraits, the scholar Dou Li said, "recently Mr. Gao Ding painted twelve portraits of me, each of which had an individual *jing*. Each spectator was surprised at these portraits and thought each painted face so resembled my real face and the complexion was so smoothed out and solemn that it completely met with its *jing*. I suspected Mr. Ding had an innate capability of painting, which could not be reached by mere learning. He answered, 'It is not so, rather it is because of the principles. Principles can be learned, but the intention beyond the principles must be understood by the heart'" (53). A portrait was usually composed within a *jing* and both sides needed to match each other. Only when the face and the *jing* were completely matched was the "real face" present in depiction. The resemblance of a portrait was not simply an imitation, but rather needed to be intended and understood by the heart.

Compared with previous dynasties, there were more discussions in the Qing dynasty about the relationship between *jing* and buildings, yet building paintings still ranked low and were looked down upon in comparison to landscape paintings. The scholar Qin Xu confirmed this: "Ancient painters painted buildings with precise measures without error. Their strokes all looked deep, distant and spatial. . . . The present painters are keen on mystical strokes and look down upon building paintings as a mere craft. Therefore, the status of building paintings is getting lower and lower" (804). There were two important qualities for a good building painting: it should look precise and deep in view. Scholars of the Qing dynasty referred repeatedly to the precise measure of ancient building paintings while at the same time pointed out that such a precise measure should not follow the rule of carpentry's lines. Therefore, the painter's understanding of precision was not based on mathematical measures and scales but rather the deep view in which the spectator could truthfully, in such "precision without error," be himself. On the use of a ruler for creating a building painting, a portrait expert explicated: "As for painting a literati painting, besides the brush, ink, form and *jing*, we should know that the ruler is intended to guide the method, border, and scale. It does not mean the wood ruler used by a carpenter for drawing a grid and straight lines. . . . Such a ruler for the literati painting implies the principles and measures of the front and back, distant and near, big and small" (J. Zheng 972). According to the author, the use of a ruler did not necessarily mean the carpenter's straight lines but rather the clear principle and measuring within the mind. A ruler was to help establish the order of a *jing*. Such discussions on building paintings in Qing theories will be important for understanding how the Qing emperor received the Western exotic *jing*, which mainly consisted of multistoried buildings and was composed through linear perspective.

Between the trends of willful mystical strokes and rigid craft-like building painting, there was another trend, which explored the depth of *jing*, but lay somewhere in the middle of the other two; this trend was primarily developed through the court paintings of the Qing dynasty. One of its representatives was the court painter, Dai Tang, who painted the Forty Scenes in the Yuanming Yuan. He stated: "A mountain looks just so from its front; it looks respectively different from its side and back. Each turn and undulation of the frontal mountain should match the posture of the frontal mountain in a moving-through *jing* [*tongjing*]. . . . If there is a bit of discrepancy, a mistake will have been made" (863). In the forty paintings of the Forty Scenes, Tang adopted a bird's-eye view but clearly differentiated the front from the side in order to depict the buildings in great detail. He discussed the scale of *jing* and continued, "Landscape painting is different from figure painting. In the latter, only a cliff, crag, or single piece of landscape is painted. This is the so-called spot *jing*. As for the complete *jing* of mountains and rivers, it is necessary to go to see real mountains" (867). The spot *jing* and the complete *jing* were two typical ways of depicting gardens in the Qing dynasty. A spot *jing* looks static, focused, detailed, and close to the scale of human body. A complete *jing* is on the scale of large landscapes and looks dynamic as a human being moves about in nature. The differentiation between the spot *jing* and the complete *jing* will be helpful to understanding why the Western exotic *jing* was first introduced as a spot *jing* in Chinese gardens and what changes it brought to the traditional *jing*.

Jing as bounded brightness

The *jing* as an integral concept of gardens and paintings enables us to explore the embodiment of the vision of Round Brightness in the emperor's garden as well as its representation. The commonality of the *jing* and the vision of Round Brightness can be described as the bounded brightness, where brightness exists as the origin of *jing* and "bounded" implies the frame of the *jing* and the border of brightness. A further study of the literature of the Forty Scenes, written by the emperors and Jesuits, will clarify how brightness was physically framed in the garden.

The end of the construction of the Yuanming Yuan was marked in 1744 by a set of forty paintings, created by the court painters Dai Tang and Yuan Shen. They painted forty scenes and called their art the Forty Scenes because those scenes were already known by that name. The original Chinese term of the "scene" in the title Forty Scenes is *jing*. Emperor Qianlong named each *jing* with a four-character poetical phrase. Such an activity in Chinese gardens was called "thematicizing a *jing*" (*tijing*), which was intended to "brighten up the *jing*" (C. Chen *Shuo yuan* 46), as each painting was paired with a poem by the emperor. The pattern of pairing the forty paintings and forty poems for the Forty Scenes at the Yuanming Yuan was intended to follow the model established at the Mountain Hamlet for Summer Coolness garden. In the postscript of a court print on the Yuanming Yuan, the court annotator confirmed: "This print imitated the poetical principle of the Mountain Hamlet for Summer Coolness, namely marking out a scenic *jing* and painting it according to its title. The emperor then prefaced and poetized it. There were thus forty poems in total" (E). It is interesting to note the procedure of the imperial pattern of poetizing a *jing*: first, the emperor established a *jing* through entitling it; second, a court painter or painters painted the titled *jing*; third, the emperor wrote a poem for the same *jing*; and finally, the court compiled the paintings and poems of the multiple *jing* into a print for appreciation. An earlier case in the history of pairing poems and paintings for a garden was offered by the twenty *jing* of poet Wei Wang's garden, Wangchuan Villa, during the Tang dynasty. Wang and his friend wrote poems on each of the twenty *jing* of his garden, although these poems were not entitled with a four-character poetical phrase. Furthermore, except for Wang's famous *Painting of the Wangchuan*, with a general view of the garden, it is unknown whether a painting was made for each of the *jing*. Like the traditional landscape painting, the forty paintings of the Forty Scenes presented no shadows and were in the bird's-eye view in which brightness flowed to and fro. One of the first Westerners to observe the Chinese inclination for brightness in their gardens and garden representations was the first British ambassador to China, George Macartney, who visited the Yuanming Yuan in 1793. According to him, cheerfulness was a principal feature of this garden that "lights up the face of the scene" (272). His secretary George Staunton concluded that the Chinese considered shadows an accidental circumstance that ought not to be carried from nature to picture, since it took away a part of the *éclat* and uniformity of coloring (309).

The eighth *jing*, Oneness of Sky and Water, was located on the northern bank of the Back Lake where the emperor would look upon the expansive water from a two-floor pavilion. In his poem on this *jing*, Qianlong expressed his emotions: "The falling rainbow strides over the lake and meanders one hundred feet. / . . . / I look over the water from the air and see the universal green with ten thousand *qing*. / My bosom cannot help swallowing the clouds like in a dream. / . . . / Above and below, the sky and the water are one color, / The water and the sky, above and below, are interconnected" ("Shangxia" 21). Referring to Dai Tang's painting of this *jing*, it is understood that the "falling rainbow" indicated the meandering walkway built over the water. The place where "I look over the water from the air" was a double-floor pavilion on the lakeshore. The "universal green," unifying the sky and water, depicted the far distance of the atmospheric perspective of the *jing*. The Chinese term for "atmosphere" is *fenwei*, which literally means the "enclosure of *qi*," where *qi* flows with one's mood. The *jing* described by the poem was the view that the emperor saw when he stood in the multistoried pavilion; while the *jing* depicted by the painting was the place where he stood. These two *jing* were unified under the same title, Oneness of Sky and Water, and fused into each other. The fact that the titled *jing* included both a view of a place and a view that was perceived from that place reveals that the interpretation of the painting of a *jing* should consider how that depicted *jing* was used in the garden. By comparing a painted *jing* and the same titled *jing* described in the poem, the connection between the brightness of the painting and the emperor's perception mode can be found. On the first *jing*, Uprightness and Brightness, Qianlong wrote, "Poetical books are as many as the trailing plants in the courtyard, / Grace is as extensive as silvery water waves. / A green grass reminds me of being thrifty, / Still mountains recall benevolence" ("Zhengda" 7). His perception shifted among different things, which in turn brightened his mind. His rambling perception, shifting to and fro, matched with the bird's-eye view of the painting of this *jing*. The buildings in this painting were arranged obliquely in a single-point perspective, but the focal point fell far beyond the upper right corner of the painting. The absence of the focal point, seen in traditional landscape paintings, reinforced the back and forth movement of the view. But the perspective convergence, unlike the parallel projection in traditional landscape paintings, resulted from the influence of the Jesuit painters in the court.

In addition to the multiple views depicted in the poem of a single *jing*, perception also unveiled itself along the path of the Forty Scenes. There is a debate on the locations of the thirtieth and thirty-sixth scenes, specifically, which came first on the emperor's poetical route of the Forty Scenes. According to an imperial anthology of Qianlong's forty poems, the thirtieth scene is Open Mind and Enlightened, and the thirty-sixth scene is Bath Body and Enhance Virtue (E). In a modern edition of the similar anthology of the forty poems, however, the Bath Body and Enhance Virtue becomes the thirtieth scene; and the Open Mind and Enlightened the thirty-sixth (Zhongguo Yuanmingyuan xuehui, *Yuanmingyuan Sishijing* 64, 76). Connecting the spot of one *jing* with the spot of the next *jing* with a straight line reveals a clear pattern in the emperor's path. In the 1887 version, the path is a clear zigzag pattern without any overlap of lines; in the 1985 version, the path overlaps around the area of the Fortunate Sea (H. Zou, "Jing of a Perspective" 315, fig. 11). The first pattern guarantees that the emperor's poetical journey did not overlap and would be a continuous process of curiosity and discovery and reveals the hidden order of the seemingly disordered path of the Forty Scenes. Along the path, the Forty Scenes were opened up to the emperor's mind, which in turn was brightened by each *jing*. Such a continuous, zigzagging path created the most expansive vision of Round Brightness within the enclosure of the garden. The journey of the Forty Scenes satisfied Qianlong's need for roaming around and appreciating expansive landscapes, which were so bright and beautiful that "nothing can surpass" them.

The concept that *jing* is a unity of mind and scene was also related to the requirement that each scene had to be recomposed in the mind to become a *jing*. When a name board for each *jing* was hung on the eave of a specific building, it did not mean the *jing* was specifically focused only on that building, but rather an intended group of buildings and their surroundings. A distant scene, for example, the West Mountain, was borrowed into the emperor's mind to compose a *jing*. In the poem "The Yuanming Yuan after a Rain," Qianlong wrote, "The frontal *jing* is so fine; I look upon the mountain, which always looks flourishing" ("Yuhou" 21). "The mountain" indicates the distant West Mountain. The "frontal *jing*" here describes a straight framed view through which the image of West Mountain was borrowed into the garden. After the rain, the view and heart were refreshed and became clear. When the view was extended into the far distance, the depth of the bosom was opened up for brightness.

In his poem "Looking from the Pavilion of Chanting Aloud on an Autumn Day," Yongzheng presented a detailed view of a similar distant *jing*: "Misty distant peaks bathe in sunset light, / Clear rays open up one after another through my watching. / The bridge strides its rainbow-like shadow over the brook, / Wind passes by, cicadas chirp across the river. / Several patches of rosy clouds and three paths of chrysanthemums, / One pool of autumn water and half a bed of clouds. / No sooner have I chanted and had summer coolness at the high pavilion, / Than I hear the golden storm wind send the flock of wild goose away" ("Qiuri" 172). The first two sentences indicate that West Mountain was included in the *jing*, yet West Mountain was not within the garden boundary. His view kept on shifting between the near and far, and finally his heart moved into the distance with the disappearing wild gooses. Furthermore, his chanting in the pavilion echoed the distant golden storm. It can thus be said that the *jing* of the Yuanming Yuan is a collection of multiple scenes, near and far, within the mind. In forming a *jing* within the mind, the emperor not only borrowed a distant view but also frequently made historical allusions. In the poem "The Jing of the Peach Blossom Sunken Bed," Yongzheng wrote: "The imperial garden is good for rainy and clear days, / The bamboo pillow and mat are cool in the remote lodge of the deep spring. / Several falling petals wake up my noon dream, / A song from a fisherman arouses my leisurely emotion. / When temporarily moving around the couch and sitting in a pine grove, / I just heard birds chanting in the bamboo groves. / Only the eastward wind knows my intention, / The pool full of tender green produces ripples" ("Taohuawu" 145). With the *jing* named Peach Blossom Sunken Bed, Yongzheng alluded to the famous "Record of the Paradise beyond the Peach Blossom Spring," an essay written by Yuanming Tao of Eastern Jin. As did Tao, Yongzheng longed for "leisurely emotion" in the garden. In the poem, the *jing* of Peach Blossom Sunken Bed seemed to be a normal *jing*, but in fact it was related to a *jing* in memory.

The allusive *jing* was a typical way for the emperor to establish the connection between the present and the past. In the poem, "Hall for Receiving the Jing [of the Lion Grove]," Qianlong wrote, "I come here occasionally for the purpose of stealing a short leisure, / It has been one year since my last poem at this same spot. / A person like me hastens to ask for a *jing*, / How could I be as lofty and leisurely as the pedantic celestial?" ("Najing" 220). The "pedantic celestial" alludes to the painter Zan Ni of the Yuan dynasty, who was said to have participated in the design of the Lion Grove garden in Suzhou, which was the inspiration for the Lion Grove garden in the Yuanming Yuan complex. In the poem, Qianlong expressed his longing for a *jing* like the Lion Grove in Suzhou. By intentionally "receiving" the *jing* of the Lion Grove, he was seeking the same "lofty and leisurely" state of the painter Ni. While Yongzheng alluded to an ancient writer for the meaning of a *jing*, Qianlong alluded to a past painter for the same purpose. While Yongzheng sought meanings of Round Brightness from classic scriptures, Qianlong was keen on expanding the visibility of Round Brightness through creating new gardens and paintings. Qianlong's strong visual approach encouraged the overlapping between a garden *jing* and a painting *jing*. In the poem "Window of Colored Painting," emperor Jiaqing, son of Qianlong, wrote:

> The area of ten *hu* is big enough to accommodate my body,
> The small window receives remote prettiness.
> Overlaid rocks are made into artificial hills,
> The spare land is used in accordance with the *jing*.
> The rugged peaks are the most singular,
> The sound of spring is like the music of *qin*.
> Pine boughs stick out of the stream valley,
> Winding water runs through the cloudy cave.
> The wonderful bounded view is like a painting,
> In my imagination crags and mountain caves are lined up.
> Sitting in front of the window can substitute for grand wandering,
> Whether it is true or not needs extensive study. ("Yanhua" 229)

The title of the poem, "Window of Colored Painting" echoed the same concept of Yu Li and was a metaphor of a specific *jing*. What is significant is that the wonderful bounded view was like a painting, and sitting in front of the window was like wandering through nature as if it were real. It is clear that this "wonderful bounded view" was actually the *jing*. Looking into the *jing*, the emperor was not sure whether he was looking at a painting or wandering through a real garden scene.

Besides the emperor's poetry and the pictorial representations, another aid to understanding the *jing* of Round Brightness is the literature left by the Western missionaries who worked in the garden. Father Matteo Ripa served as a painter in the courts of Kangxi, Yongzheng, and Qianlong. He contrasted Chinese gardens and Western gardens: "For whereas we [Europeans] seek to exclude nature by art, leveling hills, drying up lakes, felling trees, bringing paths into a straight line, constructing fountains at a great expense, and raising flowers in rows, the Chinese on the contrary, by means of art, endeavor to imitate nature" (62). He thought that creating gardens in a natural way, as the Chinese so skillfully accomplished, was to imitate nature by means of art; the natural way was to respect the original topography as much as possible. Ripa's "natural way" echoed with William Chambers's concept of nature. In his book on Chinese gardens, Chambers criticized the fact that although English gardens were intended to imitate nature, they embraced raw nature without artistic creation. The Chinese artists had nature for their general model, but they were not so attached to nature as to exclude all appearance of art. He argued: "Art must be employed not only to produce variety, but also novelty and effect: for the simple arrangements of nature are . . . too familiar to excite any strong sensation in the mind of the beholder, or to produce any uncommon degree of pleasure" (14). Chambers's criticism of a "simple arrangement of nature" was given to his peers, English garden designers. To support his argument for novel effects in gardens, he referred to the letter of the Jesuit painter, Attiret, about the Yuanming Yuan: "We are told by Father Attiret, that in one of the imperial gardens near Peking, called Yuanming Yuan, there are . . . four hundred pavilions, all different in their architecture" (31). Chambers was not only impressed by the variety of buildings, but he was also impressed by the role of buildings in composing a distant *jing*. He observed that buildings were arranged according to perspective by "giving grayish tints to the distant parts of the composition." His observation of the depth of *jing* was based on his knowledge of linear perspective, but he also noted the effects of atmospheric perspective. He found that the winding path helped introduce varied *jing* and that a *jing*, which he called "a new arrangement," could "occupy the mind agreeably" (42-45). While Chambers referred to Chinese gardens in order to express his concept of English gardens, Attiret referred to European gardens in order to understand the Yuanming Yuan. A comparative perspective was adopted in both their observations. As Attiret stated, "[In the Yuanming Yuan,] they go from one of the valleys to another, not by formal straight walks as in Europe, but by various turnings and windings" ("Letter" 8). He described these pathways as a "beautiful disorder" and thought the Chinese liked "wandering as far as possible from all the rules of art." Being "struck" and "pleased" by the "beautiful disorder," he even admitted, "My eyes and taste are grown a little Chinese" ("Letter" 36, 38).

The same *jing* impressed the French Jesuit, Michel Benoist (Chinese name, Youren Jiang), who designed the fountains of the Western garden. In a letter he wrote, "In Chinese gardens, the view is not strained at all, because it is set up in a space proportional to the field of perception. You look at a beautiful scene that strikes and enchants you; and after a few hundred feet, new objects appear to you and evoke new admiration" (178). He observed that in European gardens, though the path was straight and extended to a far distance, there were many magnificent things to see and the visitor's imagination could not focus on any one of them. By contrast, in Chinese gardens, each view was well proportioned and the beauty came from the changing views. The view "set up in a space proportional to the field of perception" indicates exactly a *jing*. Another reference regarding the *jing* of Round Brightness came from the British ambassador Macartney, who visited the garden in 1793. As for the Chinese approach of conquering while improving nature, he gave detailed descriptions: "It is indifferent to a Chinese where he makes his garden, whether on a spot favored or abandoned by the rural deities. If the latter, he invited them or compels them to return. His point is to change everything from what he formed it, to explode the old fashion of the creation and introduce novelty in every corner. . . . He undulates the surface; he raises it in hills, scoops it into valleys and roughens it with rocks" (271). It is not true that Chinese gardens, as the author described, were indifferent to the issue of site. To the contrary, a correct selection of site was a priority for Chinese gardens. However, he was quite right that in Chinese gardens, especially imperial gardens, everything could be changed in order to "introduce novelty in every corner." The "novelty" is related to the uniqueness of each *jing*. He also observed that the panoramic view of the garden was appreciable. He wrote: "Several hundreds of pavilions scattered through the grounds . . . and yet contributed to the general purpose and effect intended to arise from the whole" (95). The "general effect intended to arise from the whole" could only be observed from a bird's-eye view. This was verified by the paintings of the Forty Scenes.

    The Yuanming Yuan impressed Western visitors, but they tended to perceive a garden scene as much an objective view as the "view" represented in many eighteenth-century copperplates of European gardens. Although Attiret asserted that his eyes and taste were growing a bit Chinese, the emperor's allusive *jing* remained unknown to him and his Jesuit brothers. In the late eighteenth century, an important visual resource for Europeans to learn about the *jing* of the Yuanming Yuan was Georges-Louis Le Rouge's engraved garden encyclopedia of 1775-89. This garden encyclopedia provided detailed copperplates of French, English, and Chinese gardens throughout the world. The thirteenth volume outlined "Jardins anglo-chinois." The fourteenth to sixteenth volumes focused on "Jardin chinois," which included a complete set of the forty copperplates of the Forty Scenes of the Yuanming Yuan engraved in 1786. In addition to those forty copperplates, twenty copperplates of the Western garden of the Yuanming Yuan were engraved in Beijing during the same year (L. Yi). In Le Rouge's encyclopedia, the sequence of the forty copperplate engravings did not follow the original sequence of the Forty Scenes established by Qianlong. In contrast to the original sequence of the Forty Scenes, the appearing sequence of Le Rouge's forty copperplate engravings is (in volume 15) scenes 20, 19

... 2, 1, 40, 39 ... 34, 33; (in volume 16) scenes 32, 31 ... 22, 21. For example, the twentieth scene, Simple Life in Peaceful Surroundings, appeared as the first engraving; while the first scene, Uprightness and Brightness, became the twentieth engraving in Le Rouge's book. The discrepancy between the two sequences demonstrates that the poetical path of the Forty Scenes was unknown by him. On the first plate of volume 15, Le Rouge noted that the so-called English garden was an imitation of Chinese gardens (vol. 15, plate 1). It might be for the sake of proving this idea that he edited these two volumes on the Yuanming Yuan. On the second plate, he noted that his copperplates were intended to imitate the original Chinese woodcuts of the same garden, but he thought that landscapes would be better depicted in his copperplates. He also noted that he followed the Chinese way of using whiteness of paper for expressing distance in a *jing* (vol 15, plate 2). The Chinese woodcuts that Le Rouge imitated can be found in a late-Qing transcript of Qianlong's forty poems of the Forty Scenes (E). The woodcuts were drawn by the court painters Hu Sun and Yuan Shen and carved by unknown Chinese craftsmen. When one compares the woodcuts of various *jing* with Le Rouge's copperplates, for the most part, all the details appear to match. For other *jing*, there are some discrepancies between the Chinese woodcuts and Le Rouge's copperplates. In the woodcut of the fortieth scene, Deep and Remote Dwelling, the bottom border was depicted as flowing clouds that hinted at the Daoist fairyland. The same depiction of clouds appeared in Dai Tang's painting of this scene, but in Le Rouge's copperplate the same portion was presented as a lake and the original Daoist implication was lost. There is a high frequency of Chinese elements within European gardens, such as Jardin Chinois, Pavillon Chinois, Petit Pavillon, Palais Chinois, Maison Chinoise, Pont Chinois, Temple Chinois, pagoda, Barque Chinoise, voliere Chinoise, belvedere Chinois, Salon Chinois, Galeries Chinoises, Maison du Philosophe, grottes Chinoises and kiosq. These Chinese garden elements, as part of the trendy *folie* in French gardens (Conan 104), demonstrated the Europeans' attention to the unique form of buildings in Chinese gardens during the eighteenth century. However, in most cases, as demonstrated in Le Rouge's copperplates, these buildings existed as isolated objects in the *vûe* in European gardens. This isolation did not bring about the cohesive *jing*, where the *jing* required that the elements of the scene and the observer's bosom be combined into a depth of view.

Chapter Four

The Chinese Garden and Western Linear Perspective

The Yuanming Yuan integrated the virtue of Round Brightness and the vision of *jing*. How was this unity applied to the Western portion of the garden? The fact that the Chinese portion enclosed the Western garden has demonstrated that the Round Brightness acted as the immediate context of this exotic garden. In the Chinese portion, the embodiment of the Round Brightness is the multiple *jing*, which can be analyzed through their representations. The representation of the *jing* of the Western garden is a set of twenty copperplates, which were composed with the technique of line method (*xianfa*), the Chinese translation of Western linear perspective. As demonstrated in the paintings of the Forty Scenes, there was already a traditional perspective in Chinese landscape paintings.

    A central issue in Chinese landscape painting is the expression of depth. One of the earliest theorists on distance and depth in Chinese paintings was Bing Zong in the Southern dynasties. He wrote, "The Kunlun Mountain is too big, yet the eye is so small. If the mountain is too close to the beholder, its form cannot be seen. If it is several miles away, its form can be contained in the small eye. It is true that the longer the distance is, the smaller the size of the mountain is. . . . Therefore, the beholder should not burden himself in seeking a detailed likeness in an apparently small mountain in the painting, but rather grasp its natural propensity" (14). In Zong's thought, the greater the distance from the object, the smaller the object appeared, and this was true in both reality and painting. Another classic discourse on depth and distance was advanced by the poet and painter Wei Wang of the Tang dynasty: "In paintings, a distant person has no eye; a distant tree has no bough; a distant mountain has no stone and appears like eyebrows; and a distant body of water has no ripple. . . . These are the knack for depicting distance. To differentiate between the distant and the near, you have to separate them" ("Shanshui" 32). His theory of distance also came from his observation of nature and was close to atmospheric perspective in the modern sense. Further, in Chinese Buddhism, the transformation of scriptures from words into pictures is called *jingbian*, that is, "transformed scriptures." The Tang dynasty cave frescos at Dunhuang became an important source for studying transformed scriptures. One type of fresco, called Western Pure Land Transformation, adopted a large courtyard building as the backdrop for the depiction of Buddha. The compositions of buildings in these frescos were usually a concentrated projection of view, close to central perspective, with a bird's-eye viewpoint (Whitfield, Whitfield, and Agnew 217). These were the earliest cases of concentrated projection known in the history of Chinese painting. Although Buddhism was originally imported from India, the buildings depicted in these frescos were of classic Chinese architecture. It is interesting to note that the Dunhuang frescos were probably the first and only time that concentrated projection has been known to appear prior to the Qing dynasty. Concentrated projection in the Dunhuang frescos was most likely used to emphasize the central position of Buddha, who traditionally sat in the center of the picture.

The central perspective, with the horizon at eye level, in Renaissance art is close to the traditional "frontal view" (*zhengshi*) in Chinese paintings. In the history of Chinese landscape painting, one finds only a few rare pieces with a frontal view. In the painting entitled, "A Thatched Pavilion," by Hong Lu of the Tang dynasty (Guoli gugong bowuyuan; H. Zou, "Jing of a Perpective" 308, fig. 7), the figure in the picture looks straight towards the spectator, appearing to be in a meditation state, sitting inside a single-room house. The figure appears to be a Buddhist residing in the mountain and might be related to the spread of Buddhist temples in remote mountains at that time. The roof of thatch almost reaches the upper border of the painting, while the figure's head touches the ceiling, making his head appear to be the most distant item in the interior of the house. This piece of art is a good example of how depth in a painting was depicted, where the higher a thing was positioned, the more distant it appeared. The positioning of the inhabitant creates a straightforwardness to the inhabitant's view and is in sharp contrast to the randomness of the natural landscape in front of the house, and there is no presence of the horizon of view or the sky. The frontal view seen in this painting was quite rare during the Tang dynasty. In the gardens of the Ming dynasty, the frontal view emerged as a type of *jing*, called the head-on *jing* (*duijing*). It was either arranged on a meandering path to arouse the visitor's surprise or composed as a static picture for appreciation from the interior. But this type of *jing* did not appear in garden representation until the use of line method, a Chinese translation of Western linear perspective in the eighteenth century.

In the Song dynasty, depth in painting theory became well known, with the greatest theoretical advances made by Xi Guo of Northern Song. He theorized the "three distances" in mountain paintings: "Mountains have three distances. The expanse from the foot of the mountains looking up to the peak is called high distance; from the front mountains looking through to mountains behind is called deep distance; from near mountains looking off towards distant mountains is called level distance" (639). The first one, high distance, is vertical and the other two, deep and level distances, are horizontal. While the level distance describes the view moving forward and expanding to both sides, the deep distance indicates a straightforward movement and is obtained when one looks through mountains in the forefront towards the mountains behind. Advancing Guo's theories, Chunquan Han proposed to further define depth in painting. He worked with the concepts of expansiveness, blurriness, and seclusion. His discussion of these concepts is as follows: "There is near but expansive water, and there are expansive but distant mountains. This is called expansive distance. When there are mists and smoke, the water in wilderness cannot be seen. This is called blurred distance. When a scene is in the absolute distance and thus appears minute and dimly discernible, it is called secluded distance" (135).

Guo and Han advanced theories of atmospheric perspective in Chinese paintings. In order to study geometrical perspective, which is rare in Chinese paintings but typical in Western representation, attention needs to be paid to the depiction of buildings. Kuo Shen made well-known comments on the Song painter Cheng Li's paintings of buildings:

> In Li's paintings of pavilions, lodges, towers, and pagodas, the flying eaves were all depicted as being looked upon from the underside. His own explanation is that this looking up from below happens when a person looks upward at the ceiling and eaves while standing on the ground. His viewpoint is wrong. Usually, the principle of landscape painting is looking at a small thing from a big thing, just like looking down at an artificial hill. If adopting the principle of a real mountain and looking upward from below, you can see only a single mountain. In his way, how can you see one mountain after another? In his way, you cannot see brooks in valleys, courts of houses, and what happens in back alleys. . . . Mr. Li probably did not know the principle of looking at a small thing from a big thing where the eye moved up into the distance because of its own subtle reasons for using this principle. What is the purpose of looking at the curved roof corners from the underside? (625)

The painting model of "looking upward at flying eaves from the underside" did not begin with Li; in the Dunhuang frescos, many buildings were depicted with flying eaves, which appeared to be looked upon from underneath; such a viewpoint expressed a feeling of the high and sublime. Shen thought that since Li's paintings were of buildings that were located in mountains, a bird's-eye view should be adopted in order to introduce an expansive vision rather than Li's viewpoint from the ground. Shen's comments demonstrated that the bird's-eye view became a dominant perspective in landscape paintings during the Song dynasty and that the viewpoint from the ground was not appreciated. The differences between Shen and Li also lie in the emphasis between the view and viewer. Shen paid more attention to the view of the landscape itself, while Li emphasized the perspective of a real person standing on the ground.

Kuo Shen preferred an unrealistic bird's-eye view in order to express truthful nature. Cheng Li took a real person's viewpoint but lost the truthful view of nature: in Shen's words, he could not "see one mountain after another." This difference of views brought to light the issue of truth in landscape painting, which did not lie in a morphological imitation of nature but, rather, in a truthful understanding of nature.

The poet, Shi Su, criticizing morphological imitation, claimed that a commenter on a painting focused on the issue of resemblance had an opinion like a child's ("Dongpo" 51). But the issue of truth was not avoided in theoretical discussions. Qi Han stated that appreciating a painting had to do with seeing its ability to "close in on the real" ("Zhigui" 41). The concept of "closing in on the real," *bizhen*, means that the truth is the destination, although it is not easy to obtain and requires much effort. Interestingly, the concept of *bizhen* is similar to the Renaissance idea of approaching truth. According to Nicholas of Cusa, truth functions like an ideal that human beings can approach more or less successfully, although it can never quite be seized. This Renaissance approach has been defined as "a particular perspective" (Harries 50-51). The degrading of morphological imitation did not mean that truth in landscape, especially in the depiction of buildings, did not require the careful observation of objects. Ruoxu Guo wrote about this issue:

> When depicting buildings, the painter needs to calculate without mistakes. The brush strokes should appear balanced and sturdy. The picture should look distant and spatial. All the depicted buildings universally move into the distance in an oblique way. From the Sui, Tang, and Five Dynasties to the early Song, artists such as Zhongshu Guo and Shiyuan Wang usually painted multistoried buildings in such a way that all four roof corners appeared and brackets were depicted one by one with clear differentiation between front and back, without loss of regularity. Current painters like to use a straight ruler to complete a building painting and differentiate multiple layers of brackets. In this way, the brush strokes are miscellaneous without a sense of sublimity and elegance. (58)

To "calculate without mistakes" is to observe precisely with the mind's eye the propensity of landscapes with which the depiction of buildings should resonate. The phrase, "universally move into the distance in an oblique way" indicated a parallel projection in bird's-eye view for the depiction of buildings. Only in such a composition were the four corners of the roof shown at the same time or the front and one flank of the building body shown simultaneously. For the author, the expression of depth and spatiality in a building painting was more important than a mechanical imitation.

In the delineation of buildings in traditional Chinese paintings, there is no fixed focal point. With a single building or several buildings in a closely related group, there is no discrimination in size, and parallel lines remain parallel and equidistant throughout their length. Parallel projection looks similar to Western axonometric drawings, a form of shop drawings where a three-dimensional form is represented in a measurable scale in all its parts (March 132). The two methods of perspective should not simply be equated to each other, as Chinese parallel projection is not for measuring and control, as is the Western method, but rather is related to the expression of the depth of a *jing*. Except for some fragments, it is hard to find documentation in Chinese theories of painting regarding building drawings. However, Chunquan Han advanced the idea that "buildings should hide among mountains and forests and not appear completely. Otherwise, a painting would look like a pattern of buildings . . . especially for Buddhist temples and Daoist belvederes, it is better to locate them in secluded valleys" (141). Rendered from a distant point of view, such buildings only rarely exhibited the effect of foreshortening. Beside the atmospheric perspective and parallel projection of buildings, another way of expressing depth in Chinese paintings was the vertical composition, where the painter placed the point of view of the composition at a very high level. The line of the horizon was very high, and the various planes ranged one above the other in such a way that the glance embraced a vast space (Bushell 108-09; Petrucci 24). Chinese landscape paintings are primarily on vertical scrolls, with a large vertical area, creating a surface where the higher an object is in the composition, the more distant it appears. Viewing the painting begins at the bottom and gradually moves towards the top, thus, the view slowly extends into the distance. Corresponding with the nonfocal point, there is a movable viewpoint in Chinese paintings. Some scholars have pointed out that for the Chinese artist, man is not the measure of all things, but is a figure that has to be integrated into the landscape (see, e.g., Beurdeley 138). The concept of being in nature in order to paint real nature is expressed in Xi Guo's theory of painting: "If you put yourself in mountains and waters and then observe them, the idea of mountains and waters completely appears. . . . The shape of a mountain changes with your moving. . . . If a painting can make the idea emerge within the beholder, he must feel like being in the real mountain" (634-35). The first poet who said "Rivers and mountains are picture-like" (*jiangshan ruhua*) was Haoran Sun of the Song dynasty. The phrase came from his poem, "The Flying Away Swallow (Li ting yan)." Compared to the concept of the picturesque (*pictoresque*), which indicated a rational method of composing a view in European gardens in the eighteenth century (Conan 179), the Chinese concept of picture-like was not defined in specific terms. The pictorial images presented in landscape paintings often showed a tendency toward ambiguity and the disintegration of forms into a misty poetic mood and blurry atmosphere rather than emphasizing natural details in a landscape (Ho 365, 383). The tendency towards the picture-like suggests that the view of landscapes must be put under control by mental enclosure in order to become a significant existence—*jing*.

In the Yuan dynasty, there emerged a concept of "moving-through *jing*" (*tongjing*) to describe the type of landscape paintings that maintained a high viewpoint so that the observer could look through the whole pictorial *jing* (*Zuan zu* 1: 7, fig. 24). In the Qing imperial gardens, this concept was used to describe Western paintings that were composed in linear perspective. The commonality of Chinese and Western paintings in this respect probably lies in the intention of seeing through into the distance. In the Ming dynasty, it became popular for individuals to request artists, such as Zhengming Wen, to paint their own private gardens. Wen's paintings at first showed views of garden scenes with the horizon at eye level, as depicted in his famous set of paintings known as *Garden of an Unsuccessful Politician* in Suzhou (Barnhart figure 22). Once the viewpoint was from the ground, buildings in the garden scenes required a more detailed representation, although they remained rough and ambiguous and did not show any sign of linear perspective. Wen did admit his great difficulty with depicting buildings: "To paint a palace building is the most difficult. It is said only when the measure has no error can a painting be a good piece. Because such a painting is restricted by rules, the brush and ink cannot be used freely. If a small break of rules is made, the painting will degrade into a vulgar piece. Therefore, there has not been a master painter in this field before the Tang dynasty or until the Five Dynasties, when Xian Wei became famous in this field, but his paintings still did not reach the highest level" (Wen, "Hengshan" 713). Wen thought that a building painting had to follow certain rules to obtain correct measurement, but he did not specify what the rules were. On this issue, his peer Yin Tang stated, "Painting a building without a ruler started from Shuxian Guo [that is, Zhongshu Guo]. Using a ruler to measure a painting started with Boju Zhao. In later generations, such as that of Song Li, the method of carpentry was used to paint buildings. At that point, such paintings finally degraded to the lowest level" (712). Tang described how to measure a building in a landscape painting, noting that applying a ruler to measuring did not mean following the rigid method of carpentry, which was despised in landscape painting. The fact that a painter worked with or without a ruler to measure indicates that mathematical precision was not a criterion for judging the correctness of measurement within the painting. The correct measure originated more from the regularity of the heart than from that of mathematics. The regularity of the heart indicated more a concentration of the mind than the true view observed.

The traditional composition described by "the higher position in a painting, the more distant" began to change during the Qing dynasty, especially in court paintings that were influenced by the Jesuits, such as the Forty Scenes by Dai Tang and Yuan Shen. On painting a mountain, Tang explained that "if it is distant, it should look low; if it is near, it should look high. . . . The distance can be expressed by layers of mountains, one after another" (851). According to his theory, a distant mountain was not necessarily positioned at the top of the painting, but the peak of a near mountain could reach that top, and the front mountains should partially block the view of the back ones. A new phenomenon evolved from his theory of distance, which was the emergence of the horizon of view in perspective and the horizon of land in the depicted view. In all the paintings of the Forty Scenes, these two horizons appeared clear and matched with each other, although the spectator's viewpoint still floated in the air (Tang and Shen). In traditional landscape paintings, there was no chance for the presence of the horizon of land. In the paintings of Forty Scenes, the clear presence of the horizon of land began to draw the consciousness to the horizon of view. Compared with a contemporaneous work of another Qing imperial garden, *Thirty-Six Scenes of the Mountain Hamlet for Summer Coolness* by Weicheng Qian in 1752-54 (Bishu), the layers of mountains in Tang's paintings are clearer and more cohesive with the perspective effect of the buildings in the paintings. The expression of general propensity in Tang's paintings is thus closely related to the depiction of perspective effects.

The composition of oblique projection in the paintings of the Forty Scenes was developed from the traditional oblique-parallel projection, which advanced the concept that an object should be painted as what it should be rather than as how it appeared. The British envoy Staunton observed that in paintings displayed in the Yuanming Yuan, objects at different distances were drawn not as they appeared to the eye but in their actual size, "as determined by the judgment correcting the errors of sight" (309). Others have proposed that the oblique angle of view in Western engravings provided the Chinese "an interesting new way" to organize landscape paintings (Cahill 77). This is not completely true if one considers the oblique parallel projection of buildings in traditional landscape painting. There were many discussions in the Qing dynasty about how to typify a specific *jing* in a painting, some quite detailed. The painter Xian Gong stated: "When painting a stone, it should be noted that its upper side is bright and its lower side is dark. The bright is *yang* and the dark is *yin*. If the stone surface is flat, it will be bright. If it receives light from the sun or moon, it will also be bright. . . . The side that does not receive light from the sun or moon is in a shadow and therefore looks dark" (782). Gong was a painter who theoretically discussed and intentionally practiced the depiction of volumetric images in landscapes. He continued: "A building should appear as if it is there in that place and looks accessible. A bridge has a face and a back and if its face appears on the upper west, its back should be on the lower east. People usually paint this position in the reversed order and it is a big mistake. . . . When placing a temple, it should be in accordance with the depth of the mountain and the thickness of the forests" (786). In fact, this discussion mirrored the principles of Western linear perspective. He proposed a static viewpoint, which was in contrast with the traditional movable viewpoint of landscape painting.

The Jesuit perspective of art

In order to understand how the Jesuit perspective of art was translated into Chinese representation, it is necessary to trace its Western origin. During the Middle Ages, a belief was held based on Aristotle's thought that nature worked in the most efficient way possible. Based on that principle, Franciscan friar Roger Bacon advanced the notion that species traveled in straight paths and that vision, as the movement of species, must be demonstrated in geometrical lines. For him, the "good vision" was the "radiant pyramid," perpendicular to the eye (Bacon 131, 457). The medieval homology of perception and *perspectiva naturalis* was broken up by the Renaissance *perspectiva artificialis* where, in the Renaissance theorist Leon Alberti's words, "the eye measured quantities of things with the visual rays as with a pair of compasses" (*On Painting* 46). The conjunction "as" indicates the distinction between artificiality of perspective and the naturalness of perception. The verb "measure" implies making something that was invisible become visible through engaging in visible things. The dominant practice of the Renaissance perspective was to imitate architectural settings. To make his comic stage set look real, for example, the Renaissance architect Sebastiano Serlio noted that houses with strong projections worked well for perspective effects for backdrops on the stage. He even used perspective to create

The Chinese Garden and Western Linear Perspective

fake windows through which buildings were painted to "simulate reality" (86, 378). A 1609 edition of Serlio's book was stored in the Jesuit libraries of eighteenth-century Beijing (*Catalogue*; H. Zou, Appendix). However, artificiality of perspective was intended to reveal something that went beyond the tangible world. This invisible reality emerged in engravings by a group of craftsmen in Nürnberg, who freely used perspective to imagine ideal gardens and structures. The German engraver, Lorenz Stöer, made eleven woodcuts of perspective gardens, portraying building ruins, trees, and stereometric bodies in front of landscapes (Stöer). His intention was not to depict an actual garden, but rather to demonstrate how magical a garden made of perspective would be.

Invisible reality is approached by perspective with two visual effects, depth and foreshortening. The effect of foreshortening is created through lines converging towards a focal point. Although Alberti did not use the term "focal point," his concept of "central point" was the same as a focal point. He noted that the central point was "a point which occupies the place where the central [visual] ray strikes [on the picture plane]" (*On Painting* 56). The central point was therefore like a counter-eye through which both the viewer and the painted objects appeared to be on the same plane. As Alberti advanced the concept of central point, his peer, the architect Filippo Brunelleschi, developed the concept of perspective through a famous experiment in 1425. The application of a mirror in his experiment demonstrated that the precise geometrical center of the painting panel was made in the image of the eye. The central point as a counter-eye, even in modern times, still cannot be equated with the vanishing point. As Alberti described, the oblique lines were drawn from rather than toward the central point. In his book on painting, he only mentioned the convergence of lines once, and even this expression was uncertain. He wrote: "Thus the inscribed line indicates to me in what way, as if looking into infinity, each transverse quantity is altered visually" (*On Painting* 56). The phrase "as if" demonstrates that during the Renaissance period, the concept of "focal point" was already established, but its connection with infinity was not. The concept of the focal point acting as the counter-eye was well maintained by the Jesuit concept of perspective. This is illustrated in a treatise on linear perspective by the architect Giacomo Barozzi da Vignola, who had a close relationship with the Jesuits. In the first rule of perspective in his book, similar to German engraver Albrecht Dürer's "lute method," the perspective of a square was constructed without the use of a focal point. Although the focal point did not enter the perspective construction in the illustration of the first rule, Vignola clearly marked the focal point on the picture plane to demonstrate the projection of the viewer's eye. In the second rule of perspective, he introduced a viewing figure to mark the point of distance. This second observer, another eye, defines the distance of perspective (69, 100; Kitao). A copy of Vignola's book was stored in the Jesuit libraries of eighteenth-century Beijing (*Catalogue*; H. Zou, Appendix). Vignola's distance-point method as a two-point system prefigured the Jesuit scholar Jean Dubreuil's bifocal perspective, which was drawn with two lateral foci. Dubreuil published his book on perspective in 1648 and its English version appeared in 1672. Like Vignola, Dubreuil stuck to the monocular vision, as the thought at that time was that one could more clearly see a perspective "with one eye only" than with two. He called the focal point "the point of sight," and said that the horizon, bearing always the point of sight, showed "how much the eye is elevated from the earth." He clearly stated that perspective could not only please the eye but also "deceive the sight," and to achieve this, the horizon must always be set at the natural height (4-11, 120-23). His theories about deceiving the sight coincided with the Jesuit painter Andrea Pozzo's (1642-1709) experiment on illusory perspective.

Pozzo was a virtuoso of *trompe-l'oeil* and *quadratura*. Based on the principle of Italian perspective known as *di sotto in su* ("from below upwards"), he painted the dome of the church of San Ignazio and the altars of the church of Gesù in Rome, and transformed the interior of the church of the University of Vienna. Pozzo's perspective of *di sotto in su* was then integrated with architecture: "perspective never appears more graceful than in architecture" (30). Like Vignola's book, a 1702 edition of Pozzo's book on linear perspective was stored in the Jesuit libraries of eighteenth-century Beijing (*Catalogue*; H. Zou, Appendix). Like Dubreuil, he admitted that the art of perspective did, "with wonderful pleasure," deceive the eye. To make visual deception work, an arbitrarily located point of view was necessary in order to be "free from the incumbencies of occult lines" in perspective and to "draw all the points therefore to that true point, the glory of God" (12). With the single "true point," Pozzo defended the unifocal perspective, which maintained the hypothesis of monocular vision and unprecedentedly drew the point of view into spatially constructing a perspective. His projection method was based on the visual pyramid whose apex was the eye of the viewer and bottom was the constructed painting. In this way, perspective is "a counterfeiting of the truth," and the painter is not obliged to make it appear real when seen from any part; but, "from one determinate point only," the painted scene does appear real for spiritual epiphany. Alberti described perspective as "an open window" for looking through. Within the window, the central ray of the eye, which he called "prince of rays," was of greatest importance for the certainty of sight (*On Painting* 48, 56, 121). Renaissance perspective brought a certain transparency to vision and provided a chance to look through the painting plane, as indicated by Dürer's concept *Durchsehung* ("seeing through") (qtd. in *Jamnitzer*). Many Renaissance gardens—for example Vignola's works—were composed like architectural forms, with long vistas and a halting point. During the Baroque period, there was an accentuation of the picture-like effect, and linear perspective helped the designers grasp the totality in gardens. Dubreuil particularly connected perspective with buildings and thought the fairest pieces of perspective were made in rich and sumptuous buildings. He discussed the horizon of view, which "separates the heaven from the earth and limits the sight," and emphasized that perspective could either make counterfeit pictures or "draw to the life" (11). For Pozzo, the art of perspective does, with wonderful pleasure, deceive the eye for "the solemnity of exposing the holy sacrament" (12). At almost the same time as Dubreuil, the French architect André Félibien developed a similar idea, that linear perspective was especially useful to depicting buildings (702). In France, perspective was applied in the creation of copperplate engravings of gardens. Israël Silvestre liked to entitle his engravings as "veue en perspective de" or "veue et perspective de" (several of Silvestre's books of engravings were held in the Jesuit libraries of eighteenth-century Beijing [*Catalogue*; H. Zou, Appendix]). The expression of the horizon of land through perspective was particularly obvious in the copperplate engravings by Dutch artist Johannes Kip. Usually, he located the horizon of land high, almost touching the upper border of the picture, and left only a narrow strip of sky. However, in most of his engravings, the horizon of perspective did not match the horizon of land, so that the converged lines seemed to suddenly be truncated by the horizon of land.

While the importance of the perspective "view" was greatly enhanced during the Baroque period, the Jesuit order maintained the tradition of visualizing Christian metaphysics. This tradition originated from the *Spiritual Exercises* of Saint Ignatius, the founder of the Society of Jesus. One composition of the *Spiritual Exercises*, for example, is "seeing the place," which requires the individual prayer to see the material place through the gaze of the imagination in order to visualize the contemplated object of the prayer (Ignatius 294). The extreme attention paid by the Jesuit order to material details is also demonstrated by the order's tradition of locating churches in urban areas. St. Ignatius was the founder of the first major religious order in the history of the church to opt deliberately for complete insertion of a religious order's works and residence in the center of the urban fabric (Lucas 23). In the "modo de proceder" ("our way of proceeding") of Jesuits, Pozzo asserted that a painter was obliged to make the truth (namely, God) appear in a perspective from "one determinate point only" (221). This point as the counter-eye, in Jesuit perspective, allowed the beholder a unique frontality where invisible reality, "the truth," was encountered. Pozzo located the "true point" for spiritual epiphany yet left all the other points as distortions of perspective. It has been argued that Pozzo's geometry led to a simple representation of reality and encouraged the architect to believe that one could "design in perspective" and make "pictures" of buildings (Pérez-Gómez and Pelletier 71-72). Such a belief might have influenced the Jesuit design of the Western garden in the Yuanming Yuan. In current scholarship, Jesuit engravings that applied this concept and perspective are regarded as "tools of proselytization." Since perspective is degraded to a tool, the contemporary interpretation of Jesuit perspective tends to seek external ideas for this tool and suggests that the concept of *disegno*, promoted in the academies of Firenze and Bologna, was the preferred "style" of the Jesuit perspective (Edgerton 258). It is even suggested that the "lines" of Jesuit perspective were "the rays of spiritual energy radiating to the peoples of the world" (Kemp 139). Along this line, Vignola's distance-point method was stressed by the attempt to draw a rhetorical conclusion: that the Jesuits went to "distant" China to find their "point" (A. Chen 401). I disagree with these opinions, basically because such metaphoric inductions represent—as suggested by Jaques Derrida—a "worn-out metaphor," which is powerless to affect sense and especially poetical sense (217-19).

The Italian Jesuit Giuseppe Castiglione (Chinese name, Shining Lang) played a central role in introducing linear perspective in China. Born in Milan, he entered the Society of Jesus in 1707. During his novitiate in Genova, he was trained as a painter. By 1715, he arrived in Beijing and lived at the Jesuit church called Eastern Hall (Dong Tang; Catholic name, St. Joseph Mission). He served successively as a court painter for three emperors of the Qing dynasty: Kangxi, Yongzheng, and Qianlong. Castiglione's first known painting in China was created in the Yongzheng court in 1723. It is commonly held that he also made two large paintings for another Jesuit church, Southern Hall (Nan Tang). Two comments by eighteenth-century Chinese scholars on Castiglione's perspectival paintings in the Southern Hall church are available. Yuanzhi Yao of the Qing dynasty wrote:

> There are two Shining Lang's line-method paintings in the Southern Hall church. They were on the east and west walls of the hall. . . . Standing by the west wall and looking across at the east wall with one eye, you will see that the inner chamber extends to a great depth. . . . The southern window is half open and the sunbeams play on the ground. . . . Where the sunbeams reach, the shadows of the fans, vases, and tables are perfectly accurate. . . . A set of pillars stands in line and the stone pavement evenly shines with brightness. To the east, it appears as if a house exists, and the door seems not yet open. . . . Looking down upon the ground, it is as bright as a mirror and you are able to count all the square tiles. . . . If you step further away from the hall, there are two bedrooms. . . . When you see them at a distance, you are tempted to enter. If you touch it, you will suddenly find that it is a wall. There was no line method in our ancient times. It is so accurate that you will only regret that our ancestors had not seen it. (*Zhuyeting zaji* 66-67; Ishida 102)

Another scholar, Jingyun Zhang, most likely wrote the following regarding the same work of Castiglione: "If one leans on the west wall and looks eastward, one sees a double door and a chamber endlessly deep and wide. The interior chamber that is surrounded by more chambers seems partly open and partly closed. . . . The painter was an expert in the art of *yin* and *yang*; therefore, when viewed at a distance, things will always appear so real" (J. Zhang; Ishida 104). Both comments expressed a common impression of Castiglione's perspectival paintings, which was that the paintings exhibited a great depth and lifelike effect. For the Chinese eye, such an amazing lifelikeness resulted from the accurateness of line method and the rendering of chiaroscuro, called the art of *yin* and *yang*. When a painting draws one into the painting at such a great depth, it is indeed a feeling that the mind is drawn into the painting and wanders therein. In 1703, the Jesuit Northern Hall church (Bei Tang) was built and consecrated. An Italian painter, Giovanni Gherardini, painted the frescos of the interior. There is a description of these paintings in a Jesuit letter (Jartoux 3). One fresco depicted an illusionary open dome, which was supported by marble columns, decorated arcades, and balustrades, and the picture "Our Heavenly Father" was surrounded by a group of angels. The descriptions of the painted dome indicated that the paintings were very similar to the works of Pozzo. Gherardini was born in Modena in 1655 and moved to Bologna, where he was a pupil of Angiolo Michele Colonna, known as one of the founders of the Bolognese school of *quadratura* (Corsi 109).

The perspectives painted by the Jesuits had been displayed sporadically throughout the Yuanming Yuan. They were called the depth paintings (*shenyuan hua*), which recalled Xi Guo's concept of distance and indicated an identification of perspective with depth. On the fifteenth day of the first moon of the fourth year of the Yongzheng reign (1726), Castiglione was ordered to create six "depth paintings" for the All Season Hall. On the third day of the sixth moon, he presented a sample work to the emperor. After reviewing it, the emperor said that "this work is very excellent, but the building in the background is too high to climb and the depth of the picture is too shallow. Please make another sample work in accordance with the depth of the three-bay room" ("Neiwufu" archive 23). The Chinese had multiple names for depth or perspective paintings. One name is the "moving-through-*jing* painting" (*tongjing hua*) indicating identification with the effect of foreshortening. Another is "looking-through painting" (*touhua*), similar to Dürer's concept of *Durchsehung* ("Neiwufu" archives 227, 330, 227). Some of these names certainly existed before the advent of perspective paintings. A garden in Beijing during the Ming dynasty was named Garden of Moving-through-Jing (Tongjing Yuan), for instance (D. Liu 249). That an existing Chinese term was used for naming Western perspective paintings may help us to understand how the Chinese were impressed by the perspectival view.

On Castiglione's painting quality, a scholar of the Qing dynasty commented that "Shining Lang, a Westerner, is good at paintings of feathers and flowers. He uses the Western method. . . . A poem written by the emperor Qianlong for Lang's painting of a tribute horse says: 'Convex and concave the painting method, it circulates from the West.' Lang has his own Western painting tools and his painting method has no bone. . . . His portrait is better than any other. His paintings are based on the Western method and fused with the Chinese method. His flower paintings look vivid and real and are not what a mediocre painter produces with tools. . . . In 1740 he made an album of twelve portraits with the Western method for emperor Qianlong" (Hu 40). The phrase "his painting method has no bone" meant that Castiglione did not depend on contour lines, which were called "bone" in Chinese painting theories. With rather subtle color rendering, which was called "flesh" in painting theories, he created volumetric images. Although Castiglione applied the Western method, his paintings looked vivid and real, which were highly appreciated aspects in Chinese paintings. No records have been found about the relationship between Castiglione's paintings in China and his religious intentions, but some traces exist. Castiglione tried to publish a book of the engravings he created while in China. In a letter asking for funds from the Society of Jesus, he said that it would be a great comfort if only two Jesuit brothers were to be involved in this little undertaking so that laymen of Europe would note that the Jesuits in China "dedicated all their time to the glory of God" ("Letter" 154). Castiglione certainly used his specially developed painting method, the so-called "flesh without bones," to accommodate himself to the Chinese imperial context. He was one of the Jesuit painters who were experts at painting portraits, which was an important type of painting in the imperial court. The Jesuits applied perspective to this field in order to create a life-like representation of the imperial face. According to the records of the Qing court painters, no one could paint as real a portrait as Castiglione did (Hu 40). In the colophon of a colored painting by Castiglione, *Welcome the Arrival of Spring*, Qianlong wrote: "Shining [Castiglione], who is good at portraiture, painted so well my image when I was a teenager. But now, being an elder full of white hairs, when I enter the room and look at this painting, I cannot even recognize the painted young man" (Castiglione, *L'empereur*). The painting depicted emperor Yongzheng and his son Prince Hongli (later emperor Qianlong) talking in a garden. The emperor's calling Castiglione by his Chinese given name reveals their close relationship. The garden setting on the front is combined with a perspectival background. The figures and bamboo trees correspond to the central axis of perspective. More significant are the lifelike effects of the rock, bamboo, ground, and human bodies.

Emperors preferred to have their portraits painted in full face, which required a frontal posture, with the eyes looking straight at the spectator, because the full face was supposed to be brightest. When Jesuit painters painted a side face that cast shadows, like the Renaissance three-quarter position, the emperor usually rejected it and insisted on the frontal view, showing the face of perfect brightness. The emperor's preference for frontal portrait was noted by Attiret: "In fact, the Chinese taste prefers the frontal face portrait to the side view in Europe. It is required that the similar parts of a face appear equally in the portrait, and that there be no other difference than those introduced by shadows according to the light source. So, the portrait has always to look at the spectator. It therefore means that it is more difficult for us here in China than elsewhere to succeed in this kind of painting" ("Lettre" 400). In an illustration of portrait positions of the Ming dynasty, ten positions were classified according to the amount of face that appeared in the portrait (Q. Wang 1651). The position of the full frontal face was called the ten-degree image (*shifen xiang*). The Chinese term "ten-degree" also means "very," and the Chinese term "image" has the meaning of "resemblance." Thus, the "ten-degree image" implies "very resembling." In other words, the frontal face is the most real face. Although the use of shadows in portrait paintings was a typical technique for Jesuit painters, the Chinese considered shadows on the face as inauspicious. The Chinese dislike of shadows yet their wonder at them in portrait painting was observed by Staunton, who was the secretary of the first British ambassador to China. When several portraits by the Jesuits were exhibited in the Yuanming Yuan, the Chinese questioned the variety of shades and asked whether the right and left sides of the original face had different colors. They considered the shadow of the nose as a great imperfection in the pictures and supposed it had been placed there by accident (307). The portrait of the imperial face not only had to look perfectly bright but also had to appear in its best time of life. According to the imperial archives, the portrait painter in the court had to "observe the imperial face frequently" to form its perfect image in the mind. So, when an emperor became aged, a painter would "take the utmost care to paint the imperial face according to his memory" (Kun 18872).

The overlapping of the two kinds of frontal faces, the imperial face and the frontal face of Jesuit perspective, was best represented by a portrait of Prince Guo (that is, Hongyan), Qianlong's younger brother (*Portrait of Hongyan*). The prince sat in an armchair in front of a painting screen that depicted a Western portal. The screen in central perspective echoed his frontal posture, and his head rested exactly at the focal point. The central board of the portal was depicted in central perspective as an illusionary *jing* of a distant landscape. It is interesting to note that the painting was cut off from the original paper and remounted on another piece of paper. The thickness of the cut edge of the portal reinforces the perspective effect and paradoxically the artificiality of line method. Jesuit perspective has a close relationship with the technique of copperplate engraving. In 1688, the French Jesuits presented to Kangxi twenty engravings of "trois Fêtes de Versailles" and thirteen "Vues de Villes et de Maisons royales" engraved by Silvestre (Durand 133). These engravings of Versailles most likely influenced the emperor's understanding of French royal gardens. The earliest copperplates made in China were the Thirty-Six Scenes of the imperial retreat garden, Mountain Hamlet for Summer Coolness, in Chengde. These copperplates were engraved by Matteo Ripa in 1713. At the same time, thirty-six woodcuts of the same scenes were created by Chinese artists, and Kangxi wrote a poem for each of the thirty-six scenes. It is interesting to note that both the copperplates and woodcuts were paired with the same poems by the emperor, which showed his great interest in the differences of the landscape representation. Ripa gave a detailed account about his experience of making the copperplates of the *jing* of the Mountain Hamlet for Summer Coolness garden: "As subjects on copperplates thus prepared present a very handsome appearance, the emperor Kangxi drew a landscape, in order that I might afterwards engrave it. As soon as it was done it was shown, together with the original, to his Majesty, who expressed considerable delight and surprise at finding the copy so perfectly similar to the original without being impaired; for this was the first time that he had seen an engraving on copper" (66). The emperor was very impressed by the precise, detailed, and real-life effects of the copperplates, because such a real-life effect had never been reached in the history of Chinese painting. Ripa confirmed that his copperplates were engraved based on the paintings created by the Chinese painters (72). However, Ripa's copperplates give no clear sign of linear perspective, since they were engraved after the bird's-eye-view paintings, taken from a great distance.

In 1765, the Jesuit painters made a set of sixteen drawings depicting the victory of the Qing government in the war at the northwestern frontier (Castiglione et al., *Suite des Seize Estampe*). The first four drawings were sent to Paris in 1765 for the purpose of making copperplates and the rest were sent the following year. The first drawing was drawn by Attiret, the second by Joannes Damascenus (Chinese name, Deyi An), the third by Castiglione, the fifth by Castiglione, the sixth and seventh by Damascenus, the eighth by Ignaz Sichelbarth (Chinese name, Qimeng Ai), the eleventh by Damascenus, the fourteenth and fifteenth by Attiret, and the rest by anonymous painters. Comparing these drawings, one can see easily that Damascenus's skill at drawing was not equal to that of his Jesuit colleagues. In the second drawing, by Damascenus, all the figures appeared to have the same smiling face, although they were depicted on the battlefield. In the sixth and seventh, also by him, almost every figure, no matter whether a victor or loser, kept the same smiling face. In the eighth, by Sichelbarth, the complexions of victors and losers were depicted differently. In the third, by Castiglione, and the fifth, by Attiret, each figure had a different bearing and posture.

The Western line method of painting

The Jesuit perspective works in China indicate that linear perspective was presented to the Chinese court, but how linear perspective was translated into a Chinese approach of representation can be gleaned from the study of cultural exchange. The golden age of the Jesuit mission in China was during the Kangxi reign, with the climax being the building of the French Jesuit church, Northern Hall (Bei Tang; Catholic name, The Holy Savior) in about 1700. The emperor permitted the church to be located within the Imperial City. The property contained a library, an observatory, a garden, and the church. There was an inscription sign that read: "True Origin of All Things (Wanyou Zhenyuan)" and it was penned by the emperor and embedded in the wall over the main gate of the church. The inscription expressed Kangxi's attitude towards the Western religion, that is, he wished the religion would help reveal the truth of the world. At the same time, the search for truth in the world was also undertaken in the West. The German philosopher, Gottfried W. Leibniz, wrote the famous preface for his book *Novissima Sinica* (1697) during this period. He had a close relationship with Jesuits, such as the German Jesuit Athanasius Kircher, and both Leibniz's and Kircher's books were held in the Jesuit library in Beijing (*Catalogue*). At this time, the Jesuits held two different views in their understanding of Chinese philosophy. The Jesuit leader of the Chinese mission, Matteo Ricci, took the accommodationist position, excoriating popular Buddhism and Daoism, but cultivating the Confucian literati; his successor, Nicholas Longobardi, considered the ancient Chinese as materialists devoid of any spiritual thoughts (Cook 14). Longobardi's observation was probably correct in that Chinese thought was really of the world and not as transcendental as Western metaphysics. However, Ricci attempted to find a common ground to draw the Chinese view close to Christianity.

In the preface, Leibniz referred to both Jesuit and Chinese views in his exposition on geometry. He first took Longobardi's side by expressing his pride in Western metaphysics and the understanding of concepts abstracted from the material world. At the same time, he described Chinese philosophy as remaining content with a sort of "empirical geometry." Leibniz's position that geometry was an expression of metaphysics was extended further by his claim that geometry ought not to be regarded as the sphere of workmen but as that of philosophers, because through demonstrations of geometry the nature of eternal truth had been perceived. For Leibniz, the only way to educate individuals in the mysteries of sciences was through geometry. He described geometry as "one of the eyes" of Westerners, yet pointed out, "we have still another eye," known as First Philosophy, through which an understanding of incorporeal things was admitted. First Philosophy is the philosophy on the existence of God (Descartes, *Meditations*). Thus, God and geometry, as two eyes, were inherently related. Furthermore, the strength of geometry lay in teaching people how to reason, and this strength, according to Leibniz, had been tasted by the Chinese emperor ("Preface" 50-53). However, in another article, "Remarks on Chinese Rites and Religions," Leibniz shifted to Ricci's side by defending the idea that there was indeed something in Chinese thought that corresponded with Western metaphysics. His discussion focused on the neo-Confucianist concept, *li* (roughly, "reason"). In his correspondence with the Jesuits, he expounded *li* as "the primary matter," "the substance of things." In Chinese, *li* means in history "rule," "principle," and "Dao" (*Zhongwen*). According to Leibniz, from *li* emanated justice, wisdom, and the other virtues; from the unity of *li* and *qi* originated the five elements (gold, wood, water, fire, and earth) and physical forms. But Leibniz pointed out that, because the *li* could be united with the *qi*, Chinese spirits (e.g., heaven, or the spirits of mountains and rivers) were composed of the same substance as physical things and had a beginning and end along with the world ("Remarks" 68).

In the essay, "Discourse on the National Theology of the Chinese," Leibniz asked if *li* could be equated with prime matter in Western philosophy, with his analysis originating from geometry. He thought that since the Chinese called their *li* a circle, that is, the circle of *taiji* that integrated *yin* and *yang*, *li* coincided with the Western way of speaking of God as being a sphere whose center was everywhere and whose circumference was nowhere. He criticized Longobardi for treating *li* simply as the scholastic notion of prime matter—a passive power—and asserted that *li* was closer to Spinoza's principle of prime matter—creature as modes of God. By citing the neo-Confucianist philosopher of the Song dynasty, Xi Zhu's thoughts, Leibniz interpreted *li* as the quintessence of things and inferred that if *li* could not be equated with the prime matter of Western philosophy, it should have been conceived as the "prime form" ("Discourse" 82-133). Zhu's concept of *li* is embodied in every natural phenomenon and he finds that the mind can discern profound philosophy from the observation of simple things such as the flow of water and the growth of grass in a garden (X. Wu 186). In other words, *li* has an inherent relationship with what the world looks like. According to Leibniz, the *li* was embodied by "spiritual substances," for example, the spirits of mountains and waters, which were "clothed in subtle material bodies," like angels of Christianity ("Discourse" 148).

While Leibniz struggled with categorizing the Chinese concept of *li* as physical or metaphysical, the Jesuits observed the relation between visible and invisible as an important issue in China. In his Chinese book *Tianzhu shiyi* (*The True Meaning of the Lord of Heaven*), Ricci (Madou Li) wrote that "a foolish man thinks that what is invisible must not exist. This is like a blind man cannot see the sky and therefore does not believe the existence of sun. . . . The Dao of heaven [*tianzhu*] exists in human heart. . . . The heaven's providence has no form, but it is like a great eye that sees everything" (60). The great eye is the God's eye, which is the origin of all things. Ricci continued, "An intelligent man does not need to believe in the existence of reason [*li*] based on what he sees physically. The appearance of reason is truer than flesh eyes. The senses of ear and eye frequently make mistakes, but the being of reason must be faultless" (322). As did Leibniz, Ricci attempted to compare the neo-Confucianist concept of *li* to the Dao of heaven, the God's eye. For him, the *li* was invisible but truthful, perfect, and existing. Based on the understanding of *li* as the prime form, Leibniz connected geometry with Chinese philosophy. On the one hand, *li* was taken as the invisible law of the world; on the other hand, it was supposed to be composed of the same substance as physical things. Such an ambivalent identity does not fall into the dualism of subjective versus objective but rather fits into the demonstration of geometry, which reveals eternal truth. This finding provides a clue to understand the rooting of the Jesuit perspective in China.

Chinese scholar and official Guangqi Xu (Christian name, Paul), of the late Ming dynasty, and Ricci translated the first six volumes of Euclid's *Elements* into Chinese and published the translation, entitled *Jihe yuanben* (*Origin of Geometry*), in 1607. The scholar Shanlan Li of the late Qing dynasty and a Briton, Alexander Wylie, translated the remaining nine volumes and published the translation in 1857. The first complete translation of *Elements*, based on the Jesuit mathematician Christopher Clavius' Latin version (Rome, 1574), was published in 1865. Ricci was a member of Clavius's Academy of Mathematics at the Collegio Romano. Another Jesuit, Giulio Aleni (Chinese name, Rulue Ai), Clavius's disciple at the Academy, and Shigu Qu published *Jihe yaofa* (*Principles of Geometry*) in 1631, which emphasized the necessity of a metal pen to draw geometry accurately. Details such as this exemplify the nuances between Ricci's and Aleni's understandings of geometry: Ricci seemed to present geometry as self-sufficient and divorced from the material world (Jami 192), but in his preface of *Jihe yuanben*, there still remained a strong connection between geometry and the material world.

In the preface to *Jihe yuanben*, Xu wrote that "the origin of geometry is the beginning of degrees and numbers. It can thoroughly express the emotion of rectangular, round, level and straight things, and function as the rule and principle. Mr. Li [Ricci] has studied geometry since he was a teenager. In the West, geometry is taught by a teacher to his disciple. Li's teacher, Mr. Ding [Clavius], is an unrivaled master. . . . His theory is extremely incisive. . . . If this book were not translated, all the other Western books could not be understood. We therefore translate the first six volumes. . . . Geometry is the foundation of all uses and can be called the form of all images. . . . Mr. Ding's knowledge can be categorized into three types: the big one is for self-cultivation and serving heaven; the small one is for understanding physical things; a special part of this understanding is measures of images. . . . I start from the small one in order to make his knowledge easily convincing" (Ricci and Xu 1151). Ricci wrote:

> Confucianism always seeks thorough knowledge, which should start from understanding things. . . . Our Western countries are small, but the methods of understanding things developed in their schools are unique. . . . Those

scholars esteem only reason (*li*) and do not follow human will. . . . In this way, the obtained knowledge is deep and stable. Geometry is especially so. Geometers observe the division and limitation of things. If the division is calculated in numbers, the quantity of the thing becomes clear. If the division is measured in degrees, the size of the thing is known. . . . Geometry can measure the heights of mountains and storied buildings, the depths of valleys, the distance between two places, the extensions of fields and cities. . . . It can survey the scenery to know seasons, day and night, sunrise and sunset, and the orientation of heaven and earth. . . . It can be used for making machines to observe heaven and earth, administrate the country, perform music, announce time for daily life, and offer a sacrifice to God. It can be used for hydraulic and civil engineering, cities and building construction . . . not only for beauty but also for stability and durability. . . . Some of its uses are to survey topography, distance, symmetry, and height. According to the shape of an object, its solid volume can be drawn on a plane. The size and real form of a distant object can be measured. Though the picture is small, the depicted object appears big; though the picture is quite near, the depicted scene looks distant. If a circle is drawn, it looks like a real ball. The portrait has its depth and the painted room has its brightness and darkness. . . . Administering the country requires being familiar with its borders, the distances to other countries, and the area of the land so that bilateral friendship is available. . . . A brave general must first know geometry; otherwise, his bravery is useless. . . . The term "origin" means we must know why and what geometry is. . . . Geometry originated in our West. Hundreds of scholars have written books on it, but all of them are based on Euclid. . . . Today, there emerges a well-known scholar, Mr. Ding, who is my teacher of geometry. . . . Since I came to China, I have met some scholars who study geometry, but their theories are usually not original. . . . I therefore translate this book for these gentlemen. . . . Mr. Xu asked me to translate orally and he himself wrote down these translations. We did it again and again to catch the original meaning of the book. . . . The first six volumes were finished this spring. . . . Mr. Xu intended to finish the whole book, but I suggested we stop here and publish the finished part as soon as possible for serving our colleagues. (Ricci and Xu 1151-54)

Like Leibniz, Ricci attempted to connect geometry with the *li* of neo-Confucianism. For both Ricci and Xu, the starting point for the *li* was to understand physical things. In their prefaces, Ricci explicated how to measure things, while Xu suggested that the understanding of things could lead to emotion (*qing*). Although within the same book, the focuses of these two prefaces are quite different. Xu emphasized the importance of the original and used the terms such as "beginning," "rule," "foundation," and "form" to explicate it, while Ricci accentuated the use of this origin, such as measuring topography, surveying scenes, astronomical observation, painting, administration, and military activity. As a Chinese scholar, Xu understood how important the issue of origin meant to his country fellows; as a Western Jesuit, Ricci observed that the usefulness of geometry could draw the Chinese attention. It is worth noting that when Ricci mentioned painting, he seemed to highlight how perspective could be used freely to create desired images. His exposition echoed the seventeenth-century interest in perspective and had nothing to do with Euclidean geometry itself.

The final sentence of Ricci's preface showed that he had a close relationship with Chinese scholars and his books enjoyed a wide readership. Before going to Beijing, he lived in the Jiangnan area, which included the cities Nanjing, Suzhou, and Zhenjiang, well known as the gathering places of literati. In his communication with Chinese scholars, Ricci observed that "here in China, literary studies are cultivated to such an extent that there are very few people who are not interested in them to some degree. Their religious doctrine is promulgated by written books, rather than by the spoken words" (*China* 446). With such a wide readership, Ricci's translation of Euclid was influential. It was reprinted in 1611, published repeatedly during the Ming and Qing dynasties, and was ultimately included in the Qing imperial encyclopedia, *Siku quanshu* (*Complete Libraries of the Four Treasures*), with one complete copy held at the Multistoried Pavilion of Literary Origin (Wenyuan Ge) in the Yuanming Yuan. This imperial library was located north of the twenty-second scene, Water and Rustling Trees, and east of the twenty-third scene, Xi Lian's Wonderful Place for Study. There was a clear pool in both the front and the back of the building. The pools acted as a metaphor of the literary origin (M. Yu 3: 1360). Ricci's approach of connecting the visibility of geometry with the neo-Confucianist concept of reason (*li*) was clear to Chinese scholars. On Ricci's tomb in Beijing is inscribed:

> In 1610, Madou Li (Ricci) died and was buried respectfully west of the Jiaxing Tower, which was two miles outside the Fucheng Gate. The tombstone is different from the Chinese one. Its body is rectangular but its head is round.... Behind the tombstone there is a hall with six corners.... The four corners of the surrounding wall are all stones. On the left side is the tomb of his friend, Yuhan Deng (that is, Joannes Terrenz), who was good at the medicine in his country [Switzerland]... and died in 1630.... Western guests, they keep distance from our Daoism and Buddhism, but are close to Confucianism. The Chinese therefore call them Western Confucians. I once discussed with Madou Li's student and found his thoughts were in fact close to Moist (namely, Mozi's philosophical school).... They are good at machinery and military affairs. This matches the Moist tradition. (Liu and Yu 304)

The tombs of Ricci and other Jesuits still exist. The relocated Jesuit cemetery is now part of the campus of the Municipal Institute of the Chinese Communist Party of Beijing. The text demonstrates that the Jesuits announced publicly their preference for Confucian thoughts over Daoism and Buddhism. Importantly, the author also pointed out the similarity between the ideas of Jesuits and ancient Moists, both of whom were good at geometry and machinery. On the connection between the Jesuits and the Moists in regards to geometry, Joseph Needham commented that the Jesuits reminded the Chinese of things which they themselves had developed long before. The Euclidean definition of a geometrical point caused much admiration because neither the Jesuits nor their Chinese friends were aware that the Moists had discussed such matters before the Han dynasty (437).

It has been widely held in scholarship that through Ricci, the Western perspective and chiaroscuro began to have influence in Chinese landscape painting and portrait painting. Jing Zeng and Shaoshu Jiang were two scholars who probably communicated with Ricci. Zeng lived in Nanjing and was a respected portrait painter. Jiang wrote a well-known history book of painting, *Wusheng shi shi* (*History of Silent Poetry*), about painters of the Ming dynasty, which included Zeng. The author was once the government official Gongbulang of Nanjing. He commented on Zeng's paintings: "His building paintings depict zigzag verandahs and winding rooms, whose postures are natural and majestic and whose portrayal is as real as a mirror image. His portraits look magically real and the color of the face is saturated and moist. Although the making up of the figure is very simple, its longing eyes and smile are extremely lifelike [*bizhen*]. . . . Standing in front of the portrait and meticulously appreciating it, I forget I am a beholder. In each portrait, there are so many layers of colors. It must be done with great ingenuity and craftsmanship" (ch. 4: 15). Jiang did not specify if Zeng's work was influenced by Western perspective and chiaroscuro, but wrote a brief description of a Western painting brought to China by Madou Li (Ricci): "Madou Li brought to us a Western portrait of God. In the work, a woman holds a baby. Her complexion and clothes look as real as a mirror image. She seems to be walking and her pose is dignified and graceful. Chinese painters cannot make it" (ch. 7: 19).

In the eighteenth century, the Chinese term, "linear perspective" was *xianfa*, which literally meant "line method." The modern Chinese name "perspective" is *toushi*, which literally means "seeing through." This meaning is close to Dürer's concept *Durchsehung* (or *perspectiva* in Latin, also meaning "a seeing through"). In the history of the Chinese language, *fa* means "Dao of the world," "making a thing and using it," "image," and "foundation of measuring" (*Zhongwen*). It can be sensed that the *fa* as a method did not mean the Cartesian method but rather indicated the principle of engaging the world—the "reason" in both Leibniz and Ricci's discussions. The linguistic structure of the term "line method" gives a sense of the copresence of two entities, line and method, whose interaction creates perspective. The line is visible and the method invisible. The invisibility of the method does not necessarily mean absolutely transcendental and out of the world. The lines were the interaction between the visible and invisible; lines were put in order and the cosmos was perceived through the method as "principles." It was in the interaction of line method that the worldliness of the method became conscious. In this sense, the line method is neither a mere representation of "the idea of *disegno*" nor an Eastern transplanting of a Western idea. Unlike the modern term, "perspective," *toushi*, the meaning of line method is not close to the concept of *Durchsehung* or the window theory of *perspectiva artificialis* in the Renaissance. It was completely a Chinese interpretation of linear perspective based on Chinese cosmology in the early eighteenth century.

The earliest theoretical discussion on the concept of method (*fa*) was from Mozi, the founder of the philosophy school of Moists, of the Warring States period. He wrote: "All human undertakings must have a method, without which no undertaking can be achieved. A scholar can be an official because of a method; a craftsman can engage in his enterprise because of a method. A craftsman uses a square to draw a rectangular form; a compass, a circle; a rope, a straight line; and a pendant, a vertical line. It does not matter if he is skillful or not, he must follow these five aspects as the method. . . . Therefore, all craftsmen have a method for each engagement" (Yushu Li 17). It is obvious that for Mozi, the method meant general principles that guided human activities rather than a specific instrumental method. Based on this understanding, the method (*fa*) of line method, though roughly translated as "method," is not equal to the modern English term "method."

The term "line method" first appeared in the 1735 reprint of *Shixue* (literally, *Perception Studies*), the first Chinese book on linear perspective. Written by Xiyao Nian, the book was first published in 1729 and reprinted in 1735. In his prefaces to both editions, Nian mentioned that he received assistance from the Western scholar Mr. Shining Lang (Castiglione). It is popularly held in scholarship that *Shixue* was adapted from the Jesuit painter Pozzo's book on perspective. The edition of this book that was stored in the Jesuit libraries in eighteenth-century Beijing was a bilingual version in both Latin and Italian (1702-1723) (*Catalogue*; H. Zou, Appendix). According to a modern scholar, Qi Han, in a comparative study of the 1702 edition of Pozzo and the 1735 *Shixue* edition, the first twenty-nine drawings in *Shixue* were similar to Pozzo's, and most of these adopted drawings came from Pozzo's discussion of projection principles and did not include his complicated architectural drawings ("Shixue" 709-10). In the 1729 preface of *Shixue*, Nian wrote:

> I paid attention to the study of perception for a long time, thinking hard but unable to understand it well. Later, after talking with the Western scholar [Shining] Lang several times, I began to create a Chinese painting in the Western way. The method (*fa*) of drawing lines from a fixed point enables me to catch the fully varied appearances of things. Once the position of the point is defined, the others will follow swiftly and continuously. Each part is so precisely positioned that it cannot be exchanged with another. The pointed, oblique, level, straight, round, and rectangular forms of things are all drawn on paper, but a drawn thing looks suspended in the air and shows its different surfaces simultaneously. As for the effects of the distant skylight, oblique sunlight, flickering candlelight, distance and size, shape and shadow, zigzag, and obscurity, they all are as I wish. This might be because they originate from the nature of things. Touched by my force of eye, they appear as clear as in my heart. Then, I realize perception is a high study. For example, if an object is set in a room and its position is not suitable, it will bring uneasiness when caught in sight, and the same happens in a painting. There have been some painting theories inherited from our ancestors. One theory says: "Looking up, you can draw the flying posture of the bent eaves," and, "Looking down, you can see a deep valley" [Note: These quotes alluded to the theoretical debate between Cheng Li and Kuo Shen of the Song dynasty.] However, in such situations, the force of the eye moves up and down without a stable position. Can such a theory be a high study? On the issue of resemblance, a theory says: "Gazing into the distance, [you can see that] all oblique things appear." However, it is not

as practicable and clearly stated as this book, which is illustrated and being sent to my colleagues and diligent scholars. The understanding of the book results from its reason (*li*) [Note: The *li* is the same concept as that in Leibniz's discussions.] Based on the reason, a big thing like a high mountain and an extensive river, a small thing like a lively fish, a flower, and a bird, and all the others rooting on the ground or flying or diving can be obtained. It is obvious that truth results from a thorough revealing of subtlety and mystery. Somebody might say such a painting is real but not wonderful [Note: The original term of "real" is *zhen*, which means in Chinese "true" and "original." The original term of "wonderful" is *miao*, which means in Chinese "beautiful," "subtle," and "extremely elegant."] However, if it is first not real, how could it be wonderful? (Nian, "Shixue" 711-12)

The term *xue* in the book title *Shi-xue* literally means "studies" or "high knowledge." Indicating linear perspective, this Chinese title highlights the inherent relationship between perspective and perception. In other words, *Shixue* teaches us how to see. The *xue* means a school of high knowledge, which has its own system, as a *xue* deserves everyone's study and respect and not all knowledge can become a *xue*. A Chinese architectural scholar interpreted *Shixue* as the "method of distance" (Tong 284), but the *shi* as "perception" cannot be simply equated to "distance" in the Cartesian system but should rather be understood from the perspective of phenomenological intuition. According to his famous discussion on the differences between architectural works by several persons and by a single hand, for Descartes, the "method" is absolutely an individual approach to truth (*Discourse* 10). Compared with the Cartesian method, the *fa* as a method is more cosmologically related with the living world. According to Nian, the method of drawing lines started from a "fixed point," yet it was not specified whether the fixed point was the actual focal point. The preface connected the principle of perspective with the neo-Confucianist concept, "reason" (*li*) and pointed out that the significance of the perspectival painting lay in its truthful appearance. Such an understanding of truthfulness was new to the Chinese belief system at that time.

Nian's 1735 preface is as follows:

> The attainment of the high study of perception is endless. How could I claim to have held its quintessence? I have studied it for thirty years. It is not exaggerated that I am a good painter in this country. I can paint skillfully and freely thousands of mountains, bodies of water, deep forests, and wooded valleys. The expression of my Chinese paintings is incisive and vivid, but its appreciation unfortunately lies beyond measure and scale. As for buildings and utensils, if you want to depict them precisely without hairbreadth, it cannot be realized perfectly without the Western method. At first, I did a preliminary study with some drawings, yet this is only a small part of the study of perception. Although I have revealed my studies to the public, my understanding is still shallow. I recently met with Mr. Shining Lang several times, and reviewed the origin of the study of perception with him. The aspects of line method (*xianfa*), such as the projection of light, convergence, slanting, upside-down, and overlooking, all emerge from one point. But the reason (*li*) of one point exists not only in the West but also in China. Among

visible things, the near one looks big while the distant one, small. This is very certain. The Five Mountains are the biggest, but if we look at them from a distance, they look small. The further away they are, the smaller they look, until they shrink to a point. A mustard seed is the smallest. If I put it at a distant place and look straight at it, though it becomes invisible, at the infinity of the force of the eye, the reason of one point remains effectual. It is therefore inferred that all things can shrink to a point, and one point can produce all things. Because they emerge from one point, this point is called the head point. From points emerges a line, and from the lines emerges an object. Although one object is different from another, as points from lines, their reason is the same. Furthermore, one object appears in a size in the distance of five feet and appears in another size in the distance of ten feet. If a distance is intersected by a point, the point is called the distance point. Once the distance is decided, the reason cannot be changed. If we draw a room according to this method and arrange everything in order, the beholder might want to walk on the steps, enter the door and stand in the hall, but does not realize it is only a painting. If we draw an object and hang the painting—whose surfaces are up and down, level, slant and solid, bright in light and dark in shadows, with clear convex and concave effects—in the air, the beholder must take it as a real thing. When an object becomes convex and concave with *yin* and *yang* and a room becomes deep with mutual compliments, is this not the quintessence of the method of Western painting? It is hard to enumerate all such cases to make the method understood. However, if we remember that the distance is set up by points and lines, the volume emerges from *yin* and *yang*, and the effect of wonderful lies in borrowing sunlight, most varieties of this method will not go beyond these three aspects. I thought very hard, supplemented over fifty drawings, and wrote captions for those drawings to make this book useful. The reader himself can explore the origin of this method and become a leader in the study of perception through analyzing the changes of things and extending the movement of points and lines. In terms of such benefits, if in my spare time I could explore further the infinite attainment, ponder its quintessence, and learn from brilliant gentlemen, how great my enjoyment. ("[The second preface]" 713-15)

The term "line method" (*xianfa*) did not appear in the 1729 preface but appeared, for the first time, in the 1735 preface. The "fixed point" in the previous preface is now called the "head point," *toudian*, located at infinity. The *tou* in Chinese means the human head, origin, and the first. The head point in this context holds a double meaning: the point indicates both the eye and the origin of geometrical construction. In Chinese philosophy, the point of infinity is taken as the origin of life, which clearly identifies with Daoist thought regarding the origin of the world. Chapter 42 of *Laozi* says: "Dao produces one [primary *qi*], one produces two [heaven and earth], two produce three [*yin-qi*, *yang-qi* and their mixture], and three produces all things" (S. Zhou 69). The statement, "the reason [*li*] of one point does not only exist in the West but also in China" provides insight for the understanding of the common ground for the fusion of the Jesuit perspective and Chinese cosmology. The idea that one point is both cosmically and geometrically generative can be traced back to

Proclus (fifth century) in Western history (Casey 65). In addition, for the first time, objects in the line method are clearly specified as converging toward the central point, the head point. Since the head point is taken as the origin of life, the movement of convergence itself can be understood as a return to the truth of the world, the "primary one." The perspectival convergence recalls the Daoist sage Zhuangzi's idea of "condensation of mind" (*ningshen*), which he explicates as "fixed and stopped [on something]." In the situation of the condensation of mind, the smallest thing, like the head point, is coincident with the cosmos (F. Wang 7-8). In the primary one, there was no difference between big and small, the world and "I," and at this moment the spirit would ramble freely and happily.

There is the suggestion that there were no illustrations in the 1729 edition of *Shixue* (see Swiderski 230), yet this is questionable. In the 1729 preface, Nian stated that the book was illustrated in order to be practical for scholars. In the 1735 preface, Nian mentioned that he "supplemented over fifty drawings" to the first version, which indicated that there had already been some illustrations in the first version. He also said that he "did a preliminary study with some drawings" in the first version. Additional research shows that, in the 1735 edition, these over-fifty supplemental drawings were numbered and related to the diagrammatic demonstration of the principles of line method; yet the other drawings were not numbered and were related to the three-dimensional illustrations of building details (Q. Han "Shixue" 710). The fact that the three-dimensional architectural drawings were published in the first edition of Nian's book demonstrates his idea that the Chinese audience might be receptive in accepting such illustrations, because they appeared close to reality. Comparing the three-dimensional architectural drawings in Nian's and Pozzo's books reveals that Pozzo's drawings were more detailed and sophisticated. Qi Han attributes this difference to the less-developed technique of copperplate engraving in China ("Shixue"), yet this is only part of the picture. One of Nian's unnumbered illustrations of architecture was the view of a dome ceiling perceived by a spectator who was standing on the ground and looking upward. Regarding this drawing, Nian wrote, "If drawing the ceiling according to this method, when you look up at the ceiling, the square and circle fit appropriately; the stone columns suspend in the air; the window mullions interweave with each other. It looks like a multistoried building standing steadily above. In the openings, you seem to peep at the blue sky and see the stars. Only when the drawing skill reaches such a level can we understand the Western method, which requires detailed research and careful scrutiny. Does not the spirit appear in this drawing? How can it be only for the stroll of eyes?" ("Shixue" 813). For Nian, the view of line method not only appeared real but could also draw the spectator's mind into the "spiritual stroll," which echoed with the Daoist idea, *shenyou*. Another interesting aspect of these illustrations is the depiction of shadows. Nian used only the dotted line to mark the contour of shadows without hatching the shadowed area as Pozzo did. In a perspective drawing illustrating the method of drawing shadows, Nian simply called the point of light source the "light" (*guang*), which identified with the head point in the perspective ("Shixue" 855). Did this, in his mind, hint at the inherent relationship between the focal point, the origin of the world, and the brightness of the cosmos? Although in his book, Nian introduced both one-point and two-point perspectives, in the two prefaces he emphasized only the importance of the head point of the one-point perspective. This matched with the priority of one-point perspective in the Jesuit tradition. When the Jesuits introduced linear perspective to the Chinese and transformed it into line method, the two-point perspective had already been well developed in Europe. As Pozzo explicated, the Jesuit priority of one-point perspective was related to their understanding of the focal point as the incarnation of God's eye. For the Chinese, as Nian's book demonstrated, the same point, the so-called head point, was related to the origin of the world in the Daoist sense. Thus, the line method, as a result from the intense discussions between Nian and Castiglione, connected the Jesuits' religious metaphysics with Chinese cosmology.

In Nian's prefaces, painting was presented as the most useful field for line method. Indeed, the influence of line method to the Chinese culture first took place through landscape paintings. In the Ming dynasty, there were already some paintings that consciously applied the technique of Western perspective. In this respect, the foreshortening effect and the "pursuit of descriptive naturalism" in Hong Zhang's paintings as well as the chiaroscuro stippling of brushwork in Xian Gong's paintings were two very fine examples (Cahill 13, 169). A major influence of line method on Chinese garden representation was building delineation. Buildings occupied a prominent place in the garden and landscape paintings by the Qing painter Jiang Yuan, who once served in the Yongzheng court and had a chance to work with Jesuit painters (Dou Li 41). Although his building delineation was extremely detailed and obviously took a great deal of effort, the oblique lines in his paintings continued to remain parallel, as in the Chinese tradition, without converging towards a focal point. In Yuan's landscape paintings, the traditional atmospheric perspective became weakened because of the universal prominent image of buildings depicted in redundant details. The representation of Qing imperial gardens underwent many changes as a result of Jesuit influences. An example of this change was in the forty paintings for the Forty Scenes of the Yuanming Yuan where, with rich shades, the mountains began to appear more solid and voluminous (Tang and Shen). In similar fashion, paintings of the Forty Scenes began to be more precise by being more detailed than ever before. Compared to traditional garden representation, these paintings were a true depiction of the garden and also helped to explain the poetry on the same garden. Dai Tang, the painter of the Forty Scenes, was honored by the emperor with the title of Number One Painter. His theory on painting distant mountains stated that the size of distant mountains must be proportional with near mountains and should not look higher than near mountains, so that the beholder could extend the view to infinity ("Huishi" 859). This theory diverted from the traditional principle of distance depiction, that is, the higher a mountain was located, the more distant it appeared. His observation of distance, as his paintings of the Forty Scenes demonstrated, implied the horizon of the land, which had not yet been clearly recognized, or was hidden behind either mountains or clouds in traditional Chinese landscape painting. The oblique lines delineating the buildings in the forty paintings did not remain strictly parallel and appeared to converge towards a focal point, which, however, was located beyond the upper right corner of the painting and was not directly visible. Owing to a bird's-eye view, the foreshortening effect in the paintings of the Forty Scenes is not very apparent. A well-developed perspective effect was presented in other imperial garden paintings, for example, in Mei Leng's paintings of court ladies, as he usually put the figure in a garden setting wherein buildings, rocks, and plants were composed with the horizon at eye level and depicted in extreme details. Leng was the student of Bingzhen Jiao, a court painter in the Kangxi reign. Jiao was well known for applying Western techniques, including perspective, to his paintings. Jiao and Leng's approach was later called the Jiao-Leng Style. Compared with the parallel oblique projection in traditional building paintings, both Tang and Leng's garden paintings presented a clear one-point perspective of oblique projection.

Because of the influence of the traditional oblique projection of lines in Chinese landscape painting, the line method of Jesuit-preferred central perspective was not extensively applied to Qing imperial-garden representations until the birth of the twenty copperplates of the Western garden in the Yuanming Yuan. Like the Jesuit perspective of art, line method had a close relationship with the technique of copperplate engraving. These twenty copperplates were drawn by the Chinese painter Lantai Yi, who often worked with the Jesuits. Although Yi was not among the earliest students of Castiglione in the court, they both shared a close working relationship. According to an imperial archive, in the twelfth moon of the third year of the Qianlong reign (1738), Castiglione added colors to the background in Yi's painting of two deer in a landscape (Ju). This took place almost fifty years before the completion of the twenty copperplates. It can be imagined that Yi had enough time to learn the technique of line method from Castiglione through their collaborations in painting. Another imperial archive recorded that on the first day of the fourth moon of the fifty-first year of the Qianlong reign (1786), the twenty copperplates and their first one hundred prints (namely, five complete sets of the twenty engravings) were exhibited at the Zhai Palace ("Neiwufu" archive 820). According to the same document, Yi began to draft the drawings in the fourth moon of 1781, almost the same time that the View of Distant Sea pavilion, the final building in the Western garden, was built. He finished the first six drawings in the third moon of the next year. The titles of the copperplates indicated that, for the Chinese eye, the Western garden was in fact a garden created through line method. Examples of this include copperplate one, where the left bridge is called the Bridge of Line Method (L. Yi); copperplate eighteen, where the hill is entitled Hill of Line Method; and copperplate twenty, where the open-air stage set is entitled Walls of Line Method. Before the emperor officially named the buildings of the Western garden, they were temporarily called "buildings of line method" in general. All the titles of the twenty copperplates described the perspective view of the engravings as a "face," which was in fact the central perspective with the horizon of view close to eye level. Through the "frontal face" (*zhengmian*), composed with line method, the Chinese imperial face and the Jesuit perspective, for the first time in history, found a way to overlap.

Since all twenty copperplates were composed through line method, an analysis of perspective distortions in these engravings will be an effectual way to understand how the garden of line method was actually perceived in the Chinese mind. In copperplate twelve, for example, there is a pair of stairways descending from a roof to the ground (L. Yi). The focal point of this line-method drawing is located on the ground door with the horizon at eye level. A prominent perspective distortion is visible in the orthographic sections of the balustrades, which should converge towards the focal point and be hidden behind the front horizontal sections. The draftsman, Lantai Yi, did not appear to be clear about, or unconsciously did not strictly follow, the rule that all parallel lines should converge towards the same focal point. Although such a distortion can be judged as a perspective defect, it vividly demonstrates the motion of his mind when he exerted himself to converge his habitual roaming "force of the eye" towards the central focal point. The same problem of the focal point exists in the other copperplates, where he was able to follow the focal point within a part of the picture but could not do so for the entire picture, usually resulting in more than two focal points on the central axis. Although the twenty copperplates were the best-known application of line method in Qing garden representations, the perspective distortions in these copperplates demonstrate the experimentality of line method in the garden design of the time.

Chapter Five

The Chinese Garden and the Concept of the Line Method

The traditional Chinese term for "landscape" is *shanshui*, which literally means "mountains and waters." The Yuanming Yuan was a magnificent garden of mountains and waters for its extensively artificially made landscapes. The emperor's vision of round brightness was embodied by the multiple *jing* where his mind was brightened while his body meandered in the garden. The zigzag route of the Forty Scenes was a route along which the metaphysical brightness diffused within the garden enclosure. Once he strolled to the northeastern corner, the most remote corner of the garden compound, the winding path changed abruptly into the straight path of the Western Multistoried Buildings garden. How did the brightness in the emperor's mind diffuse along the straight path and focus on the exotic perspective views, and how did the multiple *jing* in this geometrical garden frame the Jesuits' metaphysical brightness in the Chinese context?

Labyrinths

Father Ferdinand-Bonaventure Moggi (Chinese name, Boming Li) had a broad knowledge of architecture. Imitating the altar of the St. Ignazio in Rome, he designed the high altar of the Jesuit church Eastern Hall (Dong Tang) in Beijing, whose dome fresco was painted by Giuseppe Castiglione in the Pozzo style. In 1747, Qianlong requested the best Jesuit painter in the court, Castiglione, rather than the architecturally educated Moggi, to design the Western Multistoried Buildings garden (Schulz 22). This followed the Chinese tradition that a garden should express a poetical intention like a painting (*huayi*). It also matched with the meaning of *jing* in the eighteenth century, that a garden scene should look like a painting. As a painter, Castiglione had a good working knowledge of perspective and played a key role in translating the Jesuit perspective of architecture into Chinese line method.

The application of line method in the Western Multistoried Buildings garden can first be observed by the contrast between its rigid geometrical plan and the meandering plan of the Chinese portion. This contrasting pattern, as the garden name

"Round" Brightness and the lake name "Square" River in the Western garden imply, can be characterized as the fundamental difference between circle and square. In the first-century astronomical and mathematical book *Zhoubi suanjing* (*Zhou Shadow Gauge Manual*), it was proposed that the images of all things do not go beyond circle and square. Circle appears through square, because the latter is finite and easy to measure, while the former is infinite and hard to fathom. If a polygon approaches towards the border of a circle by multiplying infinitely its edges, both will finally come to one, and a circle is formed. Square is supposed to belong to earth; and circle, heaven. Hence, "heaven is round and earth is square" (*Zhoubi suanjing* 13, 19). It is clear that the geometrical form of the "circle and square" (*fangyuan*) was the embodiment of the "heaven and earth" (*tiandi*), which signified the cosmos. It is reasonable to speculate that the "square" form of the Western garden might be an oblique way for the emperor to measure his desired "round" brightness. In his record of the garden, Qianlong expressed his desire to "encircle the cosmos and things into the round brightness." To encircle the diffusing brightness, it was necessary to measure the garden borders, of which the Western portion was the most remote. The idea of preserving full brightness in one's mind through seeking the remotest garden scenery can be related to the Daoist sage Laozi's idea that "whoever knows his brightness veils himself in his darkness" in *Laozi* (S. Zhou 45). This sentence was quoted by Heidegger in his essay "Grundsätze des Denkens" (1958). The seemingly paradoxical Daoist idea regarding brightness and darkness is quite close to Heidegger's concept of Dasein. He described the unconcealment of Dasein as the primordial brightness, which made the ontical light of an entity, for example, a building, possible. The primordial brightness cannot be understood through the ontical light, but rather through the full disclosedness of the remote "there" where care is grounded (401-02). From this perspective, it can be argued that the Western garden in the remote northeastern corner contributed effectually to the full brightness of the Yuanming Yuan.

The earliest general plan ever known regarding the Western garden was from Model Lei's collection of construction drawings. Model Lei served the Qing court for several generations as the major building contractor, and his works included the Yuanming Yuan complex. The Chinese term "plane drawing" in the Model Lei collection is *diyang*, which literally means "ground look." The Chinese term "elevation drawing" in the same collection is *liyang*, which literally means "standing look." A standing look could be either an elevation drawing in the modern sense or a traditional parallel-projection drawing, which includes the front and side views. Although the plane drawing was not a popular representation method in Chinese classic architecture and gardens, it held its special meaning. The garden treatise, *Yuan ye* states that usually in building construction, people seldom try a plane drawing, but the plane drawing represents the agreement between the owner and the builder. If a house is to be built, it should be decided how many bays in depth and how many bays in width. The designer needs to "draw a plane as a building will be." The ingenious design starts from a plane (Ji 98).

The Chinese Garden and the Concept of the Line Method

According to an imperial archive, on the eleventh day of the fourth moon of the twenty-first year of the Qianlong reign (1756), the emperor decreed: "Order Shining Lang [Castiglione] to sketch a plan of a Western garden [*xiyang yuan*] in the east of the Harmony, Wonder, and Delight pavilion of the Garden of Eternal Spring. The design should be presented for review and only after it is permitted can it be sent to the Construction Department of the Yuanming Yuan for building" ("Neiwufu" archive 419). Before the Western garden was completed, it was habitually taken as a part of the simultaneously constructed Garden of Eternal Spring. It is important to note that Qianlong called the plan a "Western garden," which is the most direct proof that the site of Western multistoried buildings was intended as a garden. The same record states that Shining Lang finished the sketch of a "Western-like and garden-like" plan and presented it. Qianlong gave approval for the construction of the garden the same day he was presented with the plan. He then decreed: "It is permitted to construct according to the design. Wherever Western paintings are needed in the garden, ask the Lodge As One Wishes [Ruyi Guan] studio to create moving-through-*jing* paintings" ("Neiwufu" archive 419). The Chinese term of "moving-through-*jing* paintings" is *tongjing-hua*. The Lodge As One Wishes was located at the fortieth scene, Deep and Remote Dwelling, where both the Jesuits' painting studio and the princes' studying studio were located. It is quite interesting to note that although the construction had not yet begun, the emperor was unable to hold himself back from seeing Western paintings in the garden. The term "Western paintings" here indicates paintings created with line method.

A general plan in the Model Lei collection published in 1932 was actually the drawing of the second construction phase of the Western garden (Lei), that is, the long rectangular area along the east-west axis starting at the Cages for Raising Birds gateway and ending at the open-air theater called Paintings of Line Method or Walls of Line Method. An important detail to note is that the five bamboo pavilions opposite The View Beyond the World pavilion were not marked in the plane drawing. This detail verifies the French scholar Maurice Adam's analysis that the bamboo pavilions were originally in the courtyard of the first-phase construction, namely, between the Harmony, Wonder, and Delight pavilion and the labyrinth. In 1771, Qianlong moved the bamboo pavilions to the south of The View Beyond the World pavilion, because they "obstructed his view" of the fountain in the courtyard (30). Another interesting detail in the same drawing is that the western gateway of the Hill of Line Method, whose image can be seen in the seventeenth copperplate, is missing. The missing gate in the general plan most likely indicates that this gate was still in the process of being designed. If this hypothesis is true, the date of this drawing can be traced to as early as 1766 when Castiglione, the chief designer of the garden, died. In addition, the fact that the bamboo pavilions are also missing in this plan supports this deduction. According to Model Lei's general plan, there were two watercourses within the Western garden, which were connected to external watercourses. The first one was a small canal that flowed southward from the outside of the northern wall of the garden. It curved towards the north, then eastward in front of The View Beyond the World pavilion and finally disappeared behind the northern wall of the garden. Three little bridges were created over the winding watercourse, which increased the feeling of depth in such a narrow site. The second watercourse was the Square River, which was the rectangular lake located to the west of the Paintings of Line Method theater. This watercourse was connected to that of the Lion Grove garden in the Garden of Eternal Spring through a small ditch. It is obvious that the water flowed from the Lion Grove into the Square River in order to create a moving body of water rather than still water, which was always avoided in Chinese gardens. Furthermore, the Lion Grove within the Garden of Eternal Spring was a replication of the Lion Grove in Suzhou, which was well known for its rockery labyrinth. The image of labyrinth in the Lion Grove mystically resonated with the overall sense of labyrinth in the Western garden in the Yuanming Yuan. In the same drawing, groves and rocks were arranged to orient the view. Two long groves on the hillocks flanked the eastern side of the Cages for Raising Birds gateway and hid the service buildings. The groves led the visitor straight to the east and framed the gorgeous façade of the gateway. When comparing the eastern and western facades of the gateway in copperplates six and seven (L. Yi), we can clearly see the difference made by the groves. Since these two groves are the only groves marked in the plane drawing of this plan, we get a strong sense of the designer's intention of orienting the viewer's movement at this spot.

There are two places where rocks were used for orienting the view in the plane drawing of the general plan. The first one was in front of the cascade west of the Hall of Peaceful Sea; the second one was at both sides of the eastern gateway of the Hill of Line Method. The first one did not appear completely in the tenth copperplate, partly because of the ascending stairways; the second one could clearly be seen in the nineteenth copperplate, where the view was led through the central arch of the gateway towards the distant illusionary but theatrical landscape appearing through the Paintings of Line Method (L. Yi). The representation of rocks in the drawing of the general plan was formed by traditional brush strokes, similar to the plane drawing of the site plan of the Walls of Line Method from the same published collection (Lei), while the groves were depicted simply with a single line, which brought a strong feeling of volume to the trees. This method of representing trees was also applied in other plane drawings and brought a sense that the trees were used as a mass material for creating space in the garden. Because the plane drawing was composed of single lines, groves were distinguished from buildings only through the shapes of the depicted objects. The buildings and fountains were universally in geometrical forms, while the groves were irregularly curved. Rocks were added on the bank of the canal to differentiate between the groves and the canal, both of which were curved shapes. The rockery bank was a typical way for Chinese gardens to symbolize water flowing through mountains in nature.

In the site plan of the Harmony, Wonder, and Delight pavilion in the published Model Lei collection (Lei), the emperor's path from the Garden of Eternal Spring to the Western garden appeared clear. He entered the Garden of Eternal Spring through the Gate of Bright Spring at the center of the western wall of the garden. The gate was named Bright Spring because it was the main connection between the Garden of Round "Brightness" and the Garden of Eternal "Spring." The name was the combination of the two characters, which came respectively from the two gardens. Upon entering the Garden of Eternal Spring, the emperor first stopped at a terraced pavilion along the western bank of the central lake. He then moved north along the bank until reaching the water mouth where a small bridge connected the western and northern banks. Standing on the bridge and looking across a small lake toward the northwest, he saw the magnificent Harmony, Wonder, and Delight pavilion and a grouping of fountains in the front yard. Flanked by dense woods on both sides, the bridge was a perfect place for a framed view of the distant fountain plaza. As shown in a general survey map of the ruined Yuanming Yuan complex of 1936 (*Shice Yuanming*), there was a small gate on the western wall of the labyrinth within the Western garden. This gate also appeared in the fifth copperplate (L. Yi). The gate enabled the emperor to enter the labyrinth directly from the twenty-ninth scene, A Wonderland in a Square Pot, in the northeastern corner of the Yuanming Yuan. In the preface of his poem on this scene, Qianlong wrote, "It is said there were three divine hills in the sea, but when a boat reached them, it was immediately led away by the wind. It is a waste of energy to talk about these hills. People should know that even the palaces made of gold and silver are not different from the human world. Since the fairyland is now in my room, why should I look for it far away? This is exactly what the name A Square Pot implies" ("Fanghu" 63). Qianlong was certainly alluding to the legendary story of the fairylands in the East Sea. According to the *fengshui* survey committed by Yongzheng, multistoried pavilions should be built in the northeast corner to correspond to Saturn ("Shandong Depingxian " 6-7). It is interesting to note that the multistoried buildings of this Daoist fairyland and the Western garden were arranged shoulder to shoulder on the both sides of a division passage. The copresence of the Daoist fairyland and the Western garden demonstrated Qianlong's principle of the whole, which intended to integrate all the beautiful scenes into his vision of Round Brightness. Another interesting phenomenon is that the twenty-ninth scene was located in the northeastern corner of the Yuanming Yuan, while the Western garden was located in the northeastern corner of the Yuanming Yuan complex. Both corners were the most remote and symbolized a far distant land. According to the Daoist cosmological idea in the *Huainanzi*, in twenty-eight years the planet Saturn completes a circuit (Major 75). The "twenty-ninth" scene located in the northeastern corner of the Yuanming Yuan not only hinted at Saturn, required by *fengshui*, but also implied its cosmic movement.

The labyrinth in the Western garden of the Yuanming Yuan can be called the first known example of a Western labyrinth built in Chinese gardens. The plan of the first phase of the Western garden was laid on a south-to-north axis whose northern end was the labyrinth. In the plane drawing of the labyrinth in the Model Lei collection (Lei), at some locations, each of the four routes that passed through the labyrinth was marked with a linear succession of dots: one went to the central hexagonal pavilion where a throne was positioned towards the south; one to the small gate on the western border wall; one to a circular fountain yard behind the throne pavilion; and one directly to a multistoried building for "delightful climbing," located on the northern border of the labyrinth. The emperor's multiple hidden paths demonstrate that the throne pavilion was not his single interest in the labyrinth. The ground floor of the multistoried building for delightful climbing was composed of a grid of nine equal squares. When the emperor meandered through the labyrinth to its northern border, climbed up to the front deck of this multistoried building, and looked back to the south, he had a pleasant panoramic view of the labyrinth. The labyrinth was called Formation of Yellow Flowers. The term "formation" hinted at the formation of troops in a war, because of the square layout of the labyrinth. Compared to the winding path in the Chinese portion, the zigzag path of the labyrinth was strictly geometrically organized. It is interesting to note that the emperor apparently accepted the straight but winding path and specifically called the labyrinth a "flower garden" (*huayuan*), as demonstrated by the title of the fifth copperplate (L. Yi). Although a labyrinth, or maze, had been a typical part of European Renaissance and Baroque gardens, both the emperor and the Chinese people likely called the exotic labyrinth a "garden" because of its zigzag movement, although the path was laid out in a line-method formation. In Chinese gardens, a winding path was believed to lead to a deep and remote area within the mind. According to the landscape theory "deep abstruseness" (*aoru*) advanced by Zongyuan Liu, a Tang landscape essayist, meandering in nature procured the "delight of abstrusity" ("Yongzhou" 26). Along the same line of thought, Gefei Li of the Song dynasty said that winding helped maintain deep thought (39). For the Jesuit Attiret, the "hundred turns and windings" formed "a beautiful disorder" ("Particular" 37-38). It can be surmised that the zigzag path of the labyrinth recalled to Chinese eyes the meandering paths in Chinese gardens. The same labyrinth was also called Lanterns of Yellow Flowers. According to an imperial archive, the tops of the brick walls of the Lanterns of Yellow Flowers were covered with turf and were watered everyday (Zhongguo diyi 1: archive 196). It is said that on the night of the Mid-Autumn Festival, when the moon was most round and its light the most perfect of the year, the emperor would watch from the central pavilion as the court ladies carried lamps of yellow flowers and meandered in the labyrinth. The name Lanterns of Yellow Flowers signified a Chinese folk tale, which was embodied by the Western labyrinth. As the traditional celebratory fireworks brightened the Chinese portion at night, the yellow-flower lanterns brightened the labyrinth. Peering down upon the circulative movement of lanterns from the central pavilion enhanced the emperor's feeling of power. The emperor's opportunity to peer down resulted from his occupation of the mystical center of the labyrinth. The emphasis on the central pavilion as a place for Qianlong to view the surroundings can be seen in copperplate four, where the front gate was perceived from the central pavilion (L. Yi); in the earliest photo of this gate in the 1870s, the central pavilion became the focal point of the perspective composition (Thiriez 41). The comparison reveals the shift of viewpoint between the copperplate and the photo.

North of the labyrinth, there was a hillock covered with dense trees, where a Chinese square pavilion was hidden. There is a sharp contrast between the forms of the labyrinth and the hillocks: regular versus irregular, open versus secluded, central versus remote, bright versus shady, and Western versus Chinese. It is meaningful for the Chinese pavilion to stand at the northern end of the axis on which the Western buildings, fountains, and gates were located. Based on the Confucian principle that an emperor must "sit in the north and face to the south" (*zuo bei chao nan*), the location of the Chinese pavilion at the northern end of the journey indicated that this Chinese pavilion was intended to provide psychological protection for the emperor's entertainment within the exotic labyrinth. One of the reasons for creating the hillock behind the flat labyrinth might have been to protect the emperor's back from being exposed to the outside of the garden as he sat in the central pavilion and faced to the south. The dense treed hillocks blocked the view to the distance and symbolically controlled the "water mouth" of the small canal flowing from the outside to the inside.

In addition to the axial and labyrinth pathways, another type of path in the garden was the bridge. We can only get a glimpse of a corner of the Bridge of Line Method (Xianfa Qiao) in the first copperplate (L. Yi). On the western side of the bridge was a Western-like portal within whose frame there was an illusionary perspective painting, which appeared behind the doorway. The illusionary portal not only extended the depth of view but also vitalized the bridge and the underneath watercourse, which flowed from the Yuanming Yuan into the Garden of Eternal Spring. This water entrance was a significant water mouth, which symbolized the connection between Qianlong's new garden and his father's old one. The Western bridge and portal framed the water mouth and hid its origin. According to a theory of Chinese landscape painting, the origin of the water mouth needs to be hidden in the painting so that the mystic and momentous sense of the watercourse can be presented; in so doing, the painter's emotional commitment and the principles of the cosmos are expressed (Z. Tang 749). Appearing real, the portal created the illusion that, from the bridge, people could step into another world. Previous research has compared the illusionary setting of this bridge with the theatrical architecture of the Bibiena family and the works of Pozzo (Schulz 42). Most significant here is the overlapping of the double depth from the Chinese and Western perspectives. While a bridge acted as a crosswalk over a watercourse, a gateway acted as a connection between two paths. In the 1936 survey map, the Cages for Raising Birds gateway within the Western garden was marked as the "Multistoried Building of Peacocks" (*Shice Yuanming*). This gateway defined the division between the first and second construction phases. An interesting feature was the double face of this gateway: its western side was Chinese-like while its eastern side maintained a Baroque face. In copperplate six (L.Yi), the colonnade on the western side was clearly depicted in the composition of line method with the focal point located on the geometrical center of the central iron gate. According to a letter from Father Martialus Cibot (Chinese name, Guoying Han), Castiglione designed this wrought-iron gate, which was forged under the supervision of the Jesuit Gilles Thébaud (Chinese name, Zixin Yang) (Schulz 25). Along the wall to the right of the portal, there was a fresco, painted by Castiglione, which depicted a ship sailing on the sea and matched perfectly the perspective effect of the portal. In the copperplate, clouds were emerging from behind the gateway and brought about a feeling that there was a mystical world behind the door. The sailing ship hinted at the Chinese legendary story that there was a fairyland in East Sea and, probably, the Jesuits' arduous journey to China. The gateway, located at the connection point of the T-square plan of the Western garden, became the only passageway between the first and the second phases of the garden. Its importance was demonstrated by its double-face images and its appearing in both copperplates six and seven. The role of the gateway as the control of the view into the mystical depth is clearly shown in a photo of the 1870s (Thiriez 42).

At the mid-point of the west-to-east axis was an imperial throne, called View the Water Method. Behind the throne, there were two side doors, the so-called Dog Head Gates, probably because the fully decorated gate looked like a dog head, which were for the emperor to secretly commute between the Western garden and the Garden of Eternal Spring and appreciate the exotic water play. The Model Lei collection contained detailed sketches of the Dog Head Gates, which were also marked as the "Western doors" (Lei). Research has indicated that these Dog Head Doors appeared similar to Bibiena's theatrical design forms, for example, the theatrical deign by Giuseppi Bibiena in Dresden in 1719 (Lancaster 282). From the Chinese characters in the drawings, it can be ascertained that they were construction sketches by Model Lei. Some of the characters marked material items such as brick and tile, but the rest of the characters were difficult to read. Since these sketches were based on the original Jesuit designs, they demonstrated the Chinese craftsmen's interpretations of the Western construction details.

In the plane drawing of the site plan of the Walls of Line Method, which is housed in the Model Lei collection, there is a small door marked with the Chinese character "door" and which is located on the southern wall close to the rocks on the right (southern) side of the Eastern Gate of the Hill of Line Method. It is unclear whether this door was also a secret entrance for the emperor, as this door appeared reasonable to this location for the the emperor to walk directly from the Lion Grove garden within the Garden of Eternal Spring to the front of the Square River lake. The secret passway door behind the rocks was well hidden yet provided a different and interesting experience for the emperor, as he would first pass through the dense rocks and trees before standing in front of the expansive Square River Lake and looking across the water at the Paintings of Line Method in the distance. The progression of experiencing a tight space before moving into an expansive view was a typical way of creating wonders in Chinese gardens. In the nineteenth copperplate (L. Yi), the only way to have a glimpse of the Square River was through the central arch of the gateway, because both flanks of the gateway were planted with dense trees and rocks. The designer intended to give the viewer a surprise by hiding the view of the lake temporarily. In his treatise, Cheng Ji described the use of "half-a-bay" space for creating "depth, mystery, meandering" and the "bounded field of fantasy" (73). In the 1936 survey map, the Eastern Gate of the Line Method Hill was marked as the "Conch Tower Gate" because of its convoluted conch-like decorations (*Shice Yuanming*), which dematerialized the stonewall and prompted a great curiosity about the view hidden behind the gateway.

To provide height along the path in the garden, stairways were constructed. There were twin stairways at several points along the path, at both the southern and northern sides of the Harmony, Wonder, and Delight pavilion; the southern side of The View Beyond the World pavilion; the western and eastern sides of the Hall of Peaceful Sea; and the southern side of the View of Distant Sea pavilion. These paired stairways provided the emperor with a slow ascent and descent while he was appreciating the fountain flanked by the stairways. All the stairways in the garden were paired and their symmetrical composition accentuated the effect of line method. The path of the garden sometimes passed through buildings, such as the five bamboo pavilions, that were connected by curved bamboo covered walkways. The Chinese term for "covered walkway" is *lang*, which was explicated by Cheng Ji in the *Yuan ye*: "The layout of ancient covered walkway was folded with the carpenter's folding ruler. The present winding covered walkway, which meanders like the character of *zhi*, turns left and right in accordance with topography and bends up and down according to the natural propensity of the site" (91). The character *zhi* is composed of zigzag strokes. In Chinese gardens, the meandering of the walkway is an embodiment of the mind searching for remoteness. The curved bamboo walkways here, which were arranged symmetrically through line method, demonstrated the gesture of enclosing. Another passing-through-building path was located at the Hall of Peaceful Sea. The emperor would enter the second floor of the building from the water-method stairway at the western end, walk over the roof of a one-floor veranda, climb to the roof of the water tank where two pavilions stood respectively at each end of the roof, then descend at the eastern end along a magnificent open-air stairway. The roof pavilions hinted at the typical terraced pavilion in Chinese gardens, although the terrace here was an exotic water tank. The image of the pavilions over a water tank also corresponded to the paradigmatic image of pavilions over water in Chinese gardens, although the water here was a hidden water body. The application of line method in the planning of the paths in the Western garden can be further demonstrated through the matching viewpoints in the garden and the frontal views of the copperplates. The path was probably, from the very beginning, designed for perfectly observing these perspective frontal faces, and the *jing* of the garden and the *jing* in perspectives had been fused together in the emperor's mind. The copperplates were intended to give Qianlong his desired views of the garden (Adam 24), and the garden was experienced as if viewing a series of separate pictures (Schulz 71, 77).

The carefully planned sequence for viewing the multiple *jing* of line method created a strong sense of time in the process of encountering the secret views one after another. The emperor's journey of searching the pictures of line method started from the Western labyrinth, went through the magical play of fountains, and ended up with the illusionary view of infinity. Each opening, hidden area, and turn on the path lured the curious mind into a specific *jing* of line method. Each *jing* completely hid the next one until the viewer's body passed through the division. Besides curiosity, the visitor on the path frequently experienced confusion, which was mostly caused by the huge discrepancy and contradiction between the façade of a building and the program hidden behind its exterior face. What was seemingly a palace building was in fact a water tank. A Chinese gateway on one side became a European Baroque portico on the other. A side door paradoxically led into a magic world of a labyrinth or fountains. When the path seemed to reach its end on the ground, it suddenly moved up to the roof of a building. An open gateway carefully framed a partial view of waters and mountains, which hinted at an expansive view of landscapes; but after passing through the gateway, one quickly realized the field was actually quite narrow. It is clear from studying the copperplates that the designer used the principle of central perspective to draw the viewer's attention towards the focal point of a view and then surprised the viewer with an unpredictable view when he reached that point. In order to anchor the viewer's mind towards the focal point, the designer clearly marked each viewing point on the straight path through architectural and garden details so that the spectator could involuntarily stop on that spot and view the *jing* of line method. The shift between the focal point and the viewing point on the path helped define the entire Western garden as a labyrinth.

Qianlong's experience in the Western garden as a labyrinth was well expressed by the title of the first *jing*, Harmony, Wonder, and Delight. One can imagine how he viewed a *jing* of line method as a wonder and became delighted at a new unpredictable *jing* when he reached the spot of that focal point. Such an unpredictable *jing* in a single view was quite rare in Chinese gardens, where a window-framed *jing* was intended to bring a symbolic view of the big world to the viewer's mind. Standing in the room and looking through the window, the Chinese viewer tended to wonder what the outside world would be, but this indirectly visible world was already expected in his mind. As Cheng Ji said, "pretty *jing* should be included" through the opening of a door or window (171).

Multistoried buildings

According to the objectives of the Society of Jesus, the more universal the good, the more divine it was and thus preference was given to influential people and places whose improvement became a cause that spread the good to others (Lucas 196). This policy was best demonstrated by the Western garden in the Yuanming Yuan. However, the interactive relationship between the garden *jing* and the representation *jing* cannot be explained simply as a direct result of the Jesuit religion. There is no absolute proof indicating that the garden was created by the Jesuits for the exact purpose of influencing the Chinese emperor with a Western religion; however, it is certain that the emperor, Jesuit builders, and other Chinese who were involved in this garden all projected their intentions into the creation of this garden. Although the Western multistoried buildings were intended to compose a garden, the title of the garden itself demonstrates that these buildings occupied prominent positions in the garden. As a type of garden building, the multistoried building, *lou*, can be traced back as early as the late Han dynasty and the Southern-Northern Dynasties period. It served as a place for viewing into the distance and itself appeared as an attractive backdrop. The multistoried building was usually located at the side or back portion of a garden (C. Zhang 185). In Jie Li's architectural treatise, *Yingzao fashi* (*The Principles and Patterns of Building*), the etymological meanings of *lou* were listed in detail. It stated: "The ancient dictionary *Er ya* says: what is narrow and curved is called *lou*. . . . The ancient history book *Shiji* says: a Daoist told the emperor Wudi of Han that Emperor Huang in the ancient time built fifty-two *lou* for the arrival of deities. Wudi thus built a divine terrace and a scaffolding *lou* in fifty *zhang* high. The ancient dictionary *Shuowen jiezhi* says: *lou* means the multistoried house. The ancient dictionary *Shi ming* says: *lou* is that between whose windows there are shooting holes which look gloomy" (4). The *Yingzao fashi* is the earliest architectural treatise known in Chinese history. In the garden treatise *Yuan ye* by Cheng Ji, similar etymological meanings of *lou* were repeated, but it further explained that the *lou* was a building "with wide open windows which are arranged in a good order" (86). The sense of order of the traditional *lou* resonates with the regulation of line method of Western multistoried buildings.

When the Western garden was under construction, those buildings were temporarily called "buildings of water method" (*shuifa fang*) ("Neiwufu" archives 345, 347), because of their close relationship with fountains. The Chinese term for "building" in this temporary title was *fang*. The etymological meanings of *fang* were cited by the *Yuan ye*: "The ancient dictionary *Shi ming* says: *fang* means to be cautious, namely, to keep privacy and to divide inside and outside" (Ji 85). The change of the building title from *fang* to *lou* indicated the change in the emperor's attitude towards the garden from early cautiousness to later acceptance and appreciation. In the Model Lei collection, the plane drawing of the View of Distant Sea pavilion indicates that there were wooden columns within the structure of the stonewalls (Lei; H. Zou, "Jesuit Perspective" 164, fig. 7). The Qing court codes for the buildings of the Yuanming Yuan complex confirmed that there were timber columns within the "Western walls" (*Yuanmingyuan damuzuo* vol. 1, ch. 3). Because the Western walls were made of stones and bricks, it is unclear whether or not these were actually load-bearing timber columns. One other possible function of these timber columns was their use by Chinese builders to arrange the plane of each Western building, because in Chinese classic architecture, the construction of a building started from arranging timber columns on the ground. This hypothesis was confirmed by the site plan of the View of Distant Sea, also in the Model Lei collection, where the plane of the building was drawn as a grid of columns in the traditional Chinese fashion (Lei).

The three divisions of the ground plan of the View of Distant Sea pavilion followed the typical division of a hall building, *tang*, in Chinese classic architecture, where the central bay was bigger than the side bays. The *Yuan ye* stated that the central bay of a *tang* should be bigger than its side bays; they cannot be evenly divided. The treatise further explained that the ancient *tang* means that its front part is open and spacious to a forward facing view, namely, to face straight towards the sunshine from the south in order to get a dignified and imposing appearance (Ji 83, 106). In the Western garden, the Hall of Peaceful Sea was a spacious building, whose interior in fact was a huge water tank, located on a massive clay terrace, which provided water to the fountains. Because the rectangular plan of the building was arranged along a west-to-east axis, there were fewer opportunities for viewing the northern and southern sides of the building. Although being named as a "hall" building, the southern face, the brightest face, of this building was not prominent in comparison with its western and eastern faces, which were engaged in fantastic water plays. Comparing the copperplates which depict the southern and northern faces of the building (L. Yi), they seem to mirror each other and the only difference between them is the floating clouds in the sky. However, one detail in the copperplates still suggests the importance of the southern face of this hall building. In the sequence of the twenty copperplates, the western face of the building was the tenth copperplate; the northern face, the eleventh; the eastern face, the twelfth; the southern face, the thirteenth. This means that after viewing the other three faces of the building, the spectator finally viewed its southern face, the brightest face. Such an organized viewing sequence created a final moment of full brightness rather than shadows.

  The frontal gesture of the hall was originally intended for the purpose of receiving sunshine from the south to match the Confucian principle that an emperor must "sit in the north and face to the south." For this reason, a hall in an imperial garden was usually used as a place for the imperial throne. Emperor Daoguang received his officials privately at the second scene, Diligent and Affectionate, of the Forty Scenes. In the summer, reception was held in the Hall of Diligent Administration in that *jing*; in spring and autumn, in a reading room west of the hall. The throne in the hall faced to the south, but the throne in the reading room originally faced to the north, due to space limitations. In the year of *dingyou* (1837), a porch was added to the south of the reading room where a southern door and a northern window were opened, creating a throne against the northern window and facing the southern door (Yao 4). As the plane drawing of the View of Distant Sea pavilion in the Model Lei collection illustrated (Lei; H. Zou, "Jesuit Perspective" 164, fig. 7), there was a throne facing to the south in the central hall of this building. In the northern part of the hall there was a screen behind the throne to protect the emperor's back. In the drawing, a Chinese character for "south" was specifically marked to accentuate the importance of the orientation to the south.

  For an important building in a Chinese garden, such as a hall building, two name boards were usually hung. One board was hung on the outer eave over the door so that people would see it when entering the building; the other board was hung on the inner eave over the central chair so that a visitor could view the board that hung over the host's head. The meaning of a name board was closely related with its location: inside or outside. The name board, Containing Clarity and Void, was hung on the outer eave of the Harmony, Wonder, and Delight pavilion in 1751. The name board, Harmony, Wonder and Delight, was hung on the inner eave of the same building in 1752, officially naming the building and the *jing* at this site. The outer board echoed with the water play of the fountains in the frontcourt, while the inner board hinted at the unifying power of the emperor by indicating the "harmony" of "wonders" and "delights." The inner board was integrated with the throne where the emperor sat and faced the fountain plaza in the south. Other examples included name boards such as the Hall of Peaceful Sea, The View beyond the World, and the View of Distant Sea, which were all hung on the inner eaves of their respective buildings and became the official names of those buildings (Z. Zhang 48). In all these cases, the name board was hung over an imperial throne.

The term "multistoried building" indicated the general type of buildings within the Western garden. Another term that indicated a special building type was the "view," *guan*, which literally meant "look" in both senses of verb and noun. Examples of the use of *guan* in building names included The View beyond the World, View of Distant Sea, and Viewing the Water Method. In the Chinese language, the *guan* also signifies a Daoist belvedere that is located in a remote landscape. Among these three "view" buildings, the first one was a two-story building; the second, a building sitting on a high terrace; and the third, an open-air imperial throne. The first two "views" indicated a distant *jing* observed from a high place. At the imperial throne, the verb form of "to view" emphasized the emperor's activity of watching the close *jing* of the Big Water Method. According to a Qing record of the name boards in the Yuanming Yuan complex (qtd. in Z. Zhang), the use of the term "view" was limited to these three Western multistoried buildings among hundreds of building names in the Yuanming Yuan complex. This detail demonstrates the extreme importance of both the "view" and the act of "viewing" in this Western garden.

Among the emperors who lived in the Yuanming Yuan, Jiaqing, son of Qianlong, wrote the greatest number of poems on the Western portion, especially on the View of Distant Sea pavilion, as this *jing* might have been his most favorite. His poetry became an important source for understanding how the Western multistoried buildings were used and how he was impressed by the "Western style" buildings. In the poem "Write on the View of Distant Sea," he wrote: "The rooms imitate the Western style, / My little heart includes the distant seas. / The benevolence extends far and wide, / The distant and near celebrate peace and harmony. / To govern the country one has to ponder deeply and extensively, / In the house I remember the difficulty of defending the achievements" ("Ti Yuanyingguan"). The term "rooms" indicates that he was sitting on the interior, most likely on his throne. Because the building was lofty and sublime, he felt as if his body was small. However, his view extended through the door and window, which came across the Big Water Method and reached the far distant lakes in the Garden of Eternal Spring from the south. It is apparent that this extensive and concentrated view opened the horizon and enhanced his feelings of power.

Like The View Beyond the World pavilion, the structure of the View of Distant Sea pavilion appeared to cater to and embrace the spectator. In this way, the imperial face was turned towards the distant south to embrace brightness. The projection of intention towards the south was attested to by the fact that the View of Distant Sea pavilion, the Viewing the Water Method throne, and the Big Water Method were all arranged on the same axis as the Gallery of Unsophisticated Transformation within the Garden of Eternal Spring. The axis began at the View of Distant Sea pavilion on the northern end, looked southwards over the Big Water Method, passed through the Hall of Wet Orchids, crossed over a huge area of water in the middle, and extended into the courtyard buildings of the Gallery of Unsophisticated Transformation, where stone tablets of classic inscriptions were stored. This viewing axis, integrating artistic waters and stones, hinted at symbolic mountains and waters—*shanshui*.

The View of Distant Sea pavilion was only one story, yet it stood on a high terrace. This positioning created the illusion of a multistoried building. On the foundation of a multistoried building in gardens, the *Yuan ye* stated, "Why not erect the foundation of a multistoried building between half a hill and half a water? It can be two or three stories. When you look at it from the bottom, it appears as a multistoried building; when you look at it at the hillside, it looks like a single floor; when you reach the top of the building, your view can reach one thousand miles away" (Ji 74). This description is an exact match to the View of Distant Sea, where the building stood on a high terrace, which imitated the "half a hill," behind the Big Water Method, which imitated the "half a water." The view from the building reached the expansive and distant landscapes in the Garden of Eternal Spring. The "view of distant sea" was so vast that it recalled Zongyuan Liu's landscape theory—vast openness (*kuangru*) ("Yongzhou" 26).

It should be noted that the View of Distant Sea was a view framed by the building composed with line method. In his poem "Chant at the View of Distant Sea," Jiaqing wrote, "Stone steps go up and down between pearl trees, / Glass windows compose beautiful views. / Widely open windows on all sides lead to cool breezes, / On the emerald-green screen the purple phoenix lingers in fragrant mists. / A room with clear views is prepared for the distant sea, / The imperial mind embraces the great world. / Look at the grand building and closely caress its structure, / Its majesty resists decay and remains full" ("Yuanyingguan ge [2]" 228). For the emperor, the *jing* of the distant lake framed by the bright room extended his mind into the cosmos, and the "grand" view expressed the "fullness" of his majesty. According to an imperial archive, the windows of this building were fitted with more than 1,200 glass plates in 1782 ("Neiwufu" archive 830), bringing light into the room and creating a "room with clear views prepared for the distant sea." The phrase, "prepared for the distant sea" indicated his southern orientation, as he would have been viewing the expansive water located within the Garden of Eternal Spring. In the emperor's mind, the Western buildings appeared exotic and maintained a strong sense of distance. In the poem "Afterthoughts on the View of Distant Sea," Jiaqing wrote, "The stone door is connected with lip windows, / The form imitates the Western" ("Yuanyingguan yougan" 23). Again, the Western style impressed him. This time he gave more details about the building. Stone took the place of wood, the typical material of Chinese classic architecture; the "lip windows" indicated the decorations on the window frames; the form was *not* Chinese. However, the sense of distance, that the building was here but appeared to be there—the West, brought joy and excitement to the emperor's mind. In the poem "View of Distant Sea," he stated, "The structure imitates the Western, / For entertainment and leisure, I occasionally come here to stroll about. / The view is like a *jing* of a painting, / My eyes are pleased and my intention remains free" ("Yuanying Guan [3]"). The poem clearly stated that the scene around the View of Distant Sea pavilion was a *jing* of a painting, where his eyes and heart met. In another sense, the exotic view itself could not cause enjoyment, rather, it had to be composed as a *jing* for appreciation. The comment, "the view is like a *jing* of a painting" immediately transformed the exotic distance into the poetic depth of the Chinese context. Penned by Qianlong, the name board, View of Distant Sea was made of glass decorated with Western lace borders and officially hung on the inner eave of the building in 1781 ("Neiwufu" archive 822). When the emperor sat on his throne and looked towards the outside, the *jing* he obtained was opposite to the *jing* expressed by the copperplate. Thus, the *jing* indicated by a name board on the inner eave and the *jing* in the copperplate with the same title were opposite to each other and complimented each other.

Jiaqing's pleasure in the "Western" *jing* of Distant Sea was also related to his image of the "Westerners" who came from a distant sea. His later poetry regarding the View of Distant Sea was about his anger towards the British envoy. One of his poems stated: "I originally had no intention to call him, / Suddenly the British envoy came. / Since he had come, but he was not obedient, / He spoke sweet words full of hypocrisies" ("Yuanyingguan shuzhi"). In this poem on the View of Distant Sea, he did not mention the "view" at all, but rather the "view" became a medium for him to reflect on diplomatic conflicts. In fact, the British had no relationship with the construction of the garden. It is interesting to note that the emperor connected the unwelcome British envoy with the "pleasurable" View of Distant Sea. This showed how the emperor's concept of the "distant sea" included the far distant sea where the "Westerners" originated. In addition, the "harmony" of "wonder" and "delight" obtained from the Western multistoried buildings was certainly part of the emperor's cosmological vision of Round Brightness. Nothing is known about Qianlong's poetry on the Western Multistoried Buildings, yet Jiaqing's poetical description that the Western structure "is like a *jing* of a painting" was well represented by an anonymous painting where the emperor, probably Qianlong, and a lady of the court sat in front of The View Beyond the World pavilion (Vanderstappen 118). This is a rare painting showing inhabitants in the garden. All the details in this painting are arranged in accordance with the focal point, which is located at the top of the ground door. The postures and positions of the figures interact with the backdrop of the building façade and the central axis of the composition. The body of the emperor is turned slightly to his side to allow the "prince of rays" (in Alberti's words), which is the line connecting the viewpoint and the focal point in perspective, to pass by. The canopy over his head and the other figures form a "window" that allows the spectator to "look through" towards the central door where the focal point is located. Furthermore, the oblique lines of the balustrades, pavement, and the inward posture of the trees all contribute to the perspectival convergence. Accentuating this effect, the original positions of the two elliptical windows are displaced inwardly toward the central door.

The same perspective distortion can also be found in the eighth copperplate, Frontal Face of the View beyond the World (L. Yi). Unlike the previous painting, a pair of open-air stairs flank the building in a curved form and two pairs of scrolled balustrades are arranged symmetrically along the central axis. All of these details enhance the perspectival convergence, which in return gives the impression that the building is opening its arms to embrace the spectator. The focal point of the copperplate is located on the balcony of the second floor. If the emperor stood on the balcony and looked into the distant south, he would have a perfect view, which would have included the bamboo pavilions with verandas that were decorated with colorful glass, a central fountain, and two lotus pools to the side. This proposed scene is best represented by the ninth copperplate, Northern Face of the Bamboo Pavilions (L. Yi), where the mists, clouds, and floating tree crowns in the background make the *jing* appear as a dreamland, which echoes the meaning of "the view beyond the world." The emperor's intention to see the *jing* of the garden through line method was also demonstrated through his request that the Jesuit painters hasten painting perspectives for the interiors of the Western multistoried buildings. On the twentieth day of the second moon of the sixteenth year of the Qianlong reign (1751), the year that the Harmony, Wonder, and Delight pavilion was completed, Castiglione was asked to paint perspectives for the eighteen bays of the eastern veranda of the pavilion. The work was mandated to be finished by the second moon of the next year. The emperor suggested that if the Jesuit painters at the Lodge As One Wishes studio could not finish on time, Chinese painting apprentices be employed to assist them. On the ninth day of the fourth moon of the forty-seventh year of the Qianlong reign (1782), the year that the View of Distant Sea pavilion was finished, the Jesuit painters Louis de Por (Chinese name, Qingtai He) and Joseph Panzi (Chinese name, Tingzhang Pan) were asked to paint Western figures for the central ceiling. The painter Lantai Yi, the draughtsman of the twenty copperplates, painted the border area. The emperor decreed that the work must be done quickly and precisely. "Because the painting assistants could not grasp line method well," despite working day and night, the Jesuit painters had difficulty meeting the deadline. They therefore asked for more assistants that were capable of line-method painting, so that the work could be finished on time ("Neiwufu" archives 356, 835).

The Western multistoried buildings played a double role in the *jing* of line method: on the one hand, they were composed as a backdrop for the water play in the garden; on the other hand, they provided a high place for peering into the distance. In the copperplates, a multistoried building appear as a focus; in the garden, the same building acts as an observation point for viewing. In European Baroque gardens, the garden designer had to work with horizontal planes by tracing a *quadratura* on the ground, which corresponded to the frame of a picture and marked the intersection of the visual pyramid with the ground level (Baridon 7). In such a position, perspective acted as a one-directional projection: the house was given a commanding position to view the garden from above, but the house itself looked very small in the large-scale garden. Meanwhile, in the Western Multistoried Buildings garden, line method maintained the traditional horizontal projection of perspective in painting and thus provided a chance of reciprocity between the viewpoint and the focal point.

Study of the counter-eye in the Jesuit perspective of art offered a way to investigate the emperor's, as well as the Jesuit designer's, intentions towards a *jing* in the garden by attending to the position of the focal point in the copperplates. The focal point in these copperplates was always on the vertical central line, and usually at a prominent place, such as a balcony, door, pavilion, portico, or throne, where the emperor would most likely have stood to appreciate a *jing*. Thus we may see that the illusionary depth in a perspective resonated with the emperor's desire for a distant view in the garden. In the imperial archives on the construction of the Western garden, the multistoried buildings were frequently called "Western multistoried buildings" (*xiyang lou*) or "palace buildings of water method" (*shuifa dian*) ("Neiwufu" archives 426, 434, 443). However, these names did not express how the buildings in the garden were actually perceived by the emperor. From the detail that the emperor was eager to see the representation of the garden *jing* depicted with line method in the copperplates, we can sense that he wanted to perceive the *jing* in the garden as the *jing* of line method. In fact, among the twenty copperplates, only a quarter of them include the image of fountains, but all the copperplates present a Western multistoried building as the center of the perspective view. Furthermore, the focal point in most of the copperplates is anchored on the central doorway of a multistoried building, which hints at the mystic world behind the door. The Western multistoried buildings seem to act as the background for the spectacular show of fountains, but in fact they were intended for the composition of the *jing* of line method. In this sense, they should be called the multistoried buildings of line method (*xianfa lou*).

Theaters

In the *jing* of line method, a central fountain was usually embraced by a Western multistoried building in the background. Such a concentrated view of dynamic water looked exotic in comparison with the expansive view of static water in Chinese gardens. For the water in gardens, Yongzheng and Qianlong had different preferences. In his record of the Yuanming Yuan, Yongzheng expressed his desire of "delight in nature" where a pool was crystal clear and the distant peaks broke into this mirror. In his later record of the Yuanming Yuan, Qianlong desired a place to roam around, where the landscapes and buildings "were beyond imagination." Although he cautioned himself not to indulge in "curiosities," in fact, his words demonstrated his strong desire for the views of a garden which could be exotic.

In his poem of the Garden of Eternal Spring, along with a preface, Qianlong explained further that his desire for brightness and remoteness could be fulfilled by spectacular views which delighted his heart and attracted his eyes. The Garden of Eternal Spring and the Western garden were built at the same time, and the poems on the former provide a good reference for the understanding of the latter. The spectacular views in his new gardens, where he strolled about leisurely and joyously, were constructed through imitating other gardens, including his ancestors' gardens, gardens in Jiangnan, and those in the West. Compared to his father's delight in nature, Qianlong's joy of gardens was more a result of his curiosity for theatrical views, which included mechanical fountains and illusionary stage design in the Western garden.

Mechanical fountains were called "water methods" (*shuifa*), about which discussion first appeared in the Chinese books written by the Jesuits during the Ming dynasty. Those books were later incorporated into the imperial encyclopedia, *Siku quanshu* (*Complete Library of the Four Treasuries*), during the Qianlong reign. One of the four original copies of the imperial encyclopedia was stored in the Multistoried Pavilion of Literary Origin in the Yuanming Yuan (E. Zhang, *Yuanmingyuan daguan* 144). The encyclopedia includes an introduction about the illustrated book, *Yuanxi qiqi tushuo* (*Illustrated Discourse of Far Western Extraordinary Machines*). The book was written during the Ming dynasty by the Jesuit Joannes Terrenz (Chinese name, Yuhan Deng) with the Chinese scholar Zheng Wang providing translation and illustrations. It is certain that the book was adapted from Agostino Ramelli's book on "skillful machines," as the illustrations in the Chinese book were almost an exact replica of Ramelli's work; however, the engraving techniques were quite different; they were created through copperplate engravings (Ramelli), while the Chinese illustrations were made through woodcuts. In Ramelli's book, in an illustration of a machine that lifted water from a well, the ground surface was opened up to show how the underground portion of the machine functioned. In the 1627 edition of Terrenz's and Wang's book, Wang illustrated the cut edge of the ground surface as Chinese lace borders, owing to his unfamiliarity with a cutout type of drawing. In the 1726 edition of this book, an anonymous Chinese illustrator developed the lace borders into blocks of clouds and the machine thus appeared as if floating in the air rather than being underground (Edgerton 277, 279, 282).

The concept of "dragon tail" appeared in another Jesuit book, *Taixi shuifa* (*Western Water Method*), during the Ming dynasty. The author, Sabbathinus de Ursis (Chinese name, Sanba Xiong), wrote that the term "dragon tail" described the image of water, which revolved and moved up slowly (Xiong 3). The term alluded to the legendary story of the Dragon King in the East Sea and demonstrated how the image of a Western hydraulic machine was transformed into a Chinese understanding. In chapter 4, "Water Method," he wrote, "It is better to locate a well at the foot of a mountain where spring water comes out; *yin* and *yang* are appropriate; and gardens and houses can be established" (2). The siting of wells was connected with the knowledge of *fengshui*: "The moon is the quintessence of *yin* and belongs to the same category of water. Wet, tender, dark, and cold things in the world are administered by the moon. Since they are in the same category, their natural propensities can correspond to each other" (7). It is interesting to read that the Jesuit author related the force of *yin*, the moon, and water together. This is an idication of his knowledge of Chinese cosmology.

The Ming concept of water method was used to signify the fountains in the Western garden of the Yuanming Yuan. Those water methods were made by the imperial Department of Clockmaking. An imperial archive recorded that on the eighteenth day of the seventh moon of the thirty-sixth year of the Qianlong reign (1772), the emperor decreed: "Order the Westerners Dahong Wang [Jean-Mathieu de Ventavon] and Hengliang Li [Western name unknown] to make water methods at the Department of Clockmaking" ("Neiwufu" archive 700). The hidden mechanism of both clocks and fountains evoked the emperors' curiosity, which was described in Yongzheng's poem, "Chant on an Automatic Clock": "The ingenious mechanism corresponds to heavenly rhythm, / *yin* and *yang* are contained by such a small body. / Gears revolve continuously, / Pointers and the dial meet precisely. / The marks of time have no errors, / Sunrise and sunset cannot be mixed. / When clear strikes report hours, / I doubt it is made by human labor" ("Yong ziming" 2). The poem shows that the emperor's understanding of clocks was closely related to his knowledge of the cosmos: he thought a certain supernatural power made the clock run in a precise order.

The concept of water method had existed in Chinese gardens long before its application to the Western hydraulic mechanism. The garden theories of the Ming dynasty discussed how to use the method for managing a watercourse or creating a ravine where the water method should procure a deep feeling and natural delight (Ji 219-20). The Garden of Solitary Joy owned by Guang Sima, a writer of the Song dynasty, presented an early example of managing watercourses within a garden. In the record of his garden, Sima stated that he "guided" and "diverted the water" around a building and this building was therefore named the House of Playing with Water (54). Managing water was a high priority in Chinese gardens, especially the water source at the site of a garden. The *Yuan ye* advises that when selecting the site of a building in a garden, it is highly valued to let it be over a water surface. Before erecting the foundation, a garden designer needs to trace the origin of water, smooth out where the water goes and observe where the water comes from (Ji 56). In the context of eighteenth-century imperial gardens, a water method could be a waterfall, yet it could also be a fountain. It is very likely that the fountain-like water method existed prior to the Western Multistoried Buildings garden. The fountain-like water method was described as a Water Bamboo Residence (Shuizhu Ju) in the Jiangnan region. In the description of a water method in the garden of the Xu family in Yangzhou, Dou Li of the Qing dynasty recorded that there was a long covered walkway that was called Water Bamboo Residence. Underneath was a half-acre pool where spring water was like splashed pearls, which could reach the height of the eaves (*Yangzhou* 385). The name Water Bamboo Residence indicated how the water method was integrated into a residence within the garden. There was also a Water Bamboo Residence in the Yuanming Yuan. In the preamble of his poem of the twenty-second scene, Clear Water and Rustling Trees, Qianlong described this Water Bamboo Residence: "Water is brought into the room through the Western water method to turn the fan. The sound of flowing water is sweet and pleasing to ears, just like sounds from heaven" ("Shuimu" 49). Here, the "Western water method" stood for hydraulics.

On the fountain-like water method in the Yuanming Yuan, Father Matteo Ripa recalled: "His Majesty [emperor Yongzheng] has taken it into his head to have a fountain constructed, which should never cease to play. We were accordingly asked by command, whether any of us were able to contrive it. A Frenchman answered to the effect that two of his countrymen had lately arrived who would understand such a work. Father Angelo . . . replied without hesitation, that he felt equal to the task" (127). A fountain "which should never cease to play" meant that the fountain was run by a mechanical system rather than human labor. The designer of these water methods was French, as the designer of the fountains in the Western Multistoried Buildings garden, Father Benoist, was also French, demonstrating that the knowledge of hydraulics was highly developed in eighteenth-century France. Father Benoist arrived in Beijing in 1745 to work as a mathematician, but two years later, he was in charge of making fountains for the emperor: "In 1745, by the order of the emperor, I arrived in Beijing under the title of mathematician. Two years later, I was asked by His Majesty [emperor Qianlong] to be in charge of the hydraulic work. . . . In the gardens of Yuanming, the emperor wanted to construct a palais européen. He considered decorating the exterior of the garden like the interior of buildings with hydraulic works" (177-80). Although the garden was called a European Palace by Father Benoist, the emperor paid as much attention to the outside of the palace as to the inside. Qianlong's interest in fountains did not necessarily mean that the importance of the garden lay only in fountains, because Western fountains, as Father Ripa witnessed, had already existed in the Yuanming Yuan. His interest in the fountains was closely related to his primary intention for the Western multistoried buildings. He wanted to view the fountains in the exterior of those buildings.

Additional proof for the cohesive relationship between the fountains and the buildings is that the fountains were typically not in operation except during Qianlong's visit. Before his planned visit, water would be prepared in the cisterns by garden servants. This is similar to what happened at Versailles when there was insufficient water pressure to permit all the fountains to function at once, with the solution being that only the fountains within the king's field of vision were made to function (Weiss 48). The concept of a mechanical water-method fountain differed from the Chinese traditional water method, as the mechanical one utilized a power-driven force and the traditional one fell naturally. In Italian gardens, the water never appeared in its natural form but rather through artificial contrivances. Water henceforth meant fountains, cascades, and basins, while a dry fountain was a dead body. In the front-page illustration of Giovanni Battista Falda's engraved book on gardens in Rome, two angels poured water from the sky into a fountain in a garden, suggesting that heavenly water ran through the fountains (*Li Giardini*). In another engraved book on fountains in Roma by the same author, a fountain typically occupied the center of the picture. With the horizon of view at eye level, the water column soared so high that it almost touched the upper border of the picture, so that its top was higher than the surrounding buildings and stood independently against the sky (*Le Fontane*). This composition most likely meant to emphasize the heavenly quality of fountain water. In George Böckler's book on fountains, a fountain sometimes appeared as a smiling human face of the sun god, or as a parasol under which a human figure stood (Böckler figures 12, 63).

The water method of a fountain was a transformation of a Western fountain and it held its own meanings through its "view" in the Chinese context. To explore the emperor's meaning of the water method in the southern plaza of the Harmony, Wonder, and Delight pavilion, the name of the *jing*, Harmony, Wonder, and Delight, needs to be understood. The phrase "harmony, wonder, and delight" first appeared in the Tang poet Juyi Bai's poem "Read Linyun Xie's Poetry." The poem stated: "If the lofty ideal is repressed and cannot be applied, / It must find a place to release itself. / To release the ideal is to write poems of mountains and waters, / Leisurely rhythm is harmonious, wonderful, and delightful" ("Du Xie Lingyun" 160). The poem shows that the concept of "harmonious, wonderful, and delightful" was related to the feeling of "leisurely rhythm" which indicated the mutual resonance between the viewer's emotions and the view of landscapes. Qianlong borrowed the concept of "harmony, wonder, and delight" to express his sense of the rhythmic sound with the movement of fountains. The building was named Harmony, Wonder, and Delight on the second day of the second moon of the sixteenth year of the Qianlong reign (1751) ("Neiwufu" archive 349). The name board, which officiated this name, was hung on the inner eave; another name board, Gushing Clarity and Void, was hung on the outer eave. Another version of the name was Containing Clarity and Void (Fang 53). The imperial throne was just under the interior name board, which was to be read only with the presence of the emperor's body. The board on the outer eave was read in the context of the exterior environment. In this way, the interior name board Harmony, Wonder, and Delight, which also signified a unified *jing*, expressed how the emperor himself felt within the environment of the fountains and multistoried buildings; the exterior name board Gushing Clarity and Void described the features of the water fountain. Since the interior name board was used to describe the outside *jing*, we get a sense that the name of the *jing* was intended to express the emperor's internal feelings at the "view" of water methods.

There was a vertical couplet that accompanied the name board Harmony, Wonder, and Delight. The left phrase said, "careful thinking" and the right phrase, "human being" ("Neiwufu" archive 349). When he read the couplet along with the horizontal name board, we can imagine how Qianlong watched the "wonder" of the water methods in great "delight," as he thought about leading the country into a "harmonic" world, just like the physical existence of water sounds and building details that were in front of his eyes. Qianlong's complicated feelings regarding the water method were expressed in the poem "Watch the Water Method at the Harmony, Wonder, and Delight" by his son Jiaqing in 1796: "Elongated multistoried buildings imitate the Western style, / Loud sounds seem to come from the bustling imperial court. / Stir up water and channel the spring to make the flow undulate, / Cast brass spouts lie on the ground and were excellently made. / Terrifying waves turn over stones as one thousand labors do. / White rains bounce into beads measured in ten thousand *hu*. / If ingenious people long to serve in distant places [as these Westerners do], / The territory of the country will be as stable as a solid gold bowl" ("Guan Xieqiqu" 228). Jiaqing first described the Western multistoried buildings that were in the background; next, his attention was drawn to the sound of water, the form of the water, and the appearance of the fountains. What attracted him was the integrated image of water columns, which seemed to him to mirror the prospective harmonic situation of the whole nation. While the feelings of wonder and delight were evoked by the fountains, the feeling of harmony was related to the architectural background. The feeling of harmony partly came from the view of four spouts in the form of sheep and ten spouts in the form of wild geese as they sprayed water together towards the center of the fountain pool. In addition, a harmonic feeling was also derived in part from the noisy sound of the fountains. Although we can borrow from Renaissance architectural theory to explain how a cohesive composition produced the beauty of harmony of this Western multistoried building (Alberti, *Ten Books* 113), from the last two sentences of the poem, we know that the emperor's feelings of harmony came from his view which integrated the exotic scenes into the perfect brightness.

To enhance the wonder of the fountains and increase the viewer's delight, as shown in the site plan of the Harmony, Wonder, and Delight in the Model Lei collection (Lei), the viewer was intentionally blocked from the exotic view of the fountains and buildings by dense woods. When he reached a bridge over the watercourse, the view suddenly became apparent. Standing on the high deck of the Harmony, Wonder, and Delight pavilion and looking over the watercourse, Qianlong might have recalled not only the close connection between his new gardens and his father's garden but also his affection for his father. As demonstrated in the first copperplate (L. Yi), the synchronic waterspouts facing the watercourse from one garden to another probably represented to the emperor the harmony between the past and the present. It is interesting to note that the water source for the fountains at the *jing* of Harmony, Wonder, and Delight was separate from the watercourse of the Garden of Eternal Spring, although both watercourses became very close to each other at the water mouth under the Bridge of Line Method. The water of the Western garden came from a canal outside the northern garden wall, while the water of the Garden of Eternal Spring flowed directly from the Yuanming Yuan. Although the water play between the fountains was quite impressive, the source of the water for the fountains was hidden and this enhanced the wonder of the water methods. The fountain water flowed from the cistern of a water-storage building behind the Harmony, Wonder, and Delight pavilion and was transferred to the fountains through underground silver ditches. An imperial archive recorded that on the twenty-second day of the second moon of the sixteen year of the Qianlong reign (1751), the emperor decreed: "As for the construction of the silver ditches of the palace of water method, order Shining Lang [Castiglione] to present a design for my permission and then give it to the Construction Department of the Imperial Households to construct" ("Neiwufu" archive 350). The hidden image of the water channel and water storage was greatly enhanced by the illusionary and brilliant line-method image of the multistoried building.

A fountain was located north of the Harmony, Wonder, and Delight pavilion at the center of a courtyard. To the west of the courtyard was the Water Storage Multistoried Building; to the north, the main gate of the labyrinth; to the east, the Raising Birds Cage gateway. The edge of the fountain pool was elevated above the ground and was similar to those in Renaissance gardens. Its regular geometrical form and central position reinforced the image of "une fontaine monumentale" (Adam 25). In another poem "Harmony, Wonder, and Delight" in 1798, Jiaqing wrote: "Water is transferred from the roof of the multistoried building, / Movement of machines must be carefully examined. / Although the circulation of water is completely wonderful, / Leakage has to be prevented. / Waves have one thousand layers, / Pearls and beads are measured in ten thousand *hu*. / The underground vein meanders into the distance, / Full water can be traced back to a distant origin. / Vastly and mightily all water returns into gullies, / At the beginning it flows little by little. / In watching the waves, wonder and delight meet, / The ultimate reason is thus concealed" ("Xie Qi Qu" 228). The first sentence indicates the water tank in the Water Storage Multistoried Building. The water channel from the tank to the fountains was hidden and triggered the emperor's curiosity. The sentences, "The underground vein meanders into the distance; full water can be traced back to a distant origin" show that the emperor was trying to understand the hidden water channel by comparing it to the watercourse in Chinese gardens. This can be seen in his describing the channel as a "vein" and endeavoring to trace the origin of the watercourse. By describing the hidden water source as the "concealed ultimate reason," the emperor established the connection between the water method and the principle of cosmos.

After passing through the gateway of the Cages for Raising Birds, the emperor would see five bamboo pavilions to the right. Here, the regular geometrical form of the water method mixed with traditional bamboo plants of Chinese gardens. In front of the bamboo pavilions, three pools included a round fountain pool flanked by two lotus pools shaped like lotus leaves and defined with low curbs. In the ninth copperplate (L. Yi), located at the top of the fountain's water column was the focal point of the line-method picture. Reinforced by the strong line-method effect of the bamboo pavilions as the backdrop, the top of this water method presented a feeling of mystical origin. The combination of water and bamboo was a typical backdrop in Chinese gardens. In his visit to the Jiangnan region in 1765, Qianlong named the garden of the Xu family in Yangzhou "Water Bamboo Residence." His poem on this garden says: "The color of water is clear and rests by the couch, / The sound of bamboo is cool and enters the window" (qtd. in Dou Li 382). Although the bamboo pavilions in the Western Multistoried Buildings garden were not bamboo groves, the combination of the bamboo pavilions, fountains, and lotus pools can be said to be yet another of the emperor's Water Bamboo Residences.

The most complicated vertically arranged water methods were located at the western side of the Hall of Peaceful Sea. At the top deck on the second floor, a fountain of two dolphins sprayed water that fell from one basin into another and thus formed the four cascade banisters of the twin stairways, which were typical of Italian gardens. Below the dolphins, more water gushed from a round hole and fell into a huge bowl-like shell. From the shell, the water welled over the edge, flowed down through an artificial hill, and ultimately reached the bottom pool. At this bottom pool was a total of twelve Chinese zodiac animal statues, with six on each side. This artificial hill most likely symbolized the legendary fairylands in the East Sea. The twelve Chinese zodiac animals were waterspouts, creating a so-called water clock (horloge d'eau) designed by Father Benoist (Adam 31). Every two hours, one animal would spout water into the fountain at the center of the pool, and at noon, all twelve animals sprayed together. This central fountain appeared as a Daoist pot, receiving and producing the primary liquid. Unfortunately, emperor Xianfeng disliked the water clock and put the brass statues into his grand treasure house, where they finally disappeared in the catastrophe of 1860. According to the tenth copperplate (L. Yi), construction details such as the symmetrical building façade, the fan-like plan of the water clock pool, the pair of curved stairways flanked by water cascades, and the waterfall on the central axis were all arranged into a cohesive line-method picture. The focal point of the picture was located at the hole, where water spurted out from the deck of the second floor. The focal point is the same as the topmost spot of the central fountain's water column. All the water outlets at this *jing* of water method acted as a water mouth, which symbolized and defined the border between mystery and play.

East of the Hall of Peaceful Sea, the Big Water Method was the climax of the water methods. At the center, a lion head spewed out water, which cascaded into a pool. In the pool, a fountain in the form of a stag sprayed water outwards toward all sides of the pool. In the site plan of the View of Distant Sea in the Model Lei collection, this stag appeared to be chased by twelve dogs, which simultaneously sprayed water towards the stag (Adam 34). Two twelve-level pyramid fountains flanked the central pool, with the base of each pyramid surrounded by a circle of small water jets, which created a very loud cascading sound. The pyramid fountains were similar to the "grand buffets" of water in Versailles (*La Vuë* plate 21). Between the pyramids stood two tall pine trees pruned into a nine-level topiary form, which framed the *jing*. The Big Water Method bordered the Hall of Wet Orchids in the Garden of Eternal Spring where the emperor could look across the division wall and view the fountains. Qianlong was fond of water methods, although he did not directly write about them. In his poem, "On the Hall of Wet Orchids" in 1795, he discussed indirectly the Big Water Method:

> The hall of reading is called Wet Orchids,
> Its plain style thanks simple and elegant colors.

Fragrant bookcases bear sunlight,
Ivy windows avoid thin coldness.
Affection of grasses repays goodwill,
Water methods show spectacular views.
Congratulations sent from the Western ambassador has just arrived,
I watched the water methods with him at the View of Distant Sea.
[Qianlong's note:] North of the Hall of Wet Orchids is the place of the Western water methods. When the Portuguese ambassador came to Beijing in 1753, I heard his country had spectacular views (*qiguan*) of water methods. Because China was a big country and the water method was simply one of ingenious makings, I thus ordered a Westerner in the capital, Shining Lang (Castiglione), to make this water method so that the ambassador could come to appreciate it. Two years ago when the English ambassador Mcartney came to Beijing, I also led him to the water methods and he deeply gasped in admiration. Last winter the provincial officials Lin Chang and Gui Zhu from the Guangdong Province reported that the Dutch ambassador came to China. When the ambassador heard that the coming year would be the sixtieth year of my reign, he asked to come to the capital for the celebration. Considering he came from far away with sincerity, I agreed to his request. He arrived in the twelfth moon of last year. I received him with a banquet in the first moon of the new year and showed him the water methods at this place (i.e., the View of Distant Sea) in order to demonstrate that his sincerity of coming here from afar was much appreciated by me. If he pays tributes, I might not regard them as precious things because China is so big and there is no wonder that China has not. ("Ti Zelantang" 223)

This is the only poem in which we can find Qianlong's comments on the views of the Western garden, although his comments were put in the note part instead of the poem itself. From these notes, we know that the emperor received the British, Portuguese, and Dutch ambassadors at the Big Water Method in front of the View of Distant Sea pavilion. The poem also notes that while standing at the Hall of Wet Orchids in the Garden of Eternal Spring, the emperor could look upon the *jing* of the Big Water Method of the Western garden across the wall between the two gardens. Qianlong described the *jing* of water methods as a spectacular view, which he was eager to show to his foreign guests in order to demonstrate that it was Chinese.

The Big Water Method stood just south of the View of Distant Sea pavilion. In the poem, "Chant at the View of Distant Sea," Jiaqing wrote, "Continuous lofty towers imitate the Western style, / Dig a pool and draw the water with detailed mechanical running. / Water meanders and pours into the movement of surging and stirring, / Three times of disappearing and three times of appearing, the vein is hidden" ("Yuanyingguan ge [1]" 12). According to the poem, there were several aspects of the fountain setting that impressed him: the lofty building in the Western style, the complex mechanism of the fountains, waterspouts, and the hidden watercourse. Noting that he described the covered water channel that led to the fountains as a "vein," we begin to understand how he was applying the concept of a watercourse in Chinese gardens to his understanding of the water method. In his poems of the View of Distant Sea pavilion, Jiaqing always integrated the view of the building with the view of the Big Water Method. In the poem of the "View of Distant Sea," he wrote, "The style of the multistoried building imitates the Western, / My father's reputation is widespread. / Distant seas all meet here, / Remote territories all send their national envoys" ("Yuanying Guan [2]"). The first sentence expressed his impression of the Western multistoried building. The poem revealed that for the emperor, the water of the Big Water Method symbolized the confluence of the distant seas. The View of Distant Sea pavilion was built on a high terrace and overlooked the fountains. Such an arrangement apparently made the emperor feel his mighty power. In another poem with the same title, he stated, "Operate the machine to transfer water and pour it into the stone pool, / Splashed jades and sprayed pearls can fill in as many as ten thousand *hu*. / I respectfully recognize my father's widespread reputation, / Scattered sand and western seas are all in the same wind" ("Yuanying Guan [1]"). The emperor developed his idea of harmony from the view that the myriad of water drops splashed and flowed into the same pool.

South of the Big Water Method there was a throne called Viewing the Water Method, which was for the primary purpose of appreciating the theatrical show of water play. Behind the throne was a curved stone screen, which was constituted of five relief panels of panoplies, arms, helmets, and breastplates. In the Chapelle du Château Royal de Versailles, there were some decorations of Trophées (De Mortain plate 11), which were similar to the trophy relief on this back screen. On each side of the throne, there was a porch called the Dog Head Gate where the emperor had a secret shortcut to the Big Water Method from the Garden of Eternal Spring. The title, Viewing the Water Method, shows that, like watching a play in a theater, this throne was specifically for viewing the fountains. Because the View of Distant Sea pavilion sat high upon a terrace, which was just behind the Big Water Method, the emperor's view from the Viewing the Water Method throne concentrated on the fountains and did not extend further towards the north. Contrasting with this limited and enclosed view, while sitting in the View of Distant Sea pavilion, the emperor extended his view far into the south towards the Garden of Eternal Spring.

The view of a water method in the garden was not an isolated image of the fountain itself; rather, it became an appreciable view because the fountain was integrated into a line-method picture. As the twenty copperplates demonstrated, the line method introduced the horizon of view at eye level with the single focal point to the Chinese traditional frontal view. It anchored the beholder's eyesight to the focal point, which acted as the counter-eye. With the frontal view of line method, the viewpoint echoed the focal point and they exchanged reciprocal roles. The throne was the focal point and the viewpoint, as well as the view and the place for active viewing. In the garden, the emperor watched the play of water from the throne; in the copperplate, the throne indicated his absent body and became the focal point. The title of the *jing*, Viewing the Water Method, implied the shift between view and viewing.

An imperial throne was always placed in the north and faced towards the south so that the emperor appeared to have a bright face. In stark contrast, the Viewing the Water Method throne faced towards the north, creating a situation where the imperial face was in the deep shadow of the back screen. This is probably why the View of Distant Sea pavilion was added to the opposite side in 1781, twenty years after all the other portions of the garden had been completed. It was built on a high terrace, overlooking the throne and returning the emperor's view towards the south. The ritual that the imperial throne was mandated to face the south corresponded to the fact that the capital of unified China was most often located in the north, so as to symbolically embrace the whole country. In Chinese historical archives, the Viewing the Water Method throne was a rare case of the imperial throne facing towards the north (He 471). Supposing that the throne was in the north and the Big Water Method was to its south, then the emperor's face would have bathed in sunshine; however, the sunshine would have impeded his view of the play of water. Hence, in order to have a perfect and bright view of the water method, he would most likely have sacrificed his brightly appearing face and sat in the shadows. When the views represented by two copperplates were opposite to each other, a short viewing distance was adopted in both of them, forming a sharp perspective effect. The sharper the convergence toward the focal point, the more widely open the view appeared and the more strongly it hinted at its counterpart. In the sixteenth copperplate (L. Yi), Frontal Face of Viewing the Water Method, the concave screen, the convex steps in front of the throne, the oblique lines of the clipped tree hedges, the radiating pavement patterns, and the strictly symmetrical composition of the picture all joined together to accentuate the centrality of the throne at the focal point. This effect strongly hinted at the viewpoint located at the Big Water Method, which in turn became the focal point of the fifteenth copperplate (L. Yi). The viewpoint and focal point relationship between the Big Water Method and the throne was clearly demonstrated in the two copperplates. The empty throne in the copperplate hinted at the involvement of the emperor's body in constituting the *jing* of water method.

In the garden, another form of water method, which was more hidden, was the water storage. There were two water-storage buildings that held tanks and provided water for the fountains. One was the Water Storage Multistoried Building on the western side of the northern courtyard of the Harmony, Wonder, and Delight pavilion, which provided water for the fountains of the first-phase area of the garden. The second water-storage building was at the Hall of Peaceful Sea and provided water for the second phase of the garden. The water of the Water Storage Multistoried Building came from a small canal running around the labyrinth, and the water of the Hall of Peaceful Sea probably came from the same water source, that is, a canal flowing on the outside along the northern garden wall. In the Water Storage Multistoried Building, the hydraulic machine occupied the ground floor and the cistern was on a neighboring terrace to the north. From the outside, the multistoried building looked like a two-story house, and it was difficult to notice that it was in fact a reservoir. Likewise, the Hall of Peaceful Sea looked like a palace building. In the copperplates, the buildings were composed into a line-method picture whose perspective effect was greatly enhanced by the short pruned topiary trees in front of the buildings.

The tank in the Hall of Peaceful Sea contained 180 cubic meters of water (Adam 31). According to the plane of Eastern Water Mill Building (the early name of the Hall of Peaceful Sea) in the Model Lei collection (Lei), the Hall of Peaceful Sea in fact contained three water tanks, with the central one being the largest and known as the Tin Sea. It was called the Tin Sea because the inside of the reservoir was covered with a layer of tin to prevent leakage and any large body of water that appeared in imperial gardens was called a sea. The reservoir was covered with glass and fish were raised in it (Adam 31). From above, the emperor appreciated the swimming fish through the glass cover. The activity of watching the "happiness of fish" evolved from the Daoist sage Zhuangzi's story. One day, while Zhuangzi and Huizi walked on a bridge over the Hao River, which was north of Fengyang County in Anhui Province, Zhuangzi said: "The white fish wander leisurely. Is it not the happiness of fish?" Huizi asked: "Since you are not a fish, how do you know its happiness?" Zhuangzi answered: "I know it because I am on the Hao River" (Fu and Lu 273). Based on this legendary story, appreciating the happiness of fish became a typical part of Chinese gardens.

Another fish pool served the same purpose in the Yuanming Yuan. The tenth scene of the Forty Scenes, Magnanimous and Big Hearted, was created based on Zhuangzi's story of the happiness of fish. In the poem on this scene, Qianlong wrote:

> Foreword: Dig a pool to create a happy kingdom of fish. My house is surrounded by the pool, where thousands of brilliant fish encounter and splash among water plants. They circulate and swim with leisure and joy. As an ancient poem says, people are like fish; the emperor knows of the happiness of fish and therefore takes care of the people:
>
> Dig a pool to watch the happiness of fish,
> I feel magnanimous and big hearted.
> Swim in the comfortable pool,
> Why will they long for rivers and lakes?
> I laugh at the silliness of Mr. Zhuangzi in the Qi Garden of Meng Kingdom,
> He debated with others on right and wrong.
> If you ask me how to answer the same question?
> I will say a fish knows its own happiness. ("Tantan" 25)

If the country was like a fish pool and the people were like fish, "knowing the happiness of fish" was a basic principle of his administration. Therefore, "watching the fish" in a fish pool became a symbolic activity in an imperial garden where the Peaceful Sea symbolized a peaceful country. Qianlong's poem provides a reference for understanding the deep meanings of the Tin Sea. What was unique about the Tin Sea was that the Hall of Peaceful Sea was the actual water tank and the emperor viewed the fish from the rooftop. Therefore, his path across the roof became a meaningful part of his journey in the garden.

The water in the Hall of Peaceful Sea was provided primarily for the fountains on the eastern and western sides of the building, which included the Big Water Method where water was transferred into and out of the tank through copper pipes. An imperial archive recorded that on the twelfth day of the third moon of the sixtieth year of the Qianlong reign (1795), "It has been checked that there are copper pipes and waterwheels for absorbing water for the water methods in the western and northern waterwheel rooms in the Hall of Peaceful Sea in the Western Multistoried Buildings garden. Because of the slowness of water absorbing, there is much waste of money. Not a long time ago, we followed His Majesty's decree to change the mechanism to carrying water through human labor. It is simpler and more convenient than before, and there is no more use of those copper pipes. . . . Following His Majesty's decree, we broke up the copper pipes in the three waterwheel rooms in the Hall of Peaceful Sea" ("Neiwufu" archive 939). When there was no water gushing from the fountain, the structure became a dead body. The slowness of the water flow through the copper pipes might have been caused by a blockage. The shift back to the operation of human labor demonstrated the backward thinking of the emperor, but water-method operation was formerly done by human laborers in the Yuanming Yuan.

In European sources of fountain illustrations, a fountain and central perspective were not always cohesively related. There were over five thousand European books in the Jesuit churches in Beijing, and many of them were about architecture and gardens (*Catalogue*; H. Zou, Appendix). The engravings in these books, such as the fountain engravings by Georg A. Böckler in Germany, were a primary reference for the Jesuit designers. In Böckler's engravings, a fountain could appear in many forms, such as the face of a sun, a flower, an umbrella, or an animal, thus creating a "new and curious" world. In the Italian Carlo Fontana's book, he actually used geometry to create the form of a fountain. In the engravings by Vredeman de Vries of the Netherlands, the top of a fountain was usually located at the focal point of a central perspective; such a composition echoed the water method composed in the line method in the Western Multistoried Buildings garden. In Giovanni B. Falda's fountain engravings, the top of the fountain was often higher than the focal point. In contrast, in the twenty copperplates of the Western Multistoried Buildings garden, the fountains were carefully inscribed into the composition of line method, where the "method" of water was fused into the "method" of lines and the top of the water spurt met the focal point. A Ming painting theory stated that when mountains and waters were understood by the heart, they appeared as a painting; the painting made by a master painter looked like real mountains and waters (S. Yang 241). In turn, it can be inferred that if a fountain in a line-method picture looked real, the water method would touch the spectator's heart.

While the water methods were carefully integrated into the line-method pictures, they also fit into the panoramic *jing* of the garden according to the emperor's mind. As soon as the first phase, which included the Harmony, Wonder, and Delight pavilion and the labyrinth, was finished, Qianlong immediately asked the court painter, Tingyan Zhang, to add "Western water methods" in a panoramic painting of the Garden of Eternal Spring ("Neiwufu" archive 441). Depicting the water methods in both the line method and traditional Chinese landscape painting demonstrated the emperor's curiosity about the varied representations of the water method. Including the water methods into a panoramic *jing* also demonstrated his intention of taking the Western portion as part of the Round Brightness. Line method was used for creating not only water methods but also the hill in the garden, called the Hill of Line Method, east of the Big Water Method. According to a story from an elderly man whose surname was Lu and who used to work in the Qing court, the hill was also called Terrace for Circulating a Horse, because Qianlong liked to walk his horse for entertainment and to appreciate winter scenes (Cheng 30). At the top of the hill, there was a hexagonal pavilion where the emperor would enjoy a distant view from the highest point in the garden.

In the general plan of the second construction phase in the Model Lei collection (Lei), the plane of the Hill of Line Method was clearly shown. The path from the bottom to the top of the hill was arranged in concentric circles, modeling a labyrinth. Though the path looked clear in the plan, it was obfuscating, because the hill was full of pine trees. Compared to a single spiral path or a straight stairway, the labyrinthine path provided the emperor with much more entertainment and an opportunity to appreciate the surrounding views. In the eighteenth copperplate, the hilltop pavilion appeared without any obstruction by the pine trees, which showed that the emperor wanted to have a clear panoramic view from the hilltop. The Hill of Line Method was artificially created. An artificial hill in Chinese gardens primarily indicated hill-like rock piles. On the making of an artificial hill, the *Yuan ye* states, "To pile up rocks, a designer must know how to occupy the sky. To heap up mud, he must know how to occupy the land" (Ji 77-78). The present ruin of the Hill of Line Method shows that the hill was certainly not made of rocks in the way of traditional Chinese rockery art, but rather was formulated based on the geometrical plan of line method, with one of its features being its elliptical spiral path. In the engravings of European gardens, we can find some cases of spiral hills that were similar to the Hill of Line Method.

A famous case of spiral hills in Italian gardens was the Montanola Parnassus at the Villa Medici, Rome (Falda and Venturini), and comparisons between this hill and Hill of Line Method have been made by some scholars (see, e.g., Schulz 68; Droguet 22). The path of the Hill of Line Method was elliptical in plan and looked spiral in elevation. According to research, the path of the mountain at the Villa Medici was not spiral but rather consisted of three parallel circles connected by a straight-up stairway. This has been demonstrated in Falda's engraving (c. 1676) and a later plan drawing of 1817. The illusion of a spiral form of the Medici Mountain might be caused by some oblique shortcuts connecting the three circles, which can be seen in some plan drawings of the nineteenth century (Galletti). One example of the spiral mountain is the Monte Parnaso in the Garden of Pratolino, but its shape is less geometric (Zangheri figs. 284-87). The eighteenth copperplate shows that the plants on the Hill of Line Method were universally pine trees of almost the same height, which matched up with the clipped short pine trees arranged in a rigid geometrical formation in the front courtyard (see figure 2). The straight pine trunks were in sharp contrast to the organic form of the plants beyond the garden walls. Enhancing the effect of line method, this type of pine tree had straight trunks and was easily clipped into geometrical forms. These three-level clipped pine trees, similar to the *bosco* of some *giardino segreto* (secret gardens) in Italian gardens, stand like soldiers in a

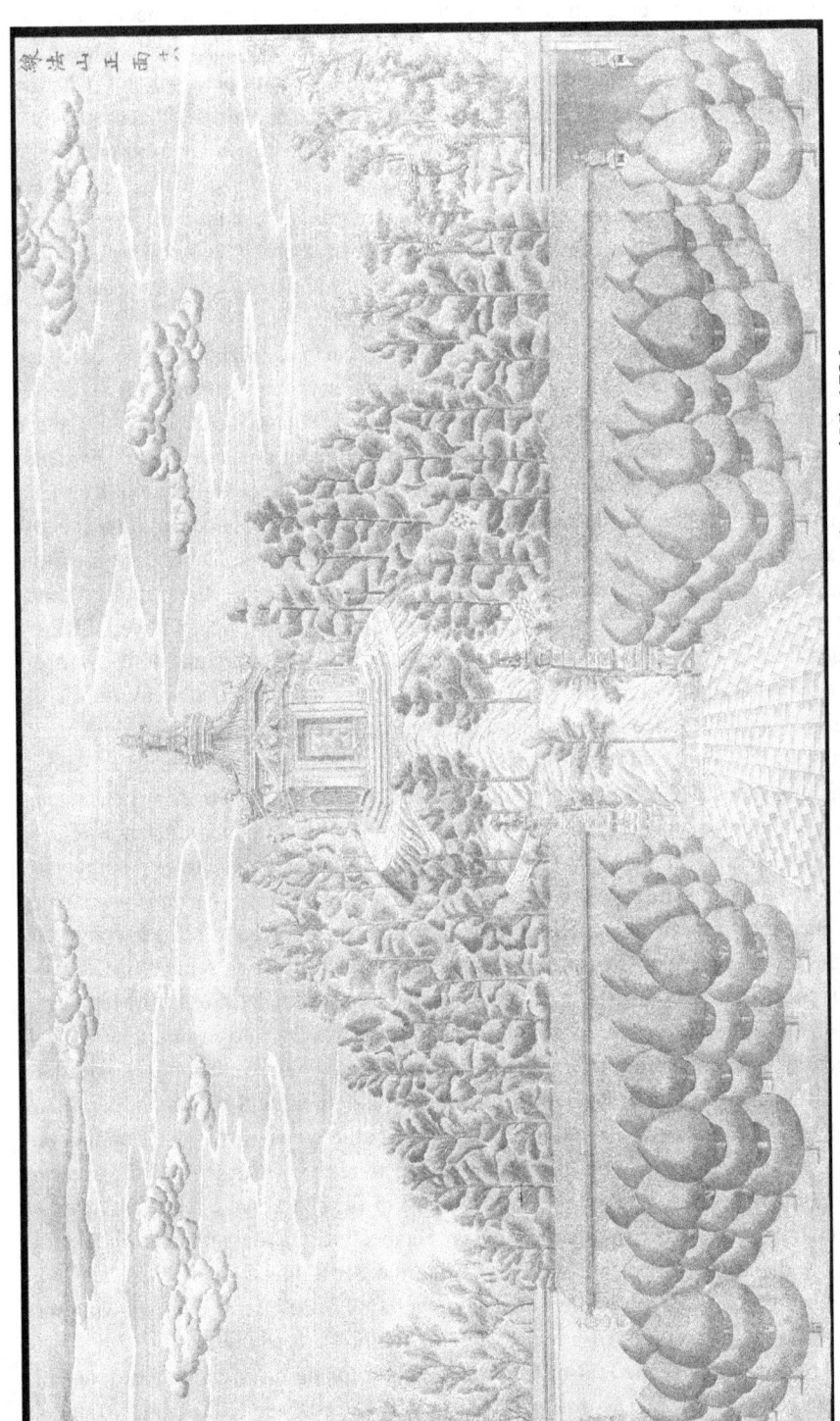

Figure 2. Copperplate of the Hill of Line Method, drawn by Lantai Yi, 1786 Yuan Ming Yuan, 1783-1786. Research Library, The Getty Research Institute, Los Angeles, California.

regular array. As the copperplate shows, the universally geometrical shapes of trees and their regular formation enhanced the convergence of central perspective towards the hill in the background. Compared to the spiral hills in European gardens, what is special at the Hill of Line Method is that the hill did not stand by itself but rather was carefully composed into the line method of the copperplate to present a "frontal face" (*zhengmian*). In all these "frontal faces," clipped pine trees constituted a significant part. In the Renaissance treatise, *Hypnerotomachia Poliphili*, plants were considered merely as a material to be used in an architectural structure, just as marble or stone would be used. In order to produce a perfect harmony and unity of vision, each plant was reduced to a prescribed size and shape (Dami 13).

The Jesuit botanist Pierre d'Incarville (Chinese name, Zhizhong Tang) served in the court as a gardener and took part in the construction of the Western garden until he died in Beijing in 1757. According to a Jesuit's letter, D'Incarville stayed in the court for three years and introduced European flowers and plant seeds to Chinese gardens (Schulz 25). In the Yuanming Yuan, some named scenes were well known for their symbolic plants, such as pine trees at the first scene, Uprightness and Brightness; peonies at the fourth scene, Carve the Moon and Open the Clouds; bamboos at the fifth scene, Natural Scenery; phoenix trees at the sixth scene, Study Room under Green Phoenix; apricot trees at the ninth scene, Wine Shop in an Apricot Flower Village; peach trees at the fourteenth scene, Spring Beauty at Wuling; orchids at the twenty-first scene, Orchid Fragrance over the Water; and lotus at both the twenty-third, Xi Lian's Wonderful Place for Study, and thirty-ninth scene, Waving Lotus in a Winery Court. In the poem on the seventeenth scene, Great Kindness and Eternal Blessing, Qianlong stated, "The surrounding area is fully covered with pine trees, which appear flourishing green and point straight towards the sky. While looking at them, awe and affection emerge [in my bosom]" ("Hongci" 39). Because the seventeenth scene was the highest place in the Yuanming Yuan, Qianlong built a Buddhist temple and stored his ancestors' portraits there. His awe and affection for the pine trees were conveyed to the older generations. A similar feeling of awe and affection related to the geometrically arranged pine trees can be sensed at the *jing* of the Hill of Line Method.

Once the hill was put into line method, it had to be viewed through the perspective of line method. In the eighteenth copperplate, there were some perspective distortions; for example, the surfaces of the spiraling path and hilltop and the floor of the pavilion on the hill should not be seen from the viewpoint of one standing on the ground. The perspective distortions demonstrate that when the painter tried to locate the hill in line method, he also intended or desired to have a bird's-eye view of the hill, which was a traditional Chinese perspective. On making an artificial hill, the *Yuan ye* states, "Take the real as artificial in order to make the artificial real" (Ji 206). In terms of the artificiality of line method, it can be inferred that viewing the hill through line method was to make the line-method image a real hill.

Climbing over the Hill of Line Method and facing towards the east, one encountered another gateway, the so-called Eastern Gate of the Hill of Line Method, through which a view of distant mountains and waters was observed. Different from the western gate of the hill, which was to enhance the centrality effect of line method, the eastern gate acted as a doorframe for drawing the mind into a distant scene, which looked like a typical "head-on *jing*" (*duijing*) in Chinese gardens. Viewing a head-on *jing* through a circular window had been described as "rambling within a mirror" (*jingyou*) in a Ming garden theory, but at that time the *jing* remained flat with a moveable point of view (Ji 205). In the Qing imperial gardens, the mirror-like view appeared deeper, clearer, and more focused. The influence of the Western vista on a straight path on Chinese gardens could be sensed from the popularization of the head-on *jing* in the imperial garden representations of the Qing dynasty. A painting of Prince Yinzhen ("Dan son"), later Yongzheng, in the Yuanming Yuan showed that the bounded brightness in a fan painting from the Southern Song dynasty had developed into a transparent and deep scene framed by a circular window. When the *jing* became a bounded view that could be operated freely through an artificial approach as in Ming and Qing gardens, the condition had become more suitable than ever for the rooting of Jesuit perspective of art, the line method, which intended to bring visual convergence and shadows to the diffused perfect brightness.

While standing in front of the eastern gate of the hill, the emperor saw the distant water and mountains. The gateway was tightly flanked by rocks and groves, with the only way to look into the distance being through the central arch of the gateway. The two side arches could not be seen through, because they were actually the windows of hexagonal rooms, as shown in the Site Plan of the Line Method Walls in the Model Lei collection. It is clear that the lake was intended to be viewed through the central arch. Due to the framing of the doorway, a spectator would not know how wide the lake was until the lake completely appeared before his eyes. The framing made the *jing* of line method appear remote and expansive. In the site plan, Model Lei marked the size of the lake as 45 *zhang* (144 meters) in length and 15 *zhang* (48 meters) in width, creating a proportion of 1:3. This meant that the lake was designed according to a mathematical proportion, which was not a method utilized in Chinese gardens. The water surface viewed through the gateway was a rectangular lake, called Square River. East of the lake, there was a stage set constituted of line-method murals on walls, which followed Pozzo's stage design. In the Model Lei plan, a small body of water came from the external canal and branched into two ditches: one moved west and passed before the eastern gateway of the hill; another moved east along the northern bank of the Square River and passed in front of the Paintings of Line Method. Both ditches acted as a symbolic boundary for marking specific territories and increased the depth of the view through the gateway towards the Paintings of Line Method. As some research has proposed, the mud excavated from making the Square River was used to create the Hill of Line Method. In addition, the existence of the Square River was mainly intended to enhance the perspective illusion of the Paintings of Line Method (Schulz 70). This is confirmed by the detail that in the title of the Lei's site plan, only the name, Walls of Line Method was mentioned. The complementary relationship between the "square" river and the "round" hill also demonstrated the Daoist cosmological idea of "heaven is round and earth is square" (Major 64)

A similar example of viewing into the distance across water in the Yuanming Yuan was the thirty-ninth scene, Waving Lotus at a Winery Court, where a longitudinal lake, rather than a rectangular form, faced the winery court. At the southern end of the lake, there was a dock from which the emperor took a boat and rowed to the northern bank. Compared with the round Back Lake to the west and the round Fortunate Sea to the east, this longitudinal lake appeared oriented to the north-south axis. As the emperor stood in the court located on the northern bank and looked across the water, which was full of lotus flowers, towards the distant southern bank, the view imitated a famous scene of the West Lake in Hangzhou. Qianlong's poem of this scene says: "With remote fragrance and fresh wind, who can understand this painting of the *jing*? / Under the standing lotus flowers twin birds are sleeping. / Stop the boat by the bank to appreciate the rich and true landscape, / Who will say only the West Lake of Hangzhou can have such a beauty?" ("Quyuan" 83). His view moved around without specifically following the north-south axis. This was quite different from the clearly oriented view at the Square River, yet in both cases, the activity of paddling and appreciating the landscape as a "painting" was the same. In comparison, the Square River was similar to the canal in the garden of Fontainebleau where there was a rectangular pool for the king's paddling (*La Vuë* plate 30). It is interesting to note that in a comparison between the thirty-ninth scene and the Square River, both lakes acted as the last stop before reaching the final destination of a poetic journey, namely the fortieth scene, Deep and Remote Dwelling, in the Yuanming Yuan and the open-air theater in the Western garden. The Paintings of Line Method were an exterior stage set, similar to the open-air theaters in the Villa Gori and Villa Geggiano, Siena (Shepherd). In Italian gardens of the seventeenth century, there was a prevalence of some "picturesque" elements. The conception as a whole was of a panoramic and perspective character (Dami 25). In the Baroque period, gardens underwent an important transformation: the *quadratura* vanished from sight and infinity became part of the garden itself. The position of the vanishing point was shifted either to the horizon or somewhere in the sky. The Baroque garden marked the triumph of the long perspective (Baridon 9, 11). Unlike those open-air theaters in Italian gardens, the theater at the eastern end of the Square River could only be appreciated by standing on the western bank of the lake or on a boat moving straight towards the eastern bank. The line method of stage-set perspective had been explicated in Xiyao Nian's *Shixue*, which, imitating Dubreuil's illusionary perspective, emphasized the position of "frontal viewing" (*zhengshi*). In Pozzo's stage design, the frontal view was one of the possible views for the audience in an amphitheater; but for the emperor, the frontal view of the Paintings of Line Method was the only view appearing to him. In the site plan of the Walls of Line Method in the Model Lei collection, unlike the oblique arrangement in Pozzo's stage design, each painted wall, depicted in its "frontal face," was arranged orthogonally with the west-to-east axis of the lake so that the general frontal face in depth, the *jing*, was literally constituted of multiple painted frontal faces.

Theaters were important buildings in Chinese imperial gardens, with more than ten theaters in the Yuanming Yuan complex. The most famous theater was the

Figure 3. Copperplate of the open-air theater, drawn by Lantai Yi, 1786
Yuan Ming Yuan, 1783-1786. Research Library, The Getty Research Institute, Los Angeles, California.

Yard of Enjoying Together at the thirty-eighth scene, Sit on a Rock and Take a Wine Cup from the Winding Stream. In the theater, the audience sat on the north and watched the stage to the south. At the open-air theater in the Western garden, the walls were for hanging paintings. Besides walls with paintings, there were an additional five rooms on each side of the stage, which were used for storing paintings. If one stood on the western bank of the Square River and looked through the eastern gateway of the hill towards the paintings across the lake, the *jing* appeared distant and real. The line-method theater was watched quietly and solitarily by the emperor himself. As the nineteenth and twentieth copperplates demonstrated, in the *jing* of line method, the point of view no longer was random and the view was fixed into an illusion of depth (see figure 3). Such a static frontal view recalls Zhuangzi's idea of "condensation of the mind" (*ningshen*), by which he meant "gaze fixedly and stop [on something]" (F. Wang 7). In the focused gaze, the smallest thing coincides with the cosmos. As shown in the twentieth copperplate, the illusionary perspective of the stage set was best perceived across the lake. This final *jing* presented the distant mountains at the infinity. Like the fortieth scene, Deep and Remote Dwelling, in the Yuanming Yuan, this illusionary *jing* of line method presented a remote dwelling for the emperor's mind. After experiencing all the real mountains and waters in the other parts of the garden, the emperor finally reached the point of perceiving the illusionary mountains and waters, which led to another imaginative world.

The theater was located at the eastern end of the Western garden, which was also the most northeastern spot of the Yuanming Yuan complex. According to the ancient cosmological graph of eight trigrams, the northeast direction was called *gen*. Beijing as the capital was located in the northeast of China. According to an explanation of the Qing dynasty, "The ancient cosmological book *Yijing* [*Book of Changes*] says: The *gen* is the cosmological mark of the northeast direction where all things end and begin. . . . The capital Beijing is located on the *gen* spot, which is a place of both the beginning and end of change . . . and can receive the return of all things. It can hold the esteem of the north and face to the brightness from the south" (M. Yu 1: 82). Following the same cosmological consideration, the location of the theater in the Western garden can be understood as a place where the journey for physical brightness ended but the journey for metaphysical brightness began. The search for the truth of the world now returned to this most remote spot of the garden. In terms of the metaphysical brightness, the theater at the eastern end of the Western garden suggested the altar of a Catholic church. It was at this *gen* spot, the most northeastern spot of the Yuanming Yuan complex that the Chinese cosmological idea of the imperial north and the Christian understanding of the eastern end fused into a unity, where the Chinese cosmological brightness interwove with the Christian metaphysical brightness.

Conclusion

The *jing* is an aesthetic concept of Chinese garden and landscape construction. The linear perspective was created in the European Renaissance and did not exist in Chinese painting until it was introduced by Jesuits working in Beijing in the seventeenth and eighteenth centuries. The encounter of *jing* and the Western linear perspective took place in the Western garden of the Yuanming Yuan. Although the ruins of Yuanming are frequently appropriated for political intentions, ideologies cannot bring to light the beauty of cultural encounters. Chinese intellectuals tend to think the Yuanming Yuan is the most forceful proof of imperialist aggressions and the reflection on this part of history can enhance patriotic spirit. For some Western Sinologists, attention is only paid to how the Chinese state makes use of the ruins as the vehicle for national expression and cultural unity. My intention is to suggest that prior to the imposition of political ideologies upon the garden ruins, it is essential to retrieve the sense of the garden itself. To seek the truthful meaning of *jing*, it is necessary to suspend monocentric cultural attitudes and conduct careful studies of Chinese literature prior to the modern age. The term *jing* can be roughly translated as "scene" in English, but the vision of *jing* as the unity of mind and scene has been transformed throughout history. *Jing* exists primarily as a view that appears bright, bounded, emotionally connected, and poetical to the mind. The brightness of *jing* and its cosmic connection had been thought and developed during the period of the Southern-Northern Dynasties. A significant move took place during the period of the Five Dynasties when the poetical dimension of *jing* was recognized, and this opened up the *jing* as an expression of the idea of the garden. The resonance between the depth of a garden *jing* and that of a painted *jing* enabled the perspective view of Western garden scenes to be rooted in the Chinese context as an exotic *jing*.

The depth of *jing* in the garden as perceived by the emperor and those working with him as the primary "builders"—both in theory and poetic conceptualization and in practice—was framed by the line-method drawings. The illusionary depth in visual representation resonated with the desire for a distant view within the garden. From the very beginning, the *jing* of the garden and the *jing* in perspective drawings had been fused. The deep and concentrated *jing* of line method opened the emperor's emotional world and enhanced his feeling of remoteness. Seeking the depth of *jing* is a typical objective in the construction of Chinese gardens, but the brightness of *jing* is seldom discussed in Chinese theories of landscape, garden, or painting, areas related closely, as I have explained. In the Yuanming Yuan, the move into visual depth was parallel with the enlightenment of the mind. The path for remoteness was the very route of the diffusion of brightness in both the view and mind. Thus, the pursuit of *jing* and the search for Round Brightness (Yuanming) became one and the same in the garden, that is, Round Brightness was *jing* itself. The combination of brightness and depth held one meaning for the emperor and another for the Jesuits. While the emperor's eyes were drawn into the concentrated depth of *jing* of line method, the Jesuits concentrated on the brightness of *jing* that resonated with the metaphysical light in their minds. The *jing* of line method demonstrates how people from different cultures and religions could collectively construct a common ground, where cultural differences merged without losing their original strength.

In contrast to the instrumental linear perspective in eighteenth-century Europe, the *jing* of line method did not employ perspective for the purpose of representation only. The mutual changeability between the focal point of the copperplates and the viewpoint within the garden shows that the linear perspective was used as a vivid expression of where the mind dwells. Such a representation centered on the mind and emotion made it possible for the emperor to identify himself with the imperial "frontal face" perspective in portrait painting and enabled the Jesuits to recognize the religious light within the cosmological light of Round Brightness. The Chinese and European collaboration with the result of several gardens—a "fusion," as it were—of significant artistic, technical, poetic, philosophical, and other components is relevant to the understanding of modern technology and its shortcomings. For example, a European photographer's pictures of the ruins of the Beijing garden of the Western Multistoried Buildings in the 1870s were not able to capture the same viewpoints as the twenty copperplates of earlier times. The free shifting of such a modern mechanical eye dissolved the frontal perspective with which the imperial face once identified, as well as the perspective depth inscribed in cosmology and time. Rather than a mere re-presentation in the modern sense, the line-method copperplates of the garden illustrates that architectural representation can be a crucial device in revealing truth that is in the world but invisible to the corporal eye. It is in respect of "infinitely approaching truth" (*bizhen*) through representation that the West and the East share a historical common ground for the shining forth of beauty.

If judged from the history of Chinese landscape and garden representation, the *jing* of line method was born at a time when the understanding of *jing* emphasized the framing of views in a garden. The same historical perspective also reveals the changes that line method brought to the concept of traditional *jing*. The illusionary depth of the perspective garden affected Chinese attitudes towards nature. The Chinese term of "nature," *ziran*, literally means "self, as such," that is, the self that is in such-and-such a condition means nature, a concept that is similar to the later notion of "In-Sein" by Heidegger. The perspective garden, being such a condition, mirrored the self and brought it to the center of *jing*. Thus, only in the self-reflected condition of the perspective garden was the emperor able to delve into the cosmos and maintain simultaneously his glorious face. In the aesthetics of Chinese landscape, the self is supposed to dissolve into a situational context: it gives way to an appearance of blending in with the landscape. The *jing* of the perspective garden woke the "self" of the body and mind up and made it realize "such" a condition of looking. The self-consciousness invoked by perspective played a role in the destruction of the medieval cosmos and the shaping of modernity in the West. This consciousness of "being-in as such," or being an individual, formed a new understanding of nature in the Chinese mind and that forged gradually the way towards a modern China.

The vision of *jing* demonstrates the Chinese philia of mountains and waters and defines the sensory horizon of Chinese religion and philosophy. Jacques Derrida proposed that there existed a sensory and material primitive meaning, the so-called "fatal materialism," hidden but erased in Western metaphysics. In dialectic materialism, the physical merely represents and is secondary to the metaphysical. Derrida's new materialism opens up "a discourse of figuration," which resists any simple definition of figures through language. The discourse of figuration must not metaphorize the figure in an economic effect to cater to arbitrary ideologies but rather to open the wider space of a discourse on figure. In this sense, the meaning of Round Brightness, Yuanming, should not be simplified under the rhetoric rubric such as the "perfect brightness" or the "lost garden" for political manipulations; rather, the interpretation of its meanings should help reveal the sensory horizon of Chinese culture through digging deeper into semantic depth. Sensory horizon was embodied in the Western Multistoried Buildings garden through the poetical *jing*, copperplates of linear perspective, fountains, and is maintained by the ruins of Yuanming. The ruins recall the distant past and a lost memory of what is no longer here. They remind consistently of the fire that destroyed the garden, as well as the brightness that enclosed the mind. In the ruins, there is something visible but scarcely readable. This mystical other materiality is related to the lost Round Brightness, whose meaning, according to Yongzheng, is extremely difficult to perceive. The Yuanming Yuan should be understood as a poetical site, whose "light without shadow" is illustrated by the paintings and copperplates of the *jing*.

The revealing of the sensory horizon in traditional China not only acts as a criticism to Western metaphysics in modern China but also defines paradoxically the historicity of materialism. In their initial encounter with Chinese culture in the seventeenth century, the Jesuits, from the Western perspective, had already considered the ancient Chinese as "materialists devoid of any spiritual thoughts." In this sense, the acceptance of dialectic materialism in modern China holds a certain historic background and should not be simplified as the importation of Western ideologies, just as line method was not a simple transplantation of linear perspective. Matteo Ricci, one of the Jesuit pioneers in China, attempted to excoriate Daoism while cultivating Confucianism for a metaphysical common ground with Christianity. This effort of seeking a common ground of truth was further expanded upon by later Jesuits through building a poetical ground, a garden, which, based on the vision of *jing*, established the connection between Christianity and Daoism.

When the Renaissance Catholic philosopher Nicholas of Cusa expounded upon the relationship between the infinity of God and the finiteness of human beings, he metaphorized it as an eternal process where the obliqueness of humanity approached responsibly the "true roundness" of divinity. He also explicated that the divine "circle" could only exist in the matter that could "shape" the circle as "the whole shines forth in all its parts." In their theoretical pondering, both Ricci and Leibniz attempted to identify the Christian image of "round brightness" with neo-Confucianist concept of reason (*li*), which they thought was closest to the transcendentality of Western metaphysics. They found the "circle" of Chinese "reason" was similar to the Christian image of circle and identified the crucial role of geometry in the religious and cultural comparability. The Jesuits in China pushed the geometrical approach into the field of perspective representation, which successfully drew the "concentration" of the Chinese mind. But the Jesuits did not find an effectual way to identify the Christian "brightness" within the Chinese context until they encountered the vision of Round Brightness in the Yuanming Yuan. In the garden, the emperor gave a free rein to his feelings and "roamed at leisure" among the *jing*. His "leisurely emotion" (*xianqing*) drifted as the diffusion of ethical brightness in the unified world. It is on such a poetical ground that the Jesuits created the perspective *jing* of "brightness without shadow," which enabled the shining forth of truth in cultural and religious encounters.

The integration of *jing* and *qing* (emotion) in Chinese gardens demonstrates that the sensory horizon in Chinese traditional culture is essentially poetical and can only be embodied through an evironment built on principles of ethics. According to Yongzheng's garden record, the meaning of Round Brightness was "deep and distant" and his approach of interpreting this concept was by referring to ancient texts, meanwhile identifying the "virtue of Round Brightness" through his personal practice. The virtuous mind cultivated in the beautiful and ethical *jing* resonates with Leibniz's "angels incarnate," which embody the "souls of virtuous people" (*Discourse* 127, 145). According to Yongzheng, the Round indicates "concentration of the mind;" and the Brightness, "extensively brightening." "Concentrating" moves the mind into depth, and "extending" brings about the sense of distance. The virtue of Round Brightness reflects the Daoist concept of "deep and distant virtue" (*xuande*) in chapter 65 of *Laozi* (S. Zhou 108). The practice of this primary virtue can lead to the ultimate harmony of full brightness by "acting opposite of the regular way," like the detour in the labyrinths of the Yuanming Yuan. Concentrating while extending seems paradoxical, but it is through such a paradoxical movement that Jesuit perspective of art and the emperor's discursive mind were harmonized into the *jing* full of wonders and delight.

The Yuanming Yuan was the emperor's residence, but its significance went far beyond the objectivity of an imperial garden. In the garden, the emperor's mind reached the Daoist ideal of happy kingdom where everyone could enjoy happiness and freedom, just like the fish in water. The garden enclosed and diffused brightness along the oblique lines of the meandering paths and linear perspective. The bounded brightness shines out from within and transcends any individual's subjectivity. It is therefore impossible to categorize Round Brightness as physical or metaphysical. The Yuanming Yuan epitomized the historical end of Chinese imperial gardens. Its destruction by foreign powers preceded the eventual collapse of the imperial system in China. The ashes of the burned wooden buildings quickly disappeared while the shambles of masonry from the Western Multistoried Buildings became the only ruins the public could view. Wars took place in rapid succession between the time of the destruction of the garden and the founding of New China. The Cultural Revolution pushed the ruins further out of the public view. When the tale of Yuanming disseminates once again throughout the nation, only the ruins of the Western buildings represent the lost Round Brightness, yet the general public does not understand the Jesuits' contribution to the garden.

The obscurity of the Yuanming Yuan mirrored the age of embracing Western metaphysics in modern China. Chinese intellectuals sought the approach that could bring the nation back to a powerful image, with a central theme of Westernized "democracy and science." At the beginning of the twentieth century, two Western ideologies, Marxism and John Dewey's pragmatism, competed intensely on the university campuses near the ruins of Yuanming. The touching prose work on the ruins quoted in chapter 1 was written by a descendant of Youlan Feng, one of Dewey's students, whose philosophical practice demonstrated the influences of both Deweyism and Marxism.

Western dialectic materialism dominated Chinese thoughts in the late twentieth century. The concept of truth based on realism quickly fused with the technological view of the world, which held that advanced science and technology, regardless of cultural differences, could make the world better. The technological outlook is accompanied with the progressive attitude of history, which values less the tradition in comparison with the newness produced by modernization. However, Walter Benjamin observed the danger that the mass movements based on mechanical reproduction liquidated the traditional value of the cultural heritage that cherished the "unique existence of the work of art" (220-21). The disappearance of poetical habitat in the forest of monotonous buildings becomes a prevalent phenomenon in Chinese contemporary urbanization.

In the late 1980s, when Western-like high-rise buildings began to emerge in Chinese cities, the Chinese tended to call the buildings a *jing* to express their curiosity and passion towards them. After decades of speedy construction, the exotic view has gradually dominated Chinese urban landscapes to become the predominant but dull view to which the concept of *jing* is no longer applied. Although the central ideology in China attempts to identify the visibility of Western buildings as the desired image of Chinese modernization, the critical voice has been heard that the regional cultural tradition is being eradicated by vulgar architectural internationalism. The loss of *jing* in Chinese contemporary urbanism indicates the withdrawal of public passion from the unethical built environment. Instead, a great number of people who live in an urban environment are shifting their attention to natural landscapes, as their ancestors did, to retrieve the "view" of poetical *jing*.

The silent stone fragments of the Western multistoried buildings are scattered around on the grass and evoke sadness in the visitor's mind. This lost garden exists as a "garden of the mind" which draws upon memories forever. The stone remnants in the wilderness comprise another type of *jing*, which cannot frame the vision of Round Brightness that implied the full moon and the perfection of virtues. The brightness encircled by the traditional *jing* is no longer evident in modern-day Beijing. The streets are now lined with the brilliance of curtained walls of high-rise buildings, yet this dazzling city skyline cannot "encircle the cosmos and enhance the virtues" as the *jing* of Yuanming once did. The loss of *jing* in Chinese urban landscapes is in fact the loss of poetical emotion. In the clusters of high-rise buildings, each building competes for visibility through height and novelty, but the vision of *jing*, that poetical visibility from which our emotion cannot be detached, that "true vision" in Merleau-Ponty's sense (*Visible* 146), is not there.

When the Western garden in the Yuanming Yuan was completed, a scholar in Suzhou gazed at the moonlight in his garden and chanted: "When the moon burst forth again in silver radiance, / Happiness once more filled our hearts" (F. Shen 17). The joy of perfect brightness gradually vanished after the god of the garden of Yuanming asked for time away from the emperor during a dream. According to Chinese thoughts, the god of the garden would rise to heaven after the death of the garden. This angel incarnate in Leibniz's sense might look down from heaven and wait for the opportunity to descend to earth. Has China realized the disappearance of the angel in its modernity, and is it ready for his return? Seeking "the returning angel," an architect wrote: "Angel come near, / So I can look into your heavenly eyes. / They are dark receding conical shapes, / Disappearing into your vanishing perspectives, / To a point of silver" (Hejduk 24). This modern poem is reminiscent of the Jesuits' encounter with the Chinese angel incarnate through the *jing* of line method while implying that poetical dwelling is the historical common ground for cultural and religious encounters.

Works Cited

Adam, Maurice. *Yuen Ming Yuen. L'Oeuvre architecturale des Anciens Jésuites au XVIIIe siècle*. Beijing: Imprimerie des Lazaristes, 1936.
Alberti, Leone B. *On Painting*. Trans. John R. Spencer. New Haven: Yale UP, 1956.
Alberti, Leone B. *Ten Books on Architecture*. Trans. James Leoni. Ed. Joseph Rykwert. London: Alec Tiranti, 1955.
Attiret, Jean Denis. "A Letter from a French Missionary in China, Peking, Nov. 1, 1743." Trans. Joseph Spence. *The English Landscape Garden*. Ed. John Dixon Hunt. New York: Garland, 1982.
Attiret, Jean Denis. "Lettre du frère Attiret à M. Papillon d'Assaut, Pekin, 1 Nov. 1743." *Lettres édifiantes et curieuses, écrites des missions étrangères*. Nouvelle édition, tome 12. Lyon, 1819.
Attiret, Jean Denis. "A Particular Account of the Emperor of China's Gardens near Pekin." Trans. Joseph Spence. *Fugitive Pieces on Various Authors*. Vol. 1. 1765.
Bacon, Roger. *The Opus Majus of Roger Bacon*. Trans. Robert Belle Burke. Philadelphia: U of Pennsylvania P, 1928.
Bai, Juyi (白居易). "Du Xie Lingyun shi (读谢灵运诗)." *Bai Juyi shixuan* (白居易诗选). Ed. Kechang Gong (龚克昌) and Chongguang Peng (彭重光). Ji'nan: Shandong daxue chubanshe, 1999.
Bai, Juyi (白居易). "Hua ji (画记)." *Zhongguo gudai hualun leibian* (中国古代画论类编). 1957. Vol. 1. Ed. Jianhua Yu (俞剑华). Beijing: Renmin meishu chubanshe, 2000. 25.
Ban, Jieyu (班婕妤). "Yong shan (咏扇)." *Wen xuan* (文选). Ed. Tong Xiao (萧统). Shanghai: Shanghai guji chubanshe, 1998.
Baridon, Michel. "The Scientific Imagination and the Baroque Garden." *Studies in the History of Garden and Designed Landscapes* 18.1 (1998): 5-19.
Barnhart, Richard. *Peach Blossom Spring: Gardens and Flowers in Chinese Paintings*. New York: The Metropolitan Museum of Art, 1983.
Beijing daxue lishixi (北京大学历史系), ed. *Beijing shi* (北京史). Beijing: Beijing chubanshe, 1999.
Beijing difangzhi bianzuan weiyuanhui (北京地方志编纂委员会), ed. *Beijing zhi: shizheng juan: yuanlin lühua zhi* (北京志：市政卷：园林绿化志). Beijing: Beijing chubanshe, 2000.
Benjamin, Walter. "The Work of Art in the Age of Mechanical Reproduction." Trans. Harry Zohn. *Illuminations: Essays and Reflections*. Ed. Hannah Arendt. New York: Schocken Books, 1968. 217-51.

Benoist, Michel. "Lettre, du père Benoist, à M. Papillon d'Auteroche, Pekin, 16 November, 1767." *Lettres édifiantes et curieuses, écrites des missions étrangères.* Tome 13: mémoires de la Chine. Nouvelle édition. Lyon, 1819.

Beurdeley, Michel, and Cécile Beurdeley. *Giuseppe Castiglione: A Jesuit Painter at the Court of the Chinese Emperors.* Trans. Michael Bullock. Rutland: C. E. Tuttle, 1971.

Bishu shanzhuang qishi'er jing bianweihui (避暑山庄七十二景编委会), ed. *Bishu Shanzhuang Qishi'er Jing* (避暑山庄七十二景). Beijing: Dizhi chubanshe, 1993.

Bo, Ti (钵提). "Ji Yuanmingyuan (记圆明园)." *Huiyizhai bi cheng : Wai shizhong* (悔逸斋笔乘：外十种). Edition Qingdai yeshi congshu (清代野史丛书). Beijing: Beijing guji chubanshe, 1999.

Böckler, Georg Andreas. *Architectura curiosa nova.* 1664.

Bushell, Stephen W. *Chinese Art.* Vol. 2. London: Wyman, 1906.

Cahill, James. *The Compelling Image: Nature and Style in Seventeenth-Century Painting.* Cambridge: Harvard UP, 1982.

Cao, Xueqin (曹雪芹), and E Gao (高鹗). *Honglou meng* (红楼梦). Changsha: Yuelu shushe, 2002.

Casey, Edward S. *The Fate of Place: A Philosophical History.* Berkeley: U of California P, 1997.

Castiglione, Giuseppe. *L'empereur Yongzheng et le jeune prince Hongli contemplent une branche de prunus devant un.* Painting. *Yuanming yuan: Le jardin de la clarté parfaite.* By Chebing Chiu. Paris: Les Editions de L'Imperimeur, 2000.

Castiglione, Giuseppe. "A Letter Dated Peking, 14 November 1729." *Giuseppe Castiglione: A Jesuit Painter at the Court of the Chinese Emperors.* By Michel Beurdeley and Cécile Beurdeley. Trans. Michael Bullock. Rutland: C.E. Tuttle, 1971.

Castiglione, Giuseppe, Jean-Denis Attiret, Ignaz Sichelbarth, and Joannes Damascenus. *Suite des seize estampes représentant les conquêtes de l'Empereur de la Chine.* 16 copperplates. 1765. Los Angeles: The Getty Research Center.

Catalogue de la Bibliothèque du Pé-tang. Beijing: Imprimerie des Lazaristes, 1949.

Chambers, William. *A Dissertation on Oriental Gardening.* London, 1772.

Chen, Arthur. "Locating the Distance Point: An Epiphany of Images, Thoughts, and Places." *Proceedings of the 85th ACSA Annual Meeting.* Washington, DC: ACSA, 1997. 401-07.

Chen, Congzhou (陈从周). *Shuo yuan* (说园). Shanghai: Tongji daxue chubanshe, 1984.

Chen, Congzhou (陈从周), ed. *Zhongguo yuanlin jianshang cidian* (中国园林鉴赏辞典). Shanghai: Huadong shifan daxue chubanshe, 2001.

Chen, Wangheng (陈望衡). *Zhongguo gudian meixue shi* (中国古典美学史). Changsha: Hunan jiaoyu chubanshe, 1998.

Chen, Zhi (陈植), ed. *Zhongguo lidai zaoyuan wenxuan* (中国历代造园文选). Hefei: Huangshan shushe, 1992.

Chen, Zhi (陈植) and Gongchi Zhang (张公驰), eds. *Zhongguo lidai minyuan ji xuanzhu* (中国历代名园记选注). Hefei: Anhui kexue jishu chubanshe, 1983.

Cheng, Yansheng (程演生), ed. *Yuanmingyuan kao* (圆明园考). Shanghai: Zhonghua shuju, 1928.

Chiu, Chebing. *Yuanming yuan: Le jardin de la clarté parfaite*. Paris: Les Editions de L'Imprimeur, 2000.

The Constitutions of the Society of Jesus and Their Complementary Norms. A complete English translation of the official Latin texts. Saint Louis: The Institute of Jesuit Sources, 1996.

Conan, Michel. *Dictionnaire Historique de L'Art des Jardins*. Hazan, 1997.

Cook, Daniel L., and Henry Rosemont. Introduction. *Writings on China*. By Gottfried Wilhelm Leibniz. Trans. Daniel L. Cook and Henry Rosemont. Chicago: Open Court, 1994.

Corsi, Elisabetta. "Late Baroque Painting in China Prior to the Arrival of Matteo Ripa: Giovanni Gherardni and the Perspective Paiting Callled Xianfa." *La misione cattolica in China tra I secoli XVIII-XIX, Matteo Ripa e il Collegio dei Cinesi*. Ed. Michele Fatica and Francesco D'Arelli. Proceedings of the International Colloquium. Collana "Matteo Ripa" XVI. Naples: Istituto Universitario Orientale, 1999. 103-22.

Cusa, Nicholas of. *The Game of Spheres*. Trans. and intro. Pauline Moffitt Watts. New York: Abaris Books, 1986.

Dami, Luigi. *The Italian Garden*. Trans. L. Scopoli. New York: Brentano's, 1925.

Dan son jardin de la Clarté parfaite. Painting. *Yuanming Yuan: Le jardin de la clarté parfaite*. By Chebing Chiu. Paris: Les Editions de L'Imperimeur, 2000.

De Mortain, Gilles. *Les Plans, Profils et Elévations des Ville et Châteaux de Versailles avec les Bosquets et Fountains*. Paris, 1714.

Deng, Yuhan (邓玉涵) (Joannes Terrez). *Yuanxi qiqi tushuo luzui* (远西奇器图说录最). Trans. and illus. Zheng Wang (王征). 1627. *Zhongguo kexue jishu dianji tonglu: jishu juan:juan yi* (中国科学技术典籍通录: 技术卷: 卷一). Ed. Jiyu Ren (任继愈). Zhengzhou: Henan jiaoyu chubanshe, 1993.

Derrida, Jacques. "White Mythology: Metaphor in the Text of Philosophy." *Margins of Philosophy*. Trans. Alan Bass. Chicago: The U of Chicago P, 1982. 207-71.

Descartes, René. *Discourse on Method and Meditations*. Trans. Laurene J. Lafleur. Indianapolis: The Library of Liberal Arts, 1960.

Descartes, René. *Meditations on First Philosophy*. Trans. Donald A. Cress. Indianapolis: Hackett Publishing, 1993.

Devine, W. *The Four Churches of Peking*. London: Burns, Oates and Washbourne, 1930.

Ding, Gao (丁皋). "Xiezhen mijue (写真秘诀)." *Zhongguo gudai hualun leibian* (中国古代画论类编). 1957. Vol. 1. Ed. Jianhua Yu (俞剑华). Beijing: Renmin meishu chubanshe, 2000. 545-69.

Droguet, Vincent. "Les Palais Européens de l'empereur Qianlong et leurs sources italiennes." *Histoire de l'Art* 25-26 (May 1994): 15-28.

Du, Xunhe (杜荀鹤). "Qiusu Qixiansi huai youren (秋宿棲贤寺怀友人)." *Quan Wudai shi* (全五代诗). Ed. Diaoyuan Li (李调元). Chengdu: Bashu shudian, 1991.

Dubreuil, Jean. *Practical Perspective*. Trans. Robert Pricke. London, 1672.

Durand, Antoine. "Restitution des Palais Européens du Yuanmingyuan." *Arts Asiatique* 43 (1988): 122-33.

E, Ertai (鄂尔泰), ed. *Yuzhi Yuanmingyuan tuyong* (御制圆明园图咏). Unpunctuated. Tianjing: Shiyin shuwu, 1887.

Edgerton, Samuel Y. *The Heritage of Giotto's Geometry: Art and Science on the Eve of the Scientific Revolution*. Ithaca: Cornell UP, 1991.

Falda, Giovanni Battista. *Li Girardini di Roma*. 1683. Facsimile. Nördlingen: Verlag Dr. Alfons UHL, 1994.

Falda, Giovanni Battista and Giovanni Francesco Venturini. *Le Fontane di Roma*. 1690. Facsimile. Nördlingen: Verlag Dr. Alfons UHL, 1996.

Fang, Yujin (方裕谨), ed. "Yuanmingyuan ge dianzuo bianming biao (圆明园各殿作匾名表)." *Yuanmingyuan xueshu lunwen ji* (圆明园学术论文集). Vol. 4. Ed. Zhongguo Yuanmingyuan xuehui (中国圆明园学会). Beijing: Zhongguo jianzhu gongye chubanshe, 1985. 39-61.

Félibien, André. *Des principes de l'architecture, de la sculpture, de la peinture, et des autres arts qui en dependent*. 1690.

Feng, Duofu (冯多福). "Yanshanyuan ji (研山园记)." *Zhongguo lidai minyuan ji xuanzhu* (中国历代名园记选注). Ed. Zhi Chen (陈植) and Gongchi Zhang (张公驰). Hefei: Anhui kexue jishu chubanshe, 1983. 78-81.

Feng, Jizhong. "Il rapporto uomo-natura: Mutual Nutrition of Man and Nature." *Spazio e società* (*Space and Society*) 57.15 (1992): 62-77.

Feng, Pengsheng (冯鹏生). *Zhongguo muban shuiyin gaishuo* (中国木板水印概说). Beijing: Beijing daxue chubanshe, 1999.

Fu, Yunlong (傅云龙) and Qin Lu (陆钦), eds. *Laozi, Zhuangzi* (老子, 庄子). Beijing: Huaxia chubanshe, 2002.

Gadamer, Hans-Georg. *The Relevance of the Beautiful and Other Essays*. Trans. Nicholas Walker. Cambridge: Cambridge UP, 1989.

Galletti, Giorgio. *Il Restauro del Giardino di Villa Medici: Masterplan*. Unpublished manuscript. 2001.

Gao, Heng (高亨), ed. *Zhouyi dazhuan jinzhu* (周易大传今注). Ji'nan: Qilu shushe, 2002.

Gao, Lian (高濂). "Yanxian qingshang jian lunhua (燕闲清赏笺论画)." *Zhongguo gudai hualun leibian* (中国古代画论类编). 1957. Vol. 1. Ed. Jianhua Yu (俞剑华). Beijing: Renmin meishu chubanshe, 2000. 121-24.

Gong, Suncheng (公孙乘). "Yue fu (月赋)." *Quan Han fu* (全汉赋). Ed. Zhengang Fei (费振刚). Beijing: Beijing daxue chubanshe, 1993.

Gong, Xian (龚贤). "Gong Anjie xiansheng huajue (龚安节先生画诀)." *Zhongguo gudai hualun leibian* (中国古代画论类编). 1957. Vol. 2. Ed. Jianhua Yu (俞剑华). Beijing: Renmin meishu chubanshe, 2000. 782-89.

Gu, Dadian (顾大典). "Xieshangyuan ji (谐赏园记)." *Zhongguo lidai minyuan ji xuanzhu* (中国历代名园记选注). Ed. Zhi Chen (陈植) and Gongchi Zhang (张公驰). Hefei: Anhui kexue jishu chubanshe, 1983. 108-12.

Gu, Kaizhi (顾恺之). "Hua Yuntaishan ji (画云台山记)." *Zhongguo gudai hualun leibian* (中国古代画论类编). 1957. Vol. 1. Ed. Jianhua Yu (俞剑华). Beijing: Renmin meishu chubanshe, 2000. 581-82.

Guo, Qingfan (郭庆藩), ed. *Zhuangzi ji shi* (庄子集释). Beijing: Zhonghua shuju, 1982.

Works Cited

Guo, Ruoxu (郭若虚). "Guohua jianwen zhi xulun: lun zhizuo kaimo (国画见闻志叙论: 论制作楷模)." *Zhongguo gudai hualun leibian* (中国古代画论类编). 1957. Vol. 1. Ed. Jianhua Yu (俞剑华). Beijing: Renmin meishu chubanshe, 2000. 57-58.

Guo, Xi (郭熙). "Linquan gaozhi (林泉高致)." *Zhongguo gudai hualun leibian* (中国古代画论类编). 1957. Vol. 1. Ed. Jianhua Yu (俞剑华). Beijing: Renmin meishu chubanshe, 2000. 631-52.

Guoli gugong bowuyuan (国立故宫博物院), ed. *Yuanlin minghua tezhan tulu* (园林名画特展图录). Taibei: Guoli gugong bowuyuan, 1986.

Hai, Zhongxiu (海忠秀), ed. *Chengdefu zhi* (承德府志). 1887. Taipei: Chengwen chubanshe, 1966.

Han, Chunquan (韩纯全). "Shanshui Chunquan ji (山水纯全集)." *Lidai lunhua mingzhu lubian* (历代论画名著录编). Ed. Zicheng Shen (沈子丞). Beijing: Wenwu chubanshe, 1982.

Han, Qi (韩琦). "Shixue tiyao (视学提要)." *Zhongguo kexue jishu dianji tonglu: shuxue juan: juan si* (中国科学技术典籍通录: 数学卷, 卷四). Ed. Jiyu Ren (任继愈). Zhengzhou: Henan jiaoyu chubanshe, 1993. 709-10.

Han, Qi (韩琦). "Zhigui lunhua (稚圭论画)." *Zhongguo gudai hualun leibian* (中国古代画论类编). 1957. Vol. 1. Ed. Jianhua Yu (俞剑华). Beijing: Renmin meishu chubanshe, 2000. 41.

Han, Qi (韩琦). "Zhongqiu ye (中秋夜)." *Song shi chao* (宋诗钞). Ed. Zhizhen Wu (吴之振). Beijing: Zhonghua shuju, 1996.

Hanyu da cidian (汉语大词典). Shanghai : Shanghai cishu chubanshe, 1989.

Harries, Karsten. *Infinity and Perspective*. Cambridge: MIT Press, 2001.

He, Chongyi (何重义) and Zhaofen Zeng (曾昭奋). *Yuanmingyuan yuanlin yishu* (圆明园园林艺术). Beijing: Kexue chubanshe, 1995.

Heidegger, Martin. *Being and Time*. Trans. John Macquarrie and Edward Robinson. New York: Harper and Row, 1962.

Hejduk, John. "The Returning Angel." *Lines: No Fire Could Burn*. New York: The Monacelli Press, 1999. 24.

Ho, Wai-Kan. "The Literary Concepts of 'Picture-like' [*ruhua*] and 'Picture-Idea' [*huayi*] in the Relationship between Poetry and Painting." *Words and Languages: Chinese Poetry, Calligraphy, and Painting*. Ed. Alfred Murck and Wen C. Fong. New York: The Metropolitan Museum of Art, 1991.

Hong, Shi (洪适). "Panzhou ji (盘州记)." *Zhongguo lidai minyuan ji xuanzhu* (中国历代名园记选注). Ed. Zhi Chen (陈植) and Gongchi Zhang (张公驰). Hefei: Anhui kexue jishu chubanshe, 1983. 65-72.

Hou, Renzhi (侯仁之). "Yuanming Yuan (圆明园)." *Yuanmingyuan: lishi, xianzhuang, lunzheng (*圆明园：历史，现状，论争*)*. Vol. 1. Ed. Daocheng Wang (王道成). Beijing: Beijing chubanshe, 1999. 119-24.

Hölderlin, Friedrich. *Hymns and Fragments*. Trans and intro. Richard Sieburth. Princeton: Princeton UP, 1984.

Hu, Jing (胡敬). *Guochao yuanhua lu* (国朝院画录). 1816. *Xuxiu Siku quanshu* (续修四库全书). Vol. 1082. Ed. Xuxiu siku quanshu bianzuan weiyuanhui (续修四库全书编纂委员会). Shanghai: Shanghai guji chubanshe, 1995.

Huang, Gongwang (黄公望). "Lun shanshui shushi (论山水树石)." *Lidai lunhua mingzhu lubian* (历代论画名著录编). Ed. Zicheng Shen (沈子丞). Beijing: Wenwu chubanshe, 1982.

Huang, Gongwang (黄公望). "Xie shanshui jue (写山水决)." *Zhongguo gudai hualun leibian* (中国古代画论类编). 1957. Vol. 2. Ed. Jianhua Yu (俞剑华). Beijing: Renmin meishu chubanshe, 2000. 700-05.

Husserl, Edmund. *The Idea of Phenomenology*. The Hague: Martinus Nijhoff, 1964.

Ignatius of Loyola. *The Spiritual Exercises*. *Saint Ignatius of Loyola: Personal Writings*. Trans. Joseph A. Munitiz and Philip Endean. London: Penguin Books, 1996.

Ishida, Mikinosuke. "Biographical Study of Giuseppe Castiglione [Lang Shih-ning]: A Jesuit painter in the court of Peking under the Ch'ing Dynasty." *Memoirs of the Research Department of the Toyo Bunko* 19 (1960): 79-121.

Jami, Catherine. "From Clavius to Pardies: The Geometry Transmitted to China by Jesuits [1607-1723]." *Western Humanistic Culture Presented to China by Jesuit Missionaries (XVII-XVIII Centuries)*. Ed. Fedrico Masini. Proceedings of the Conference held in Rome. Rome: Institutum Historicum S. J., 1996. 175-99.

Jamnitzer, Lencker, Stöer: Drei Nürnberger Konstruktivisten des 16. Jahrhunderts. Ausstellung der Albrecht Dürer Gesellschaft im Fembohaus vom 20 April bis 1 June 1969. Nürnberg: der Albrecht Dürer Gesellschaft, 1969.

Jartoux. "P. Jartoux to J. de Fontaney on Aug. 20, 1704." *Lettres édifiantes et curieuses, écrites des missions étrangères*. Nouvelle édition. Tome 10. Lyon, 1819.

Ji, Cheng (计成). *Yuanye zhushi* (园冶注释). Ed. Zhi Chen (陈植). Beijing: Zhongguo jianzhu gongye chubanshe, 1997.

Jiaqing (嘉庆). "Guan Xieqiqu shuifa (观谐奇趣水法)." *Yuanmingyuan bianqian shi tanwei* (圆明园变迁史探微). By Enyin Zhang (张恩荫). Beijing: Beijing tiyu chubanshe, 1993.

Jiaqing (嘉庆). "Ti Yuanyingguan (题远瀛观)." *Renzong yuzhi shi chuji* (仁宗御制诗初集). Ch. 35. *Qing liuchao yuzhi shiwen ji* (清六朝御制诗文集). Ed. Xin Yi (奕訢). 1876.

Jiaqing (嘉庆). "Xie Qi Qu (谐奇趣)." *Yuanmingyuan bianqian shi tanwei* (圆明园变迁史探微). By Enyin Zhang (张恩荫). Beijing: Beijing tiyu chubanshe, 1993.

Jiaqing (嘉庆). "Yanhua chuang (罨画窗)." *Yuanmingyuan bianqian shi tanwei* (圆明园变迁史探微). By Enyin Zhang (张恩荫). Beijing: Beijing tiyu chubanshe, 1993.

Jiaqing (嘉庆). "Yuanju shuzhi (园居述志)." *Renzong yuzhi shi chuji* (仁宗御制诗初集). Ch. 30. *Qing liuchao yuzhi shiwen ji* (清六朝御制诗文集). Ed. Xin Yi (奕訢). 1876.

Jiaqing (嘉庆). "Yuanying Guan (远瀛观) [1]." *Renzong yuzhi shi chuji* (仁宗御制诗初集). Ch. 19. *Qing liuchao yuzhi shiwen ji* (清六朝御制诗文集). Ed. Xin Yi (奕訢). 1876.

Jiaqing (嘉庆). "Yuanying Guan (远瀛观) [2]." *Renzong yuzhi shi chuji* (仁宗御制诗初集). Ch. 23. *Qing liuchao yuzhi shiwen ji* (清六朝御制诗文集). Ed. Xin Yi (奕訢). 1876.

Jiaqing (嘉庆), "Yuanying Guan (远瀛观) [3]." *Renzong yuzhi shi sanji* (仁宗御制诗三集). Ch. 34. *Qing liuchao yuzhi shiwen ji* (清六朝御制诗文集). Ed. Xin Yi (奕訢). 1876.

Jiaqing (嘉庆). "Yuanyingguan ge (远瀛观歌) [1]." *Renzong yuzhi shi chuji* (仁宗御制诗初集). Ch. 12. *Qing liuchao yuzhi shiwen ji* (清六朝御制诗文集). Ed. Xin Yi (奕訢). 1876.

Jiaqing (嘉庆). "Yuanyingguan ge (远瀛观歌) [2]." *Yuanmingyuan bianqian shi tanwei* (圆明园变迁史探微). By Enyin Zhang (张恩荫). Beijing: Beijing tiyu chubanshe, 1993.

Jiaqing (嘉庆). "Yuanyingguan shuzhi (远瀛观述志)." *Renzong yuzhi shi sanji* (仁宗御制诗三集). Ch. 40. *Qing liuchao yuzhi shiwen ji* (清六朝御制诗文集). Ed. Xin Yi (奕訢). 1876.

Jiaqing (嘉庆). "Yuanyingguan yougan (远瀛观有感)." *Renzong yuzhi shi sanji* (仁宗御制诗三集). Ch. 23. *Qing liuchao yuzhi shiwen ji* (清六朝御制诗文集). Ed. Xin Yi (奕訢). 1876.

Jiang, Shaoshu (姜绍书). *Wusheng shi shi* (无声诗史). 7 juan. Changxiu shuwu.

Jiang, Yikui (蒋一葵). *Chang'an ke hua* (长安客话). Beijing: Beijing guji chubanshe, 1980.

Jing, Hao (荆浩). "Bifa ji (笔法记)." *Zhongguo gudai hualun leibian* (中国古代画论类编). 1957. Vol. 1. Ed. Jianhua Yu (俞剑华). Beijing: Renmin meishu chubanshe, 2000. 605-15.

Ju, Deyuan (鞠德源), ed. "Qing gongting huajia Lang Shining nianpu: jian zaihua Yesuhui shi shishi jinian (清宫廷画家郎世宁年谱：兼在华耶稣会士史事稽年)." *Gugong bowuyuan yuankan* (故宫博物院院刊) (February 1988).

Jullien, François. *The Propensity of Things: Toward a History of Efficacy in China.* Trans. Janet Lloyd. New York: Zone Books, 1999.

Kangxi (康熙). "Bishu Shanzhuang ji (避暑山庄记)." *Zhongguo lidai zaoyuan wenxuan* (中国历代造园文选). Ed. Zhi Chen (陈植). Hefei: Huangshan shushe, 1992.

Kangxi (康熙). "Shengzu renhuangdi yuzhi Changchunyuan ji (圣祖仁皇帝御制畅春园记)." *Rixia jiuwen kao* (日下旧闻考). Vol. 2. Ed. Minzhong Yu (于敏中). Beijing: Beijing guji chubanshe, 2001. 1268-70.

Kangxi (康熙). "Shengzhu yuzhi Bishu Shanzhuang ji (圣祖御制避暑山庄记)." *Chengdefu zhi* (承德府志). 1887. Ed. Zhongxiu Hai (海忠秀). Taipei: Chengwen chubanshe, 1966.

"Kao gong ji (考工记)." *Zhongguo kexue jishu dianji tonglu: jishu juan: juan yi* (中国科学技术典籍通录：技术卷：卷一). Ed. Jiyu Ren (任继愈). Zhengzhou: Henan jiaoyu chubanshe, 1993.

Kemp, Martin. *The Science of Art: Optical Themes in Western Art from Brunelleschi to Seurat.* New Haven: Yale UP, 1990.

Kerby, Kate. *An Old Chinese Garden: A Three-fold Masterpiece of Poetry, Calligraphy and Painting.* Shanghai: Zhonghua shuju, 1922.

Kip, Johannes. *Nouveau Théâtre de la Grande Bretagne.* 1714-16.

Kitao, Timothy K. "Prejudice in Perspective: A Study of Vignola's Perspective Treatise." *The Art Bulletin* 44 (1962): 173-94.

Kong, Yanshi (孔衍栻). "Hua jue (画决)." *Lidai lunhua mingzhu lubian* (历代论画名著录编). Ed. Zicheng Shen (沈子丞). Beijing: Wenwu chubanshe, 1982.

Kun, Gang (昆冈), ed. *Da Qing huidian shili* (大清会典实例). 1899. *Qinding da Qing huidian* (钦定大清会典). Taibei: Xingwenfeng chubanshe, 1976.

La Vuë, et Elevations, de Ville, et Château de Versailles, avec les Bosquets et Fontaines. A copy in the Dumbarton Oaks Collections, Washington, DC.

Lancaster, Clay. "The European Palaces of Yuan Ming Yuan." *Gazette des Beaux-Arts* 34 (October 1948): 261-88, 307-14.

Le Rouge, George Louis. *Détails des Nouveaux Jardins à la Mode*. 1776-88.

Lei, Yangshi (样式雷). Construction drawings of the Western garden of the Yuanming Yuan. *Guoli Beiping Tushuguan guankan* (国立北平图书馆馆刊) 7.3/4 (May-August 1932).

Leibniz, Gottfried W. *Discourse on the National Theology of the Chinese*. Trans. Henry Rosemont and Daniel J. Cook. Honolulu: The UP of Hawaii, 1977.

Leibniz, Gottfried W. "Discourse on the National Theology of the Chinese." *Writings on China*. Trans. Daniel J. Cook and Henry Rosemont. Chicago: Open Court, 1994. 75-138.

Leibniz, Gottfried W. "Preface to the Novissima Sinica." *Writings on China*. Trans. Daniel J. Cook and Henry Rosemont. Chicago: Open Court, 1994. 45-60.

Leibniz, Gottfried W. "Remarks on Chinese Rites and Religions." *Writings on China*. Trans. Daniel J. Cook and Henry Rosemont. Chicago: Open Court, 1994. 67-74.

Lettres édifiantes et curieuses, écrites des missions étrangères. Nouvelle édition. Tome 10. Lyon: J. Vernarel Libraire, 1819.

Li, Chengsou (李澄叟). "Hua shanshui jue (画山水诀)." *Zhongguo gudai hualun leibian* (中国古代画论类编). 1957. Vol. 1. Ed. Jianhua Yu (俞剑华). Beijing: Renmin meishu chubanshe, 2000. 620-24.

Li, Daoyuan (郦道元). *Shuijing zhu* (水经注). Ed. Shuchun Tan (谭属春). Changsha: Yuelu shushe, 1995.

Li, Diaoyuan (李调元), ed. *Quan Wudai shi* (全五代诗). Chengdu: Bashu shudian, 1991.

Li, Dou (李斗). *Yangzhou huafang lu* (扬州画舫录). Beijing: Zhonghua shuju, 1997.

Li, Gefei (李格非). "Luoyang mingyuan ji (洛阳名园记)." *Zhongguo lidai minyuan ji xuanzhu* (中国历代名园记选注). Ed. Zhi Chen (陈植) and Gongchi Zhang (张公驰). Hefei: Anhui kexue jishu chubanshe, 1983. 38-55.

Li, Jie (李诫). *Yingzao fashi* (营造法式). Unpunctuated. 1103. Rpt. Beijing: Zhongguo shudian, 1995.

Li, Rihua (李日华). "Zhulan lunhua (竹懒论画)." *Zhongguo gudai hualun leibian* (中国古代画论类编). 1957. Vol. 1. Ed. Jianhua Yu (俞剑华). Beijing: Renmin meishu chubanshe, 2000. 491.

Li, Shan (李山), ed. *Shijing xin zhu* (诗经新注). Ji'nan: Qilu shushe, 2000.

Li, Yu (李渔). *Xianjing ou ji* (闲情偶寄). *Liyu quanji* (李渔全集). Vol. 3. Hangzhou: Zhejiang guji chubanshe, 1992.

Li, Yushu (李渔叔), ed. *Mozi jinzhu jinyi* (墨子今注今译). Taipei: Taiwan shangshu yinshuguan, 1997.

Li, Zhong (李中). "Ting wei (庭苇)." *Quan Wudai shi* (全五代诗). Ed. Diaoyuan Li (李调元). Chengdu: Bashu shudian, 1991.

Liang, Qichao (梁启超), ed. *Mojing jiaoshi* (墨经校释). *Mozi jicheng* (墨子集成). Vol. 19. Ed. Lingfeng Yan (严灵峰). Taibei: Chengwen chubanshe, 1977.

Lin, Youlin (林友麟). *Suyuan shi pu* (素园石谱). 1613. *Zhongguo kexue jishu dianji tonglu: dili juan: juan san* (中国科学技术典籍通录: 地理卷: 卷三). Ed. Jiyu Ren (任继愈). Zhengzhou: Henan jiaoyu chubanshe, 1995. 35-129.

Liu, Baonan (刘宝楠), ed. *Lunyu zhengyi* (论语正义). Shijiazhuang: Hebei renmin chubanshe, 1992.

Liu, Dianjue (刘殿爵), ed. *Huainanzi zhuzi suoyin* (淮南子逐字索引). Xianggang: Shangwu yinshuguan, 1992.

Liu, Dianjue (刘殿爵), ed. *Laozi zhuzi suoyin* (老子逐字索引). Xianggang: Shangwu yinshuguan, 1996.

Liu, Dong (刘侗). "Chengguogong Yuan (成国公园)." *Zhongguo lidai minyuan ji xuanzhu* (中国历代名园记选注). Ed. Zhi Chen (陈植) and Gongchi Zhang (张公驰). Hefei: Anhui kexue jishu chubanshe, 1983. 248-49.

Liu, Dong (刘侗) and Yizheng Yu (于奕正). *Dijing jingwu lüe* (帝京景物略). Ed. Xiaoli Sun (孙小力). Shanghai: Shanghai guji chubanshe, 2001.

Liu, Hongzhang (刘宏章) and Qingju Qiao (乔清举), eds. *Lunyu, Mengzi* (论语, 孟子). Beijing: Huaxia chubanshe, 2002.

Liu, Jian (刘兼). "Gui you (贵游)." *Quan Wudai shi* (全五代诗). Ed. Diaoyuan Li (李调元). Chengdu: Bashu shudian, 1991.

Liu, Shaojin (刘绍瑾). *Zhuangzi yu Zhongguo meixue* (庄子与中国美学). Changsha: Yuelu shushe, 2007.

Liu, Yiqing (刘义庆). "Yanyu (言语)." *Shishuo xinyu* (世说新语). Changchun: Shidai wenyi chubanshe, 2001.

Liu, Yuxi (刘禹西). "Xi-xin-ting ji (洗新亭记)." *Zhichi shanlin: yuanlin yishu wencui* (咫尺山林：园林艺术文粹). Ed. Xiaoli Sun (孙小力). Shanghai: Dongfang chubanshe, 1999. 29-31.

Liu, Zongyuan (柳宗元). "Lingling chun wang (零陵春望)." *Liu Zongyuan ji* (柳宗元集). Ed. Xinding Yi (易新鼎). Beijing: Zhongguo shudian, 2000.

Liu, Zongyuan (柳宗元). "Yongzhou Longxingsi dongqiu ji (永州龙兴寺东丘记)." *Zhichi shanlin: yuanlin yishu wencui* (咫尺山林：园林艺术文粹). Ed. Xiaoli Sun (孙小力). Shanghai: Dongfang chubanshe, 1999. 26-28.

Lucas, Thomas Martin. *Landmarking: City, Church and Jesuit Urban Strategy*. Chicago: Loyola Press, 1997.

Luo, Gun (罗衮). "Qingming Chishuisi ju 清明赤水寺居." *Quan Wudai shi* (全五代诗). Ed. Diaoyuan Li (李调元). Chengdu: Bashu shudian, 1991.

Lü, Buwei (吕不韦), ed. "Youshi (有始)." *Lüshi chunqiu* (吕氏春秋). Changsha: Yuelu shushe, 1993.

Ma, Hongtu (马鸿图). "Ye tan 'sanshan wuyuan' (也谈'三山五园')." *Jinghua yuanlin congkao* (京华园林丛考). Ed. Beijingshi yuanlinju (北京市园林局). Beijing: Beijing kexue jishu chubanshe, 1996.

Macartney, George. *An Embassy to China: Lord Macartney's Journal 1793-94*. Hamden: Archon Books, 1962.

Major, John S. *Heaven and Earth in Early Han Thought: Chapters Three, Four, and Five of the Huainanzi*. Albany: State U of New York P, 1993.

March, Benjamin. "Linear Perspective in Chinese Painting." *Eastern Art* 3 (1931): 112-39.

May, Reinhard. *Heidegger's Hidden Sources: East Asian Influences on His Work*. Trans. Graham Parkes. London: Routledge, 1996.

Meng, Haoran (孟浩然). "Su Zhongnanshan Cuiweisi (宿终南山翠微寺)." *Meng Haoran ji* (孟浩然集). *Wang Wei quanji* (王维全集). Ed. Zhongfu Cao (曹中孚). Shanghai: Shanghai guji chubanshe, 1997. Appendix.

Meng, Haoran (孟浩然). "Zaofa Yuputan (早发渔浦潭)." *Meng Haoran ji* (孟浩然集). *Wang Wei quanji* (王维全集). Ed. Zhongfu Cao (曹中孚). Shanghai: Shanghai guji chubanshe, 1997.

Merleau-Ponty, Maurice. *Phenomenology of Perception*. Trans. Colin Smith. London: Routledge, 1962.

Merleau-Ponty, Maurice. *The Visible and the Invisible*. Trans. Alphonso Lingis. Evanston: Northwestern UP, 1968.

Mo, Shilong (莫是龙). "Hua shuo (画说)." *Zhongguo gudai hualun leibian* (中国古代画论类编). 1957. Vol. 2. Ed. Jianhua Yu (俞剑华). Beijing: Renmin meishu chubanshe, 2000. 716-22.

Mungello, D. E. *The Forgotten Christians of Hangzhou*. Honolulu: U of Hawai'i P, 1994.

Needham, Joseph. *Science and Civilization in China*. Vol. 3. *Mathematics and the Sciences of the Heavens and the Earth*. Cambridge: Cambridge UP, 1970.

"Neiwufu Zaobanchu ge zuocheng zuohuoji qingdang (内务府造办处各作成作活计清档)." *Yuanmingyuan Qingdai dang'an shiliao* (圆明园清代档案史料). Vol. 2. Ed. Zhongguo diyi lishi dang'an'guan (中国第一历史档案馆). Shanghai: Shanghai guji chubanshe, 1991.

Nian, Xiyao (年希尧). "Shixue bianyan (视学弁言)" (1729). *Shixue* (视学). *Zhongguo kexue jishu dianji tonglu: shuxue juan: juan si* (中国科学技术典籍通录: 数学卷, 卷四). Ed. Jiyu Ren (任继愈). Zhengzhou: Henan jiaoyu chubanshe, 1993. 711-12.

Nian, Xiyao (年希尧). "[The second preface]." (1735). *Shixue* (视学). *Zhongguo kexue jishu dianji tonglu: shuxue juan: juan si* (中国科学技术典籍通录: 数学卷, 卷四). Ed. Jiyu Ren (任继愈). Zhengzhou: Henan jiaoyu chubanshe, 1993. 713-15.

Ouyang, Xiu (欧阳修). "Zuiwengting ji (醉翁亭记)." *Xiugu qingyun: shanshui sanwen jingxuan* (秀谷清韵：山水散文精选). Ed. Jing Li (李静). Nanjing: Nanjing chubanshe, 1995.

Panofsky, Erwin. *Perspective as Symbolic Form*. Trans. Christopher S. Wood. New York: Zone Books, 1991.

Pei wen yun fu (佩文韵府). Taipei: Taiwan shangwu yinshuguan, 1937.

Pérez-Gómez, Alberto and Louise Pelletier. *Architectural Representation and the Perspective Hinge*. Cambridge: MIT P, 1997.

Petrucci, Raphaël. *Chinese Painters: A Critical Study*. Trans. Frances Seaver. New York: Brentano's, 1920.

Portrait of Hongyan. Painting. Late-Eighteenth century. Collected by Freer Gallery, Smithsonian Institution, Washington, DC.

Works Cited

Pozzo, Andrea. *Perspective in Architecture and Painting*. Unabridged reprint of the English and Latin edition of the 1693 *Perspectiva pictorum et architectorium*. New York: Dover Publications, 1989.

Qi, Biaojia (祈彪佳). "Yushan zhu (寓山注)." *Zhongguo lidai minyuan ji xuanzhu* (中国历代名园记选注). Ed. Zhi Chen (陈植) and Gongchi Zhang (张公驰). Hefei: Anhui kexue jishu chubanshe, 1983. 259-95.

Qianlong (乾隆). "Dongtian Shenchu (洞天深处)." *Yuanmingyuan Sishijing tuyong* (圆明园四十景图咏). Ed. Zhongguo Yuanmingyuan xuehui (中国圆明园学会). Beijing: Zhongguo jianzhu gongye chubanshe, 1985.

Qianlong (乾隆). "Fanghu Shengjing (方壶胜景)." *Yuanmingyuan Sishijing tuyong* (圆明园四十景图咏). Ed. Zhongguo Yuanmingyuan xuehui (中国圆明园学会). Beijing: Zhongguo jianzhu gongye chubanshe, 1985.

Qianlong (乾隆). "Gaozong yuzhi Bishu Shanzhuang houxu (高宗御制避暑山庄后序)." *Chengdefu zhi* (承德府志). 1887. Ed. Zhongxiu Hai (海忠秀). Taipei: Chengwen chubanshe, 1966.

Qianlong (乾隆). "Hongci Yonghu (鸿慈永祜)." *Yuanmingyuan Sishijing tuyong* (圆明园四十景图咏). Ed. Zhongguo Yuanmingyuan xuehui (中国圆明园学会). Beijing: Zhongguo jianzhu gongye chubanshe, 1985.

Qianlong (乾隆). "Jiashan (假山) [1]." "Qing wuchao yuzhiji zhong de Yuanmingyuan shi [xu er] (清五朝御制集中的圆明园诗[续二])." Ed. Jiajin Zhu (朱家溍) and Yanqin Li (李艳琴). *Yuanmingyuan xueshu lunwen ji* (圆明园学术论文集). Vol. 4. Ed. Zhongguo Yuanmingyuan xuehui (中国圆明园学会). Beijing: Zhongguo jianzhu gongye chubanshe, 1985.

Qianlong (乾隆). "Jiashan (假山) [2]." In "Qing wuchao yuzhiji zhong de Yuanmingyuan shi [xu er] (清五朝御制集中的圆明园诗[续二])." Eds. Jiajin Zhu (朱家溍) and Yanqin Li (李艳琴). *Yuanmingyuan xueshu lunwen ji* (圆明园学术论文集). Vol. 4. Ed. Zhongguo Yuanmingyuan xuehui (中国圆明园学会). Beijing: Zhongguo jianzhu gongye chubanshe, 1985.

Qianlong (乾隆). "Kuoran Dagong (阔然大公)." *Yuanmingyuan Sishijing tuyong* (圆明园四十景图咏). Ed. Zhongguo Yuanmingyuan xuehui (中国圆明园学会). Beijing: Zhongguo jianzhu gongye chubanshe, 1985.

Qianlong (乾隆). "Lian Xi Lechu (廉溪乐处)." *Yuanmingyuan Sishijing tuyong* (圆明园四十景图咏). Ed. Zhongguo Yuanmingyuan xuehui (中国圆明园学会). Beijing: Zhongguo jianzhu gongye chubanshe, 1985.

Qianlong (乾隆). "Lin wu (林屋)." In "Qing wuchao yuzhiji zhong de Yuanmingyuan shi (清五朝御制集中的圆明园诗)." Ed. Jiajin Zhu (朱家溍) and Yanqin Li (李艳琴). *Yuanmingyuan xueshu lunwen ji* (圆明园学术论文集). Vol. 2. Ed. Zhongguo Yuanmingyuan xuehui (中国圆明园学会). Beijing: Zhongguo jianzhu gongye chubanshe, 1983.

Qianlong (乾隆). "Louyue Kaiyun (镂月开云)." *Yuanmingyuan Sishijing tuyong* (圆明园四十景图咏). Ed. Zhongguo Yuanmingyuan xuehui (中国圆明园学会). Beijing: Zhongguo jianzhu gongye chubanshe, 1985.

Qianlong (乾隆). "Najing Tang (纳景堂)." *Yuanmingyuan bianqian shi tanwei* (圆明园变迁史探微). By Enyin Zhang (张恩荫). Beijing: Beijing tiyu chubanshe, 1993.

Qianlong (乾隆). "Qianlong sanshiwu nian yuzhi Changchunyuan tiju youxu (乾隆三十五年御制长春园题句有序)." *Rixia jiuwen kao* (日下旧闻考). Vol. 3. Ed. Minzhong Yu (于敏中). Beijing: Beijing guji chubanshe, 2001. 1379-81.

Qianlong (乾隆). "Quyuan Fenghe (曲院风荷)." *Yuanmingyuan Sishijing tuyong* (圆明园四十景图咏). Ed. Zhongguo Yuanmingyuan xuehui (中国圆明园学会). Beijing: Zhongguo jianzhu gongye chubanshe, 1985.

Qianlong (乾隆). "Shan'gao Shuichang (山高水长)." *Yuanmingyuan Sishijing tuyong* (圆明园四十景图咏). Ed. Zhongguo Yuanmingyuan xuehui (中国圆明园学会). Beijing: Zhongguo jianzhu gongye chubanshe, 1985.

Qianlong (乾隆). "Shangxia Tianguang (上下天光)." *Yuanmingyuan Sishijing tuyong* (圆明园四十景图咏). Ed. Zhongguo Yuanmingyuan xuehui (中国圆明园学会). Beijing: Zhongguo jianzhu gongye chubanshe, 1985.

Qianlong (乾隆). "Shizi Lin (狮子林) [1]." In "Qing wuchao yuzhiji zhong de Yuanmingyuan shi [xu er] (清五朝御制集中的圆明园诗[续二])." Ed. Jiajin Zhu (朱家溍) and Yanqin Li (李艳琴). *Yuanmingyuan xueshu lunwen ji* (圆明园学术论文集). Vol. 4. Ed. Zhongguo Yuanmingyuan xuehui (中国圆明园学会). Beijing: Zhongguo jianzhu gongye chubanshe, 1985.

Qianlong (乾隆). "Shizi Lin (狮子林) [2]." In "Qing wuchao yuzhiji zhong de Yuanmingyuan shi [xu er] (清五朝御制集中的圆明园诗[续二])." Ed. Jiajin Zhu (朱家溍) and Yanqin Li (李艳琴). *Yuanmingyuan xueshu lunwen ji* (圆明园学术论文集). Vol. 4. Ed. Zhongguo Yuanmingyuan xuehui (中国圆明园学会). Beijing: Zhongguo jianzhu gongye chubanshe, 1985.

Qianlong (乾隆). "Shui men (水门)." In "Qing wuchao yuzhiji zhong de Yuanmingyuan shi [xu er] (清五朝御制集中的圆明园诗[续二])." Ed. Jiajin Zhu (朱家溍) and Yanqin Li (李艳琴). *Yuanmingyuan xueshu lunwen ji* (圆明园学术论文集). Vol. 4. Ed. Zhongguo Yuanmingyuan xuehui (中国圆明园学会). Beijing: Zhongguo jianzhu gongye chubanshe, 1985.

Qianlong (乾隆). "Shuimu Mingse (水木明瑟)." *Yuanmingyuan Sishijing tuyong* (圆明园四十景图咏). Ed. Zhongguo Yuanmingyuan xuehui (中国圆明园学会). Beijing: Zhongguo jianzhu gongye chubanshe, 1985.

Qianlong (乾隆). "Tantan Dangdang (坦坦荡荡)." *Yuanmingyuan Sishijing tuyong* (圆明园四十景图咏). Ed. Zhongguo Yuanmingyuan xuehui (中国圆明园学会). Beijing: Zhongguo jianzhu gongye chubanshe, 1985.

Qianlong (乾隆). "Tanzhen Shuwu (探真书屋)." In "Qing wuchao yuzhiji zhong de Yuanmingyuan shi [xu er] (清五朝御制集中的圆明园诗[续二])." Ed. Jiajin Zhu (朱家溍) and Yanqin Li (李艳琴). *Yuanmingyuan xueshu lunwen ji* (圆明园学术论文集). Vol. 4. Ed. Zhongguo Yuanmingyuan xuehui (中国圆明园学会). Beijing: Zhongguo jianzhu gongye chubanshe, 1985.

Qianlong (乾隆). "Ti Zelantang." *Yuanmingyuan bianqian shi tanwei* (圆明园变迁史探微). By Enyin Zhang (张恩荫). Beijing: Beijing tiyu chubanshe, 1993.

Qianlong (乾隆). "Ti Shizilin Shiliujing (题狮子林十六景)." In "Qing wuchao yuzhiji zhong de Yuanmingyuan shi [xu er] (清五朝御制集中的圆明园诗[续二])." Ed. Jiajin Zhu (朱家溍) and Yanqin Li (李艳琴). *Yuanmingyuan xueshu lunwen ji* (圆明园学术论文集). Vol. 4. Ed. Zhongguo Yuanmingyuan xuehui (中国圆明园学会). Beijing: Zhongguo jianzhu gongye chubanshe, 1985.

Qianlong (乾隆). "Xifeng Xiuse (西峰秀色)." *Yuanmingyuan Sishijing tuyong* (圆明园四十景图咏). Ed. Zhongguo Yuanmingyuan xuehui (中国圆明园学会). Beijing: Zhongguo jianzhu gongye chubanshe, 1985.

Qianlong (乾隆). "Xuti Shizilin ba jing (续题狮子林八景)." In "Qing wuchao yuzhiji zhong de Yuanmingyuan shi [xu er] (清五朝御制集中的圆明园诗[续二])." Ed. Jiajin Zhu (朱家溍) and Yanqin Li (李艳琴). *Yuanmingyuan xueshu lunwen ji* (圆明园学术论文集). Vol. 4. Ed. Zhongguo Yuanmingyuan xuehui (中国圆明园学会). Beijing: Zhongguo jianzhu gongye chubanshe, 1985.

Qianlong (乾隆). "Yinshui Lanxiang (印水兰香)." *Yuanmingyuan Sishijing tuyong* (圆明园四十景图咏). Ed. Zhongguo Yuanmingyuan xuehui (中国圆明园学会). Beijing: Zhongguo jianzhu gongye chubanshe, 1985.

Qianlong (乾隆). "Yuhou Yuanmingyuan (雨后圆明园)." In "Qing wuchao yuzhiji zhong de Yuanmingyuan shi (清五朝御制集中的圆明园诗)." Ed. Jiajin Zhu (朱家溍) and Yanqin Li (李艳琴). *Yuanmingyuan xueshu lunwen ji* (圆明园学术论文集). Vol. 2. Ed. Zhongguo Yuanmingyuan xuehui (中国圆明园学会). Beijing: Zhongguo jianzhu gongye chubanshe, 1983.

Qianlong (乾隆). "Yuzhi Bishu Shanzhuang houxu (御制避暑山庄后序)." *Yuzhi Bishu Shanzhuang shi* (御制避暑山庄诗). By Kangxi (康熙) and Qianlong (乾隆). 1741.

Qianlong (乾隆). "Yuzhi Jingyiyuan ji (御制静宜园记)." *Rixia jiuwen kao* (日下旧闻考). Vol. 3. Ed. Minzhong Yu (于敏中). Beijing: Beijing guji chubanshe, 2001. 1437-39.

Qianlong (乾隆). "Yuzhi Wangquanzhuang ji (御制万泉庄记)." *Rixia jiuwen kao* (日下旧闻考). Vol. 2. Ed. Minzhong Yu (于敏中). Beijing: Beijing guji chubanshe, 2001. 1313-14.

Qianlong (乾隆). "Yuzhi Wangshoushan Kunminghu ji (御制万寿山昆明湖记)." *Rixia jiuwen kao* (日下旧闻考). Vol. 3. Ed. Minzhong Yu (于敏中). Beijing: Beijing guji chubanshe, 2001. 1392.

Qianlong (乾隆). "Yuzhi Wangshoushan Qingyiyuan ji (御制万寿山清漪园记)." *Rixia jiuwen kao* (日下旧闻考). Vol. 3. Ed. Minzhong Yu (于敏中). Beijing: Beijing guji chubanshe, 2001. 1393-94.

Qianlong (乾隆). "Yuzhi Xiaoyoutian Yuan ji (御制小有天园记)." *Rixia jiuwen kao* (日下旧闻考). Vol. 3. Ed. Minzhong Yu (于敏中). Beijing: Beijing guji chubanshe, 2001. 1384-85.

Qianlong (乾隆). "Yuzhi Yuquanshan tianxia diyi quan ji (御制玉泉山天下第一泉记)." *Rixia jiuwen kao* (日下旧闻考). Vol. 1. Ed. Minzhong Yu (于敏中). Beijing: Beijing guji chubanshe, 2001. 122-26.

Qianlong (乾隆). "Yuanmingyuan houji (圆明园后记)." *Yuzhi Yuanmingyuan tuyong* (御制圆明园图咏). Ed. Ertai E (鄂尔泰). Unpunctuated. Tianjing: Shiyin shuwu, 1887.

Qianlong (乾隆). "Zaoshen Yude (澡身浴德)." *Yuanmingyuan Sishijing tuyong* (圆明园四十景图咏). Ed. Zhongguo Yuanmingyuan xuehui (中国圆明园学会). Beijing: Zhongguo jianzhu gongye chubanshe, 1985.

Qianlong (乾隆), "Zhengda Guangming (正大光明)." *Yuanmingyuan Sishijing tuyong* (圆明园四十景图咏). Ed. Zhongguo Yuanmingyuan xuehui (中国圆明园学会). Beijing: Zhongguo jianzhu gongye chubanshe, 1985.

Qian, Xuan (钱玄), ed. *Zhouli* (周礼). Changsha: Yuelu shushe, 2001.

Qing shi lu (清实录). 60 vols. Qing dynasty. Beijing: Zhonghua shuju, 1985.

Quanmingshi bianzuan weiyuanhui (全明诗编纂委员会), ed. *Quan Ming shi* (全明诗). Shanghai: Shanghai giji chubanshe, 1990.

Ramelli, Agostino. *Le diverse et artificiose machine*. 1588.

Rao, Ziran (饶自然). "Huizong shi'er ji (绘宗十二忌)." *Zhongguo gudai hualun leibian* (中国古代画论类编). 1957. Vol. 2. Ed. Jianhua Yu (俞剑华). Beijing: Renmin meishu chubanshe, 2000. 695-99.

Ricci, Matteo. *China in the Sixteenth Century: The Journals of Matthew Ricci 1583-1610*. Ed. Nicolas Trigault. Trans. Louis J. Gallagher. New York: Random House, 1953.

Ricci, Matteo. *The True Meaning of the Lord of Heaven: T'ien-chu shih-i*. English-Chinese version. Trans. Douglas Lancashire and Peter Hu Kuo-chen. Taibei: Institute Ricci, 1985.

Ricci, Matteo, and Guangqi Xu (徐光启). *Jihe yuanben* (几何原本). 1607. *Zhongguo kexue jishu dianji tonglu: shuxue juan: juan wu* (中国科学技术典籍通录: 数学卷: 卷五). Ed. Jiyu Ren (任继愈). Zhengzhou: Henan jiaoyu chubanshe, 1993.

Ricoeur, Paul. *History and Truth*. Trans. Charles A. Kelbley. Evanston: Northwestern UP, 1965.

Ripa, Matteo. *Memoirs of Father Ripa during Thirteen Years Residence at the Court of Peking*. London: John Murray, 1846.

Ronan, Charles E., ed. *East Meets West: The Jesuits in China, 1582-1773*. Chicago: Loyola UP, 1988.

Sartre, Jean-Paul. *Being and Nothingness*. New York: Washington Square, 1992.

Schulz, Alexander. *His Yang Lou. Untersuchunger zu den "Europäischen Bauten" des Kaisers Chien-lung*. Isny: Schmidt Schulz, 1966.

Serlio, Sebastiano. *Sebastiano Serlio on Architecture*. Vol. 1. Trans. Vaughan Hart and Peter Hicks. New Haven: Yale UP, 1996.

"Shandong Depingxian Zhixian Zhang Zhongzi deng chakan Yuanmingyuan fengshui qi (山东德平县知县张钟子等查看圆明园风水启)." *Yuanmingyuan Qingdai dang'an shiliao* (圆明园清代档案史料). Vol. 1. Ed. Zhongguo diyi lishi dang'an'guan (中国第一历史档案馆). Shanghai: Shanghai guji chubanshe, 1991.

Shen, Fu (沈复). *Chapters from a Floating Life: The Autobiography of a Chinese Artist*. Trans. Shirley M. Black. Translation of *Fu sheng liu ji* (浮生六记) (c. 1809). London: Oxford UP, 1960.

Shen, Kuo (沈括). "Mengxi bitan lun hua shanshui (梦溪笔谈论画山水)." *Zhongguo gudai hualun leibian* (中国古代画论类编). 1957. Vol. 1. Ed. Jianhua Yu (俞剑华). Beijing: Renmin meishu chubanshe, 2000. 625-66.

Shen, Zhou (沈周). "Ji xueyue zhi guan (记雪月之观)." *Xiugu qingyun: shanshui sanwen jingxuan* (秀谷清韵：山水散文精选). Ed. Jing Li (李静). Nanjing: Nanjing chubanshe, 1995.

Shen, Zhou (沈周). "Shitian lun hua shanshui (石田论画山水)." *Zhongguo gudai hualun leibian* (中国古代画论类编). 1957. Vol. 2. Ed. Jianhua Yu (俞剑华). Beijing: Renmin meishu chubanshe, 2000. 711.

Shen, Zicheng (沈子丞), ed. *Lidai lunhua mingzhu lubian* (历代论画名著录编). Beijing: Wenwu chubanshe, 1982.

Shepherd, J.C., and G.A Jellicoe. *Italian Gardens of the Renaissance*. New York: Charles Scriber's Sons, 1925.

Shice Yuanming, Changchun, Wanchunyuan yizhi xingshi tu (实测圆明，长春，万春园遗址形势图). A survey map of the Yuanming Yuan, drawn by Beiping Shizhengfu Gongwuju (北平市政府公务局). 1936. Stored in the National Library of China in Beijing.

Silvestre, Israel. *Chateau de Rue*. 1690.

Silvestre, Israel. *Le Chateau de Tanlay*. Bound pamphlet in the Dumbarton Oaks Collections, Washington, DC.

Sima, Guang (司马光). "Duleyuan ji (独乐园记)." *Zhongguo lidai minyuan ji xuanzhu* (中国历代名园记选注). Ed. Zhi Chen (陈植) and Gongchi Zhang (张公驰). Hefei: Anhui kexue jishu chubanshe, 1983. 24-28.

Sima, Qian (司马迁). *Shiji* (史记). Beijing: Jinghua chubanshe, 2002.

Sima, Xiangru (司马相如). "Shanglin fu (上林赋)." *Wen xuan* (文选). Ed. Tong Xiao (萧统). Shanghai: Shanghai guji chubanshe, 1998.

Sima, Xiangru (司马相如). "Zixu fu (子虚赋)." *Wen xuan* (文选). Ed. Tong Xiao (萧统). Shanghai: Shanghai guji chubanshe, 1998.

Song, Yu (宋玉). "Zhao hun (招魂)." *Chuci* (楚辞). Ed. Guangping Wu (吴广平). Changsha: Yuelu shushe, 2001.

Staunton, George. *An Authentic Account of An Embassy from the King of Great Britain to the Emperor of China*. London, 1797.

Stöer, Lorenz. *Geometria et perspectiva*. 1567. Frankfurt: Biermann + Boukes, 1972.

Su, Shi (苏轼). "Dongpo lunhua (东坡论画)." *Zhongguo gudai hualun leibian* (中国古代画论类编). 1957. Vol. 1. Ed. Jianhua Yu (俞剑华). Beijing: Renmin meishu chubanshe, 2000. 47-51.

Su, Shi (苏轼). "Meizhou Yuanjinglou ji (眉州远景楼记)." *Su Shi wenxue sanwen xuan* (苏轼文学散文选). Ed. Yuhua Sun (孙育华). Taiyuan: Shanxi gaoxiao lianhe chubanshe, 1991.

Sun, Xidan (孙希旦), ed. *Liji jijie* (礼记集解). 2 vols. Taipei: Wenshizhe chubanshe, 1990.

Sun, Xiaoli (孙小力), ed. *Zhichi shanlin: yuanlin yishu wencui* (咫尺山林：园林艺术文粹). Shanghai: Dongfang chubanshe, 1999.

Swiderski, Richard M. "The Dragon and the Straightedge, Part Three: Porcelains, Horses, and Ink Stones—The Ends of Acceptance." *Semiotica* 82.3/4 (1990): 211-68.

Sze, Mai-Mai, ed. *The Way of Chinese Painting: Its Ideas and Technique*. Trans. of *Jieziyuan huapu* (芥子园画谱). New York: Vintage Books, 1956.

Tang, Dai (唐岱). "Huishi fawei (绘事发微)." *Zhongguo gudai hualun leibian* (中国古代画论类编). 1957. Vol. 2. Ed. Jianhua Yu (俞剑华). Beijing: Renmin meishu chubanshe, 2000. 847-69.

Tang, Dai (唐岱) and Yuan Shen (沈源). Paintings of the Forty Scenes of the Yuanming Yuan. 1744. *Yuanming yuan: Le jardin de la clarté parfaite*. By Chebing Chiu. Paris: Les Editions de L'Imperimeur, 2000.

Tang, Mingbang (唐明邦), ed. *Zhouyi pingzhu* (周易评注). Beijing: Zhonghua shuju, 1997.

Tang, Xianzu (汤显祖). *Mudan ting* (牡丹亭). Beijing: Renmin wenxue chubanshe, 1998.

Tang, Yin (唐寅). "Liuru lun hua shanshui (六如论画山水)." *Zhongguo gudai hualun leibian* (中国古代画论类编). 1957. Vol. 2. Ed. Jianhua Yu (俞剑华). Beijing: Renmin meishu chubanshe, 2000. 712.

Tang, Zhiqi (唐志契). "Huishi weiyan (绘事微言)." *Zhongguo gudai hualun leibian* (中国古代画论类编). 1957. Vol. 2. Ed. Jianhua Yu (俞剑华). Beijing: Renmin meishu chubanshe, 2000. 735-53.

Tao, Yuanming (陶渊明). "Shi yun (时韵)." *Tao Yuanming quanji* (陶渊明全集). Shanghai: Shanghai guji chubanshe, 1998.

Tao, Yuanming (陶渊明). "Xianqing fu (闲情赋)." *Tao Yuanming quanji* (陶渊明全集). Shanghai: Shanghai guji chubanshe, 1998.

Teng, Gu (腾固). *Yuanmingyuan oushi gongdian canji* (圆明园欧式宫殿残迹). Shanghai: Shangwu yinshuguan, 1933.

Thiriez, Régine. *Barbarian Lens: Western Photographers of the Qianlong Emperor's European Palaces*. Amsterdam: Gordon and Breach, 1998.

Tong, Jun (童寯). "Beijing Chang-chun-yuan xiyang jianzhu (北京长春园西洋建筑)." *Yuanmingyuan: lishi, xianzhuang, lunzheng* (圆明园：历史，现状，论争). Vol. 1. Ed. Daocheng Wang (王道成). Beijing: Beijing chubanshe, 1999. 264-85.

Tötösy de Zepetnek, Steven. "The New Humanities: The Intercultural, the Comparative, and the Interdisciplinary." *Globalization and the Futures of Comparative Literature*. Ed. Jan M. Ziolkowski and Alfred J. López. Special Issue of *The Global South* 1.2 (2007): 45-68.

Tötösy de Zepetnek, Steven. "From Comparative Literature Today toward Comparative Cultural Studies." *Comparative Literature and Comparative Cultural Studies*. Ed. Steven Tötösy de Zepetnek. West Lafayette: Purdue UP, 2003. 235-67.

Vanderstappen, Harrie. "Chinese Art and the Jesuits in Peking." *East Meets West: The Jesuits in China, 1582-1773*. Ed. Charles E. Ronan. Chicago: Loyola UP, 1988.

Vignola, Giacomo Barrozzi da. *Le due regole della prospettiva pratica*. Roma, 1583.

Wang, Daocheng (王道成), ed. *Yuanmingyuan: lishi, xianzhuang, lunzheng* (圆明园：历史，现状，论争). 2 vols. Beijing: Beijing chubanshe, 1999.

Wang, Fuzhi (王夫之), ed. *Zhuangzi jie* (庄子解). 1681. Xianggang: Zhonghua shuju, 1989.

Wang, Jiamo (王嘉谟). "Haidian wang Xishan (海淀望西山)." *Dijing jingwu lüe* (帝京景物略). By Dong Liu (刘侗) and Yizheng Yu (于奕正). Ed. Xiaoli Sun (孙小力). Shanghai: Shanghai guji chubanshe, 2001.

Wang, Jian (王鉴). "Ranxiang'an ba hua (染香庵跋画)." *Lidai lunhua mingzhu lubian* (历代论画名著录编). Ed. Zicheng Shen (沈子丞). Beijing: Wenwu chubanshe, 1982.

Wang, Kaiyun (王闿运). "Yuanmingyuan ci (圆明园词)." *Yuanmingyuan: lishi, xianzhuang, lunzheng (*圆明园：历史，现状，论争). Vol. 2. Ed. Daocheng Wang (王道成). Beijing: Beijing chubanshe, 1999. 1124-29.

Wang, Lu (王路). *Huashi zuo bian* (花史左编). 1615. *Xuxiu Siku quanshu* (续修四库全书). Vol. 1117. Ed. Xuxiu siku quanshu bianzhuan weiyuanhui (续修四库全书编纂委员会). Shanghai: Shanghai guji chubanshe, 1995.

Wang, Mian (王冕). "Chuan shang (船上)." *Quan Ming shi* (全明诗). Ed. Quanmingshi bianzuan weiyuanhui (全明诗编纂委员会). Shanghai: Shanghai giji chubanshe, 1990.

Wang, Mian (王冕). "Ci Shentuzi di yun (次申屠子迪韵)." *Quan Ming shi* (全明诗). Ed. Quanmingshi bianzuan weiyuanhui (全明诗编纂委员会). Shanghai: Shanghai giji chubanshe, 1990.

Wang, Mian (王冕). "Deng Zhufeng (登竺峰)." *Quan Ming shi* (全明诗). Ed. Quanmingshi bianzuan weiyuanhui (全明诗编纂委员会). Shanghai: Shanghai giji chubanshe, 1990.

Wang, Mian (王冕). "Dui jing (对景)." *Quan Ming shi* (全明诗). Ed. Quanmingshi bianzuan weiyuanhui (全明诗编纂委员会). Shanghai: Shanghai giji chubanshe, 1990.

Wang, Qi (王圻), ed. *San cai tu hui* (三才图汇). 1607. Taibei: Chengwen chubanshe, 1974.

Wang, Shizhen (王世贞). "Yiyuan [?]yan lunhua (艺苑[?]言论画)." *Zhongguo gudai hualun leibian* (中国古代画论类编). 1957. Vol. 1. Ed. Jianhua Yu (俞剑华). Beijing: Renmin meishu chubanshe, 2000. 115-17.

Wang, Wei (王维). "Fengji Wei Taishou zhi (奉寄韦太守陟)." *Wang Wei quanji* (王维全集). Ed. Zhongfu Cao (曹中孚). Shanghai: Shanghai guji chubanshe, 1997.

Wang, Wei (王维). "Huaxue mijue (画学秘诀)." *Wang Wei quanji* (王维全集). Ed. Zhongfu Cao (曹中孚). Shanghai: Shanghai guji chubanshe, 1997.

Wang, Wei (王维). "Lu chai (鹿柴)." *Wang Wei quanji* (王维全集). Ed. Zhongfu Cao (曹中孚). Shanghai: Shanghai guji chubanshe, 1997.

Wang, Wei (王维). "Shanshui lun (山水论)." *Lidai lunhua mingzhu lubian* (历代论画名著录编). Ed. Zicheng Shen (沈子丞). Beijing: Wenwu chubanshe, 1982.

Wang, Wenkao (王文考). "Lulingguang-dian fu yishou (鲁灵光殿赋一首)." *Wenxuan quanyi* (文选全译). Ed. Qicheng Zhang (张启成). Guiyang: Guizhou renmin chubanshe, 1994.

Wang, Yuanqi (王原祈). "Yuchuang manbi (雨窗漫笔)." *Zhongguo gudai hualun leibian* (中国古代画论类编). 1957. Vol. 1. Ed. Jianhua Yu (俞剑华). Beijing: Renmin meishu chubanshe, 2000. 169-73.

Wang, Yuanzhi (王元之). "Shuzi quan (庶子泉)." *Song shi chao* (宋诗钞). Ed. Zhizhen Wu (吴之振). Beijing: Zhonghua shuju, 1996.

Wang, Yuanzhi (王元之). "Yuebolou yonghuai (月波楼詠怀)." *Song shi chao* (宋诗钞). Ed. Zhizhen Wu (吴之振). Beijing: Zhonghua shuju, 1996.

Wang, Zhou (王周). "Zaochun Xiyuan (早春西园)." *Quan Wudai shi* (全五代诗). Ed. Diaoyuan Li (李调元). Chengdu: Bashu shudian, 1991.

Wei, Jianxun (魏鉴勋), ed. *Yongzheng shiwen zhujie* (雍正诗文注解). Shenyang: Liaoning guji chubanshe, 1996.

Wei, Yingwu (韦应物). "Jingshe naliang (精舍纳凉)." *Quan Tang shi* (全唐诗). 25 vols. Beijing: Zhonghua shuju, 1985.

Weiss, Allen S. *Mirrors of Infinity: The French Formal Garden and Seventeenth-Century Metaphysics*. New York: Princeton Architectural Press, 1995.

Wen, Zhengming (文征明). "Hengshan lun hua shanshui (衡山论画山水)." *Zhongguo gudai hualun leibian* (中国古代画论类编). 1957. Vol. 2. Ed. Jianhua Yu (俞剑华). Beijing: Renmin meishu chubanshe, 2000. 713-14.

Wen, Zhengming (文征明). "Wangshi Zhuozhengyuan ji (王氏拙政园记)." *Zhongguo lidai minyuan ji xuanzhu* (中国历代名园记选注). Ed. Zhi Chen (陈植) and Gongchi Zhang (张公驰). Hefei: Anhui kexue jishu chubanshe, 1983. 98-104.

Whitfield, Roderick, Susan Whitfield, and Neville Agnew, eds. *Cave Temple of Mogao: Art and History on the Silk Road*. Los Angeles: The Getty Conservation Institute, 2000.

Wu, Xin. "Yuelu Academy: Landscape and Gardens of Neo-Confucian Pedagogy." *Studies in the History of Gardens and Designed Landscapes* 25.3 (2005): 156-90.

Wu, Zhenyu (吴振棫). "Yuanmingyuan, Changchunyuan, Qichunyuan (圆明园, 长春园, 绮春园)." *Yuanmingyuan: lishi, xianzhuang, lunzheng* (圆明园：历史, 现状，论争). Vol. 2. Ed. Daocheng Wang (王道成). Beijing: Beijing chubanshe, 1999. 876-81.

Wu, Zhizhen (吴之振), ed. *Song shi chao* (宋诗钞). Beijing: Zhonghua shuju, 1996.

Xiao, Tong (萧统), ed. *Wen xuan* (文选). Shanghai: Shanghai guji chubanshe, 1998.

Xie, Haofan (谢浩范), ed. *Guanzi quanyi* (管子全译). Guiyang: Guizhou renmin chubanshe, 1996.

Xie, Lingyun (谢灵运). "Nanlou zhong wang suo chi ke (南楼中望所迟客)." *Tao Yuanming quanji: Fu Xie Lingyun ji* (陶渊明全集: 附谢灵运集). Ed. Minggang Cao (曹明纲). Shanghai: Shanghai guji chubanshe, 1998.

Xie, Lingyun (谢灵运). "Ni Weitaizi ye zhong jishi ba shou bing xu: Weitaizi (拟魏太子邺中集诗八首并序: 魏太子)." *Tao Yuanming quanji: Fu Xie Lingyun ji* (陶渊明全集: 附谢灵运集). Ed. Minggang Cao (曹明纲). Shanghai: Shanghai guji chubanshe, 1998.

Xie, Lingyun (谢灵运). "Shanju fu (山居赋)." *Zhichi shanlin: yuanlin yishu wencui* (咫尺山林：园林艺术文粹). Ed. Xiaoli Sun (孙小力). Shanghai: Dongfang chubanshe, 1999. 13-17.

Xiong, Sanba (熊三拔) (Sabbathinus de Ursis) and Guangqi Xu (徐光启). *Taixi shuifa* (泰西水法). 1612. In *Siku quanshu zhenben congshu* (四库全书珍本丛书). Part 12. Vol. 50. Ed. Yunwu Wang (王云五). Taibei: Shangwu yinshuguan, 1969.

Xu, Gan (徐干). "Tuanshan fu (团扇赋)." *Quan Han fu* (全汉赋). Ed. Zhengang Fei (费振刚). Beijing: Beijing daxue chubanshe, 1993.

Xu, Hongzu (徐宏祖). *Xu Xiake youji* (徐霞客游记). Ed. Wenjiang Ding (丁文江). Beijing: Shangwu yinshuguan, 1986.

Xu, Kuangyi (许匡一), ed. *Huainanzi quanyi* (淮南子全译). Guiyang: Guizhou renmin chubanshe, 1993.

Xu, Qin (徐沁). "Minghualu lun hua gongshi shanshui (明画录论画宫室山水)." *Zhongguo gudai hualun leibian* (中国古代画论类编). 1957. Vol. 2. Ed. Jianhua Yu (俞剑华). Beijing: Renmin meishu chubanshe, 2000. 804-05.

Works Cited

Xu, Xuan (徐铉). "Fenghe You-sheng-pu-she Xiting gaowo zuo (奉和右省仆射西亭高卧作)." *Song shi chao* (宋诗钞). Ed. Zhizhen Wu (吴之振). Beijing: Zhonghua shuju, 1996.

Yan, Zhitui (颜之推). "Yanshi jiaxun lunhua 颜氏家训论画." *Zhongguo gudai hualun leibian* (中国古代画论类编). 1957. Vol. 1. Ed. Jianhua Yu (俞剑华). Beijing: Renmin meishu chubanshe, 2000. 15.

Yang, Hongxun (杨鸿勋). "Luelun Yuanmingyuan zhong biaotiyuan de bianti chuangzuo (略论圆明园中标题园的变体创作)." *Yuanmingyuan: lishi, xianzhuang, lunzheng (*圆明园：历史，现状，论争*)*. Vol. 1. Ed. Daocheng Wang (王道成). Beijing: Beijing chubanshe, 1999. 191-97.

Yang, Shen (杨慎). "Hua pin (画品)." *Lidai lunhua mingzhu lubian* (历代论画名著录编). Ed. Zicheng Shen (沈子丞). Beijing: Wenwu chubanshe, 1982.

Yang, Xuanzhi (杨炫之). *Luoyang qielan ji* (洛阳伽兰记). Ed. Jiegen Han (韩结根). Ji'nan: Shandong youyi chubanshe, 2001.

Yao, Yuanzhi (姚元之). *Zhuyeting zaji* (竹叶亭杂记). Beijing: Zhonghua shuju, 1997.

Ye, Xianggao (叶向高). "Guo Mi Zhongzhao Shaoyuan (过米仲诏勺园)." *Dijing jingwu lüe* (帝京景物略). By Dong Liu (刘侗) and Yizheng Yu (于奕正). Ed. Xiaoli Sun (孙小力). Shanghai: Shanghai guji chubanshe, 2001.

Yi, Lantai (伊兰泰). Twenty copperplates of the Western garden of the Yuanming Yuan. 1786. *Palais, pavillons et jardins construits par Giuseppe Castiglione: dans le domaine impérial du Yuan Ming Yuan au Palais d'Été de Pékin: 20 planches gravées, de 1783 a 1786*. Paris: Jardin de Flore, 1977. A copy in the Dumbarton Oaks Collections, Washington, DC.

Yi, Xin (奕訢), ed. *Qing liuchao yuzhi shiwen ji* (清六朝御制诗文集). 1876.

Yin, Zhenhuan (殷振环). *Boshu Laozi shixi* (帛书老子释析). Guiyang: Guizhou renmin chubanshe, 1995.

Yongzheng (雍正). "Changchunyuan shaoyaohua kai zuo (畅春园芍药花开作)." *Yongzheng shiwen zhujie* (雍正诗文注解). Ed. Jianxun Wei (魏鉴勋). Shenyang: Liaoning guji chubanshe, 1996.

Yongzheng (雍正). "Chi bian (池边)." *Yongzheng shiwen zhujie* (雍正诗文注解). Ed. Jianxun Wei (魏鉴勋). Shenyang: Liaoning guji chubanshe, 1996.

Yongzheng (雍正). "Huanxiu Shanfang duiyue (环秀山房对月)." *Yongzheng shiwen zhujie* (雍正诗文注解). Ed. Jianxun Wei (魏鉴勋). Shenyang: Liaoning guji chubanshe, 1996.

Yongzheng (雍正). "Huixinchu shibi (会心处试笔)." *Yongzheng shiwen zhujie* (雍正诗文注解). Ed. Jianxun Wei (魏鉴勋). Shenyang: Liaoning guji chubanshe, 1996.

Yongzheng (雍正). "Jinyu chi (金鱼池)." *Yongzheng shiwen zhujie* (雍正诗文注解). Ed. Jianxun Wei (魏鉴勋). Shenyang: Liaoning guji chubanshe, 1996.

Yongzheng (雍正). "Jingyan jiangyi (经筵讲义)." *Yongzheng shiwen zhujie* (雍正诗文注解). Ed. Jianxun Wei (魏鉴勋). Shenyang: Liaoning guji chubanshe, 1996. 266-69.

Yongzheng (雍正). "Miaogao Tang (妙高堂)." *Yongzheng shiwen zhujie* (雍正诗文注解). Ed. Jianxun Wei (魏鉴勋). Shenyang: Liaoning guji chubanshe, 1996.

Yongzheng (雍正). "Mudan Tai (牡丹台)." *Yongzheng shiwen zhujie* (雍正诗文注解). Ed. Jianxun Wei (魏鉴勋). Shenyang: Liaoning guji chubanshe, 1996.

Yongzheng (雍正). "Penglaizhou yonggu (蓬莱洲咏古)." *Yongzheng shiwen zhujie* (雍正诗文注解). Ed. Jianxun Wei (魏鉴勋). Shenyang: Liaoning guji chubanshe, 1996.

Yongzheng (雍正). "Pinghu Qiuyue (平湖秋月)." *Yongzheng shiwen zhujie* (雍正诗文注解). Ed. Jianxun Wei (魏鉴勋). Shenyang: Liaoning guji chubanshe, 1996.

Yongzheng (雍正). "Qiuri deng Langyin'ge yumu (秋日登朗吟阁寓目)." *Yongzheng shiwen zhujie* (雍正诗文注解). Ed. Jianxun Wei (魏鉴勋). Shenyang: Liaoning guji chubanshe, 1996.

Yongzheng (雍正). "Shenliu dushu Tang (深柳读书堂)." *Yongzheng shiwen zhujie* (雍正诗文注解). Ed. Jianxun Wei (魏鉴勋). Shenyang: Liaoning guji chubanshe, 1996.

Yongzheng (雍正). "Shizong xianhuangdi yuzhi Yuanmingyuan ji (世宗宪皇帝御制圆明园记)." 1725. *Yuzhi Yuanmingyuan tuyong* (御制圆明园图咏). Ed. Ertai E (鄂尔泰). Unpunctuated. Tianjing: Shiyin shuwu, 1887.

Yongzheng (雍正). "Taohuawu jijing (桃花坞即景)." *Yongzheng shiwen zhujie* (雍正诗文注解). Ed. Jianxun Wei (魏鉴勋). Shenyang: Liaoning guji chubanshe, 1996.

Yongzheng (雍正). "Xiari Qinzhengdian guan xinyue zuo (夏日勤政殿观新月作)." *Yongzheng shiwen zhujie* (雍正诗文注解). Ed. Jianxun Wei (魏鉴勋). Shenyang: Liaoning guji chubanshe, 1996.

Yongzheng (雍正). "Xing li lun (性理论)." *Yongzheng shiwen zhujie* (雍正诗文注解). Ed. Jianxun Wei (魏鉴勋). Shenyang: Liaoning guji chubanshe, 1996. 228-29.

Yongzheng (雍正). "Yongdi shiji xu (雍邸诗集序)." *Yongzheng shiwen zhujie* (雍正诗文注解). Ed. Jianxun Wei (魏鉴勋). Shenyang: Liaoning guji chubanshe, 1996. 235-36.

Yongzheng (雍正). "Yong ziming zhong (咏自鸣钟)." *Yongzheng shiwen zhujie* (雍正诗文注解). Ed. Jianxun Wei (魏鉴勋). Shenyang: Liaoning guji chubanshe, 1996.

Yongzheng (雍正). "Yuhou duiyue oucheng (雨后对月偶成)." *Yongzheng shiwen zhujie* (雍正诗文注解). Ed. Jianxun Wei (魏鉴勋). Shenyang: Liaoning guji chubanshe, 1996.

Yongzheng (雍正). "Yuhou Jiuzhou Qingyan wang Xishan (雨后九州清宴望西山)." *Yongzheng shiwen zhujie* (雍正诗文注解). Ed. Jianxun Wei (魏鉴勋). Shenyang: Liaoning guji chubanshe, 1996.

Yongzheng (雍正). "Yuexia xianbu (月下闲步)." *Yongzheng shiwen zhujie* (雍正诗文注解). Ed. Jianxun Wei (魏鉴勋). Shenyang: Liaoning guji chubanshe, 1996.

Yongzheng (雍正). "Yuexin ji xu 悦心集序." *Yongzheng shiwen zhujie* (雍正诗文注解). Ed. Jianxun Wei (魏鉴勋). Shenyang: Liaoning guji chubanshe, 1996. 258-59.

Yongzheng (雍正). "Zhongqiu (中秋)." *Yongzheng shiwen zhujie* (雍正诗文注解). Ed. Jianxun Wei (魏鉴勋). Shenyang: Liaoning guji chubanshe, 1996.

Yongzheng (雍正). "Ziming zhong (自鸣钟)." *Yongzheng shiwen zhujie* (雍正诗文注解). Ed. Jianxun Wei (魏鉴勋). Shenyang: Liaoning guji chubanshe, 1996.

Yu, Jianhua (俞剑华), ed. *Zhongguo gudai hualun leibian* (中国古代画论类编). 1957. 2 vols. Beijing: Renmin meishu chubanshe, 2000.

Yu, Minzhong (于敏中), ed. *Rixia jiuwen kao* (日下旧闻考). 4 vols. Beijing: Beijing guji chubanshe, 2001.

Yuan, Mei (袁枚). "Shuiyuan ji 随园记." *Zhongguo lidai minyuan ji xuanzhu* (中国历代名园记选注). Ed. Zhi Chen (陈植) and Gongchi Zhang (张公驰). Hefei: Anhui kexue jishu chubanshe, 1983. 359-61.

Yuan, Qi (袁起), "Shuiyuan tushuo (随园图说)." *Zhongguo lidai minyuan ji xuanzhu* (中国历代名园记选注). Ed. Zhi Chen (陈植) and Gongchi Zhang (张公驰). Hefei: Anhui kexue jishu chubanshe, 1983. 362-70.

Yuanmingyuan damuzuo dingli (圆明园大木作定例). Qing transcript. Copy in the Library of Congress, Washington, DC.

Zangheri, Luigi. *Pratolino: il giarddino delle meraviglie*. Firenze: Edizioni Connelli, 1987.

Zaobanchu Huojiku ge zuocheng zuohuoji qingdang (造办处活计库各作成作活计清档). 1747. Copy in The First Historical Archive of China, Beijing.

Zhang, Cheng'an (张承安), ed. *Zhongguo yuanlin yishu cidian* (中国园林艺术辞典). Wuhan: Hubei renming chubanshe, 1994.

Zhang, Dainian (张岱年), ed. *Kongzi da cidian* (孔子大辞典). Shanghai: Shanghai cishu chubanshe, 1993.

Zhang, Enyin (张恩荫). "'Sanshan wuyuan' bianxi ('三山五园'辩析)." *Jinghua yuanlin congkao* (京华园林丛考). Ed. Beijingshi yuanlinju (北京市园林局). Beijing: Beijing kexue jishu chubanshe, 1996.

Zhang, Enyin (张恩荫). *Yuanmingyuan bianqian shi tanwei* (圆明园变迁史探微). Beijing: Beijing tiyu chubanshe, 1993.

Zhang, Enyin (张恩荫). *Yuanmingyuan daguan hua shengshuai* (圆明园大观话胜衰). Beijing: Zijincheng chubanshe, 1998.

Zhang, Enyin (张恩荫). "Zaixi 'sanshan wuyuan' (再析'三山五园')." *Jinghua yuanlin congkao* (京华园林丛考). Ed. Beijingshi yuanlinju (北京市园林局). Beijing: Beijing kexue jishu chubanshe, 1996.

Zhang, Heng (张衡). "Xijing fu (西京赋)." *Wen xuan* (文选). Ed. Tong Xiao (萧统). Shanghai: Shanghai guji chubanshe, 1998.

Zhang, Jingyun (张景运). *Qiuping xinyu* (秋坪新语). 1792(?).

Zhang, Qicheng (张启成), ed. *Wenxuan quanyi* (文选全译). Guiyang: Guizhou renmin chubanshe, 1994.

Zhang, Yanyuan (张彦远). "Lidai minghua ji xulun (历代名画记叙论)." *Zhongguo gudai hualun leibian* (中国古代画论类编). 1957. Vol. 1. Ed. Jianhua Yu (俞剑华). Beijing: Renmin meishu chubanshe, 2000. 27-40.

Zhang, Zhongge (张仲葛), ed. "Yuanmingyuan bian'e (圆明园匾额)." *Yuanmingyuan xueshu lunwen ji* (圆明园学术论文集). Vol. 2. Ed. Zhongguo Yuanmingyuan xuehui (中国圆明园学会). Beijing: Zhongguo jianzhu gongye chubanshe, 1983. 47-53.

Zhao, Erzhuan (赵尔巽), ed. *Qing shi gao* (清史稿). Beijing: Zhonghua shuju, 1996.

Zhao, Ji (赵佶) (Huizong [徽宗]). "Genyue ji (艮岳记)." *Zhichi shanlin: yuanlin yishu wencui* (咫尺山林：园林艺术文粹). Ed. Xiaoli Sun (孙小力). Shanghai: Dongfang chubanshe, 1999. 63-68.

Zhao, Xinghua (赵兴华). *Beijing yuanlin shihua* (北京园林史话). Beijing: Zhongguo yuanlin chubanshe, 2000.

Zheng, Ji (郑绩). "Menghuanju huaxue jianming lun shanshui (梦幻居画学简明论山水)." *Zhongguo gudai hualun leibian* (中国古代画论类编). 1957. Vol. 2. Ed. Jianhua Yu (俞剑华). Beijing: Renmin meishu chubanshe, 2000. 949-80.

Zheng, Xuan (郑玄), ed. *Daxue, Zhongyong* (大学, 中庸). Shanghai: Shanghai guji chubanshe, 2003.

Zhongguo diyi lishi dang'an'guan (中国第一历史档案馆), ed. *Yuanmingyuan Qingdai dang'an shiliao* (圆明园清代档案史料). 2 vols. Shanghai: Shanghai guji chubanshe, 1991.

Zhongguo Yuanmingyuan xuehui (中国圆明园学会), ed. *Yuanmingyuan Sishijing tuyong* (圆明园四十景图咏). Beijing: Zhongguo jianzhu gongye chubanshe, 1985.

Zhongguo Yuanmingyuan xuehui (中国圆明园学会), ed. *Yuanmingyuan xueshu lunwen ji* (圆明园学术论文集). 5 vols. Beijing: Zhongguo jianzhu gongye chubanshe, 1981-1992.

Zhongwen da cidian (中文大辞典). Taibei: Zhonghua xueshuyuan, 1982.

Zhoubi suanjing (周髀算经). In *Siku quanshu zhenben congshu* (四库全书珍本丛书). Ed. Yunwu Wang (王云五). Part 11. Vol. 115. Taibei: Shangwu yinshuguan, 1969.

Zhou, Dunyi (周敦颐). *Taiji tushuo, tong shu, (Shao Yong) guan wu pian* (太极图说, 通书, [邵雍] 观物篇). Shanghai: Shanghai guji chubanshe, 1992.

Zhou, Shengchun (周生春), ed. *Baihua Laozi* (白话老子). Xi'an: Sanqin chubanshe, 1994.

Zhou, Weiquan (周维全). "Yuanmingyuan de xingjian jiqi zaoyuan yishu qiantan (圆明园的兴建及其造园艺术浅谈)." *Yuanmingyuan: lishi, xianzhuang, lunzheng* (圆明园：历史, 现状, 论争). Vol. 1. Ed. Daocheng Wang (王道成). Beijing: Beijing chubanshe, 1999. 125-50.

Zhou, Weiquan (周维全). *Zhongguo gudian yuanlin shi* (中国古典园林史). Beijing: Tsinghua daxue chubanshe, 1999.

Zhu, Boxiong (朱伯雄) and Chengzhang Cao (曹成章), eds. *Zhongguo shuhua mingjia jingpin dadian* (中国书画名家精品大典). 4 vols. Hangzhou: Zhejiang jiaoyu chubanshe, 1997.

Zhu, Jiajin (朱家溍) and Yanqin Li (李艳琴), eds. "Qing wuchao yuzhiji zhong de Yuanmingyuan shi [xu er] (清五朝御制集中的圆明园诗[续二])." *Yuanmingyuan xueshu lunwen ji* (圆明园学术论文集). Vol. 4. Ed. Zhongguo Yuanmingyuan xuehui (中国圆明园学会). Beijing: Zhongguo jianzhu gongye chubanshe, 1985. 62-100.

Zhu, Jingxuan (朱景玄). "Tangchao minghua lu xu (唐朝名画录序)." *Zhongguo gudai hualun leibian* (中国古代画论类编). 1957. Vol. 1. Ed. Jianhua Yu (俞剑华). Beijing: Renmin meishu chubanshe, 2000. 22-24.

Zhu, Sheng (朱升). "Ciyun Wang Bogong zongguan yilan (次韵汪伯恭总管一览)." *Quan Ming shi* (全明诗). Ed. Quanmingshi bianzuan weiyuanhui (全明诗编纂委员会). Shanghai: Shanghai giji chubanshe, 1990.

Zong, Bing (宗炳). "Hua shanshui xu (画山水序)." *Lidai lunhua mingzhu lubian* (历代论画名著录编). Ed. Zicheng Shen (沈子丞). Beijing: Wenwu chubanshe, 1982.

Zong, Pu (宗璞). "Feixu zai zhaohuan (废墟在召唤)." *Yuanmingyuan ziliao ji* (圆明园资料集). Ed. Mu Shu (舒牧). Beijing: Shumu wenxian chubanshe, 1984.

Zou, Diguang (邹迪光). "Yugonggu cheng (愚公谷乘)." *Zhongguo lidai minyuan ji xuanzhu* (中国历代名园记选注). Ed. Zhi Chen (陈植) and Gongchi Zhang (张公驰). Hefei: Anhui kexue jishu chubanshe, 1983. 187-96.

Zou, Hui. Appendix: Books on Architecture and Gardens in the Jesuit Libraries in Beijing. "The *jing* of a Perspective Garden." *Studies in the History of Gardens and Designed Landscapes* 22.4 (2002): 317-20.

Zou, Hui. "Jesuit Perspective in China." *Architectura. Zeitschrift für Geschichte der Baukunst / Journal of the History of Architecture* 31.2 (2001): 145-68.

Zou, Hui. "The *jing* of a Perspective Garden." *Studies in the History of Gardens and Designed Landscapes* 22.4 (2002): 293-326.

Zou, Hui. "*Jing*: A Phenomenological Reflection of Chinese Landscape and *Qing*." *Journal of Chinese Philosophy* 35.2 (2008): 353-68.

Zuan zu ying hua (纂组英华). Published under the order of The Manchoukuo National Museum (满洲国立博物馆藏版). 2 vols. Tokyo: Zauho, 1935.

Appendix

1

Kangxi's record of the Garden of Uninhibited Spring

The town of Shallow Lakes (Haidian) is situated twelve miles away from the Xizhi Gate of the capital. There are lakes to the north and to the south. Springs gush out from the ground at the Village of Ten Thousand Springs (Wanquan Zhuang) in the south, flow speedily and melodiously, and converge into the Red-Hill Lake in the north. The lake is so vast that its surface can be counted in one hundred *qing*. Lush wilderness is juxtaposed with flat agricultural fields, and clear waves with distant hills. Their colors intermingle like gorgeous embroideries. What a god-blessed scenic place! Since I inherited the throne, day and night administration has prevented me from having any leisure. A long period of fatigue and overwork has gradually made me sick. Getting free on some occasions, I traveled here for a rest. Tasting the spring water and finding it sweet, I looked around and appreciated the place. As cool breezes slowly rose, my low spirit and illness suddenly disappeared. No wonder a distant imperial relative of the Ming dynasty, Wei Li, the Marquis of Wuqing, built a villa here in accordance with the pleasant topography. The landscape of that time, as magnificent as the Weiqu landscape, can still be distinctly perceived. After the villa collapsed and was abandoned, the ruined area still has a circumference of ten miles. Although the garden has disintegrated into scattered remains with the passing of time, the original conditions can still be traced. I look at a building with its eaves that seem to fly in the air and stroll along a winding balustrade by the water. Ancient trees and dark green vines are still alive.

I thus called upon the officials of imperial households to make moderate adjustments, transforming higher places into hills and lower places into pools. The natural lay of the topography was appraised and the original stones and bricks were reused. Better use and value were achieved without recruiting much labor. The humble buildings and garden are sufficient for my contemplating and resting. Virtuous thrift is cherished forever, and sumptuous carvings avoided. Although only sixty or seventy percent of the old pavilions, terraces, hillocks, gullies, forests, trees, springs and rocks of Li's garden survive, the beauty of expansive ripples and the momentum of watercourses are as attractive as before.

Appendix

Layer-upon-layer hillocks reveal distant water shores, and morning haze is followed by evening mists. Fragrant flowers bloom in all seasons, and rare birds sing among the people. When crops yield a rich harvest, and the fields are fragrant with sweet smells, I can engage with beautiful scenes coming from all directions, and my heart projects into the distance. But sometimes, when crops are ruined and sun and rain come at a wrong time, I stand on a footpath in the fields feeling compassion for the farmers, or open the window to check the ditches, which irrigate the fields. I look for signs of rain with ardent hopes and pray anxiously to the sky. It seems the whole country can be seen from my window.

On a good day in spring or autumn when the sky is clear and refreshing, or in the humid high summer when sunlight is hot and dazzling, I come here, taking a short break from public affairs, to improve and care about my health and to roam around. This makes me feel younger and quieter, and does away with my concerns and the heat; it also puts my heart at ease and makes my complexion healthy. I sway back and forth, enjoying a good time and the joy of heaven. The hall for holding audience is bright and high, and the winding chamber with deep eaves stores ancient books. The thatched cottages are covered with thistles without any decoration. Wherever necessary, a bridge or a boat is used for crossing the water, a hedge for dividing places, and a wall for enclosing a place. Things are as simple and natural as that.

After the garden was built, it was named Uninhibited Spring (Changchun), but not because it particularly fitted springtime. In the calendars of the three successive dynasties Xia, Shang, and Zhou, the Zhou dynasty took the *zi* character as the spring of heaven; the Shang dynasty took the *chou* character as the spring of earth, and the Xia dynasty took the *yin* character as the spring of human being. The classic book *Yijing* says that when the *qian*, the primary one, unifies the world, all the four virtues become the primary one and all four seasons are spring. Previous emperors relied upon this principle to raise things at the right time, to let all people have their appropriate places and all animals live according to their nature. Under the heaven there is plenty of happiness and brightness; winds blow together from eight directions and the six movements, the six *qi*, reach everywhere. This is why I named the garden Uninhibited Spring.

The Qin dynasty had the Efang Palaces; the Han dynasty had the Shanglin Park; the Tang dynasty had the beautiful landscapes of the Embroidered Mountain Ranges (Xiu Ling); the Song dynasty had the Genyue garden. Their luxurious building decorations and huge areas including hills and valleys are certainly beyond my means and wish. I dare not imitate the ancients and compete with models from the past; I am rather satisfied with humble buildings, and I avoid spending money for sumptuous terraces. I only wish to act according to proper time and help the flow of things, support and wait upon my mother, and stay in good health. I long for peace of all creatures and wish for the harmony of the world. I think of each person and each thing all the time. How could my affection for them stop? I therefore write the record and accompany it with a poem:

The Xia people in the past,
Were strictly thrifty and lived in humble palaces.
King Wen of Zhou is acclaimed,
For his not hastening for material gains.
If ancient instructions are examined,
These two should be respected and admired.
Inscribing them as my admonition,
I practice them myself day and night.

The establishment of my residence,
Is based on the previous dynasty.
Cliffside lodges with rosy clouds,
Eaves project into blue mists.
I construct and maintain it,
So as not to let it be ruined.
There are hot springs,
Deep and diffuse here.
I travel to the western suburb,
Set up colorful banners of camp.
I draw sweet waters from there,
Carefully devise this plan.

The water is like a mirror of crystal,
Meandering as a fragrant stream.
I pace up and down by the river,
Roam here and stroll there.
Height comes from the hills,
Depth emerges from the valleys.
I consult there and construct here,
But would not say it is to transform.
Pine galleries and thatched halls,
Are suitable only to myself.
There are some plain carvings,
I feel sorry about them.

Construction began at an auspicious time,
The garden was built within a few days.
Though not specifically for strolling and enjoying,
I am delighted in this construction.
Respecting and serving my mother,
How could I live high and bright?
Gazing leisurely and looking over,
I only wish to entertain my temperament.

Lots of books and classics,
All are stored in a continuous belvedere.
Only this big veranda,
Can be compared to red embroidered collars.
Flourishing agrarian fields,
Are cultivated regularly.

Without borrowing human labor,
There are vague cloudy gullies.
Boat moves like a water bird,
Bridge spans like a rainbow.
Sailing or crossing,
I stroll around free of care.
Literature or martial arts,
I practice at different times.

I retreat to reflect upon my administration,
No mistake is to be allowed.
It is said that the virtue of a gentleman,
Cannot be but kindheartedness.
Take the primary one as the principle for administration,
It is as the springtime of seasons.
I wish all things,
Return to their plainness and purity.
The meaning of Uninhibited Spring,
Is thus proclaimed here for my officials.

Note: This translation is based on Kangxi's punctuated text "Shengzu renhuangdi yu-zhi Changchunyuan ji." The Garden of Uninhibited Spring (Changchun Yuan) was the first Qing imperial garden built in the northwestern suburb of Beijing. Kangxi died in this garden in 1722. The Xizhi Gate was a northwestern gate of Beijing. The Town of Shallow Lakes was further northwest of the gate and ten miles northwest of the Sorghum Bridge (Y. Jiang, 69; Dong and Yu 320). The Village of Ten Thousand Springs was southwest of the Town of Shallow Lakes. Wei Li's villa was called Garden of Delicate Brilliance (Qinghua Yuan). His daughter was the mother of the Ming emperor, Yijun Zhu of the Wanli reign (1573-1620). The Weiqu was in the southern suburb of the Tang capital, Chang'an, and was well known for its pretty landscapes. Kangxi's garden was designed by Tao Ye, a court painter from the Jiangnan region. The construction was supervised by Ran Zhang, a rockery art craftsman from Jiangnan. The Garden of Uninhibited Spring was smaller than the Garden of Delicate Brilliance. The water of the garden came from the River of Ten Thousand Springs in the south and flew into the future Yuanming Yuan in the north. There were three flower dikes at the middle of the garden, that is, the lilac, orchid, and peach dikes. Kangxi sometimes invited his officials for appreciating flowers together. At the southwestern corner of the garden, there were vegetable plots and rice fields. It was Kangxi that first introduced an audience hall into an imperial garden, and this was imitated by later emperors.

The garden should have been built by 1690, because it was in this year that the first general manager of the garden was appointed (E. Zhao). The Chinese calendar uses the combinations of ten characters of *tian'gan* and twelve characters of *dizhi* to mark dates. The *zi*, *chou*, and *yin* are, respectively, the first, second, and third characters of *dizhi*. Signifying heaven, the *qian* character marks one of the eight divinatory symbols of the cosmological graph, eight trigrams. The "four virtues" are *yuan*, *heng*, *li*, and *zhen*, originating from the divinatory symbol of *qian*. The *yuan* means the origin of the world; the *heng*, the growth of the world; the *li*, the maturity of the world; the *zhen*, the accomplishment of the world (M. Tang 1). According to the chapter "Youshi" of *Lüshi chunqiu* (*Mister Lü's Spring and Autumn Annals*), the "winds of eight directions" are the *yan* wind in northeast, the *tao* wind in the east, the *xun* wind in the southeast, the *ju* wind in the south, the *qi* wind in the southwest, the *yi* wind in the west, the *li* wind in the northwest, and the *han* wind in the north (Lü). The "six *qi*" are the *qi* of morning, noon, evening, midnight, heaven, and earth. Another ancient annotation indicates that the six *qi* are *yin*, *yang*, wind, rain, darkness, and brightness (Fu and Lu 88). Northeast of the Tang capital, Chang'an, the "Embroidered Mountain Ranges" were the region where the imperial retreat garden, Huaqing Palace, was located. The "virtue of a gentleman" alluded to Confucius's statement that "a good man cherishes virtue" (H. Liu 35).

2

Kangxi's record of the Mountain Hamlet for Summer Coolness

The Golden Mountain issues into a range of mountains, where a warm river divides into springs. Cloudy gullies are juxtaposed with still, deep, and expansive waters; rocky bottomed ponds, with blue-green mists. The territory is vast, filled with fertile grassland and spared from natural disasters damaging the fields. The wind is fresh and the summer weather is invigorating; the environment is suitable for taking good care of myself. The place is born of the encounter of heaven and earth; all the things here belong to the creation of nature.

    I have traveled along the Great Canal several times and know well how beautiful the southern country is. I visited twice the Qinlong region and came to appreciate even better the openness of the western land. I headed north across the desert and toured the Changbai Mountain in the east. As for the grandeur of mountains and rivers and the sincerity of people in those areas, I cannot possibly do justice to it in writing, and it falls beyond my grasp. Now Rehe is close to the capital. A trip back and forth takes less than two days, and the site is wild and uncultivated. How would it impinge upon national affairs?

    I went on surveying the high and the low, the far and the close, and opened myself to the sublimity of the distant ranges. Relying on pine trees to form a chapel brought in the moisture and greenery of the cliffs. Leading the water into a pavilion brought in the bushes from the valleys. Making such scenes as these two is well beyond human power. I borrow the lush grass patch to assist my residence, forgoing carving and painting, and enjoying the greenery amidst springs and woods. I quietly observe the world and examine all creatures. Elegant waterfowl play on the green water and do not flee; deer flock together in the light of the setting sun. Birds soar and fish jump. High or low, they follow their own nature. The purple atmosphere in the distance leads into beautiful scenes, high and low. I wander for a while and then stop for enjoyment, free from the hardship of toil. Dining late or getting up at daybreak, I never forget the vicissitudes of history told by ancient books. Encouraging working in the field, I long for bamboo baskets filled with copious crops. When the autumn harvest arrives, I celebrate the cooperative four seasons, rain and sunshine. This is the general situation of my residence in the Mountain Hamlet for Summer Coolness garden.

Admiring immortal mushrooms and orchids brings appreciation of virtuous behavior; viewing pines and bamboo brings about longing for chastity; being close to clear brooks brings up the value of integrity; looking over creeping grass brings about scorn for filthy and greedy persons. This is how the ancients identified with natural things to evoke ideas and emotions. It should be known that the resources of an emperor come from his people. I would be confused if I did not love my people. I therefore inscribe this love into the record forever unchanged. I hereby express my respect and sincerity.

Written in the second half of the sixth moon in the fiftieth year of the Kangxi reign (1711).

Note: This translation is based on Kangxi's punctuated and annotated text "Bishu Shanzhuang ji." It also refers to the unpunctuated text, "Shengzhu yuzhi Bishu Shanzhuang ji." The Golden Mountain is fifty miles away in the northwest of Chengde. It is opposite to the Black Mountain in the northeast. All the other mountains in the Rehe area derived from these two mountains (Hai 572). Chengde is northeast of Beijing and belongs to today's Hebei Province. The "warm river" used to be called Rehe. It is called Wulie River today. It enters the garden at the northeastern corner as the major water source. The Great Canal starts from Beijing, passes through the Hebei, Shandong, Jiangsu Provinces and ends at Hangzhou in Zhejiang Province. The term Qinlong designates the present territory of Shaanxi and Gansu Provinces. The construction of the Mountain Hamlet for Summer Coolness (Bishu Shanzhuang) garden began in 1703, just after Kangxi's visit to the Jiangnan region in that spring. The phrase, "the ancients identified with natural things to evoke ideas and emotions" alluded to Confucius's concept of comparative virtue (*bide*) that "an intelligent man delights in waters; a humane man, in mountains" (H. Liu 51; W. Chen 91).

3

Qianlong's later record of the Mountain Hamlet for Summer Coolness

My grandfather Emperor Kangxi built the Mountain Hamlet for Summer Coolness in the year of *xinmao* (1711). The thirty-six scenes were painted and described in poems, with a preface written by him. I was just born that year. It is hard to understand whether there was any connection between the two events. After ascending to the imperial throne, I began my annual hunting tour in the year of *xinyou* (1741). I came to the Mountain Hamlet, pacing up and down, full of memories and admiration, and

I therefore wrote poems following the original rhythm of my grandfather's poems in order to express my reverence. In the year of *jiaxu* (1754), I wrote poems for another thirty-six scenes, which included those to which my grandfather had given a name but had not ordered to paint; as to those scenes that I have visited, I occasionally give a name, but these names do not exceed the standard form adopted by my grandfather. So my poem on the scene of House of Eternal Tranquility says: "It has already been a jade epistle from the Daoist paradise; I inherit this blessed site to carry on Daoist scriptures." The title of House of Eternal Tranquility was penned by my grandfather.

Since his previous garden record has been perfect and has reached for all details, why do I write a record? It is because I was born on the same year that the Mountain Hamlet was created. It is also because I began to serve my grandfather in the year of *renyin* (1722), and the current year is *renyin* (1782) too. I have to stress my deep feelings towards my grandfather during these sixty years, and I should keep reminding myself and my offspring of these feelings. In the Mountain Hamlet, I live in fearful respect of heaven and learn from my grandfather's diligent administration, his kindness to his people, and his maintaining peace close and far. I cannot account for all such significant traits appearing in poem and prose. How could I have not yet expressed my deep feelings? Speaking when there is nothing to say is cheating myself; remaining silent when there is something to say is cheating others.

My grandfather built the Mountain Hamlet to improve military control in the north, show support to the people in this distant territory, and pay respect to simple life and love to nature. Appearing in his garden record, these ideas are deep and far ranging. My father, emperor Yongzheng, did not follow the ritual established by my grandfather during the thirteen years of his reign. He often explained this to me: "Busy administration is my excuse for not going to Mountain Hamlet for Summer Coolness and the hunting field of Mulan, but it was my mistake to indulge in leisure and deprecate taking the life of animals. My children should follow their grandfather's example, practicing the martial arts in Mulan, and should not forget family rules." His brilliant instruction was heard simultaneously by me, Prince He (Hongzhou), and the Grand Minister of State. The other two have all passed away. If I do not write of it, my offspring will never know of my father's instruction and sagely intentions. Furthermore, in the past several years, I found some interesting places on my daily walks in the Mountain Hamlet. Besides the scenes previously established by my grandfather, I also built up others, such as the Chapel of Creation and Gain, the Hall of Admonishment and Enhancement, etc. There are at least twenty newly established places. Since reflecting on history can teach me some lessons and I have not completely presented my viewpoints, I must instruct them to my offspring.

After the Han and Tang dynasties, which emperor did not have his retreat palaces and gardens? This being so, nevertheless, they wasted much labor and resources to satisfy their own lust. In the worst cases, it even led to the ruin of the country and destruction of the royal families. Such examples should be kept in mind and should not be followed. For example, the present Mountain Hamlet is located in the wilderness outside of the capital. Originally, it was intended for martial exercise rather than for literature study. Today it has its own school and actively promotes literary studies. The poet Fu Du said: "A general needs not be fond of martial activity and a child can always be taught about literature." Although I once studied this sentence and found it meaningful in some circumstances, if people take it as a criterion of perfection, there is still something lacking. As for those servants who accompany me here, they serve for several months starting early in the morning. Ancient emperors therefore sympathized with their servants, and I should not forget this. Humble men know the importance of what they do. If rewarded from time to time, they work hard without complaint. To seek only for my own pleasure but forget others' hardship is not what a humane man does. Lofty mountains and steep mountain ranges, the appearance of waters and forests, roaming cranes and deer, happy birds and fish, as well as chapels on rocks, belvederes by brooks, fragrant grass and old trees, all such things provide natural delight, and one forgets the worries of this dusty age. When compared with the retreat palaces and gardens of the Han and Tang, the Mountain Hamlet for Summer Coolness surpasses them and there is none that can match it. If I indulge myself here by forgetting everything, the Mountain Hamlet will entrap me and I will do wrong to my ancestors.

Such apprehension has been in my heart for a long time without my being willing to acknowledge it. Now I am getting old and have to speak out. Therefore, I write it here as a warning to myself and my offspring. If my offspring forgets my words, then those faithful vassals and righteous councilors can admonish him. If he is admonished but does not follow and even punishes his advisers, the country will not be blessed by heaven. If this really were to happen, I do not know what I can do otherwise.

Note: This translation is based on Qianlong's unpunctuated text, "Yuzhi Bishu Shanzhuang houxu." It also refers to another unpunctuated version, "Gaozong yuzhi Bishu Shanzhuang houxu." The thirty-six scenes of the Mountain Hamlet for Summer Coolness were first named and poetized in 1710 by Kangxi. The paintings of these scenes were painted by Yu Shen. Based on the paintings, under the commission of Kangxi, the woodblocks were carved by Gui Zhu and Yufeng Mei in 1711, and the copperplates were made by the Italian missionary Matteo Ripa in 1713. Qianlong's thirty-six poems on the old thirty-six scenes adopted the same titles that Kangxi gave them. To be differentiated from the four-character titles of Kangxi's thirty-six scenes, the titles of Qianlong's new thirty-six scenes were phrased in three characters. Thus, he showed deference to his grandfather. In 1752-54, Qianlong committed an official Weicheng Qian to paint the old and new thirty-six scenes (Bishu). Among Qianlong's new thirty-six scenes, sixteen ones were originally titled by Kangxi and the scene of House of Eternal Tranquility (Yongtian Ju) was one of them. During the Qing dynasty, many Mongolian tribes submitted to the central government. The founding of the Mountain Hamlet for Summer Coolness showed the emperor's concern to that distant territory. Although this intention was expressed by Qianlong's record, it was ambiguous in Kangxi's.

4

Qianlong's record of the Village of Ten Thousand Springs

The name of the Village of Ten Thousand Springs (Wanquan Zhuang) does not appear in the two Qing books, *Rixia jiuwen* (*Current Records of Old Stories*) and *Chunming mengyu lu* (*Records after Dreams in the Bright Spring*), but when you pass through the area and point to the village, everybody knows it is the Village of Ten Thousand Springs. As for the Red-Hill Lake, its name does appear in both books; but when you pass by the area and point at it in the village to inquire from local people, they are utterly ignorant of it. I therefore sigh when realizing that ancient recorders wrote history according to hearsay and seldom from personal testimony. Hence, many records do not match facts. Then I think that the cause for error is their lack of patient scrutiny, extensive investigation, and lack of determination and endurance in seeking for the truth. However, starting from such records, we can examine their rights and wrongs and distinguish their mistakes. In this respect, records based on hearsay rather than personal testimony can still to some extent be helpful to later generations and should not be blamed further.

Discussing the Red-Hill Lake, the records of the two books are almost the same, stating that water originates from the Ba Ditch and arrives at the Sorghum Bridge. But it is at this point that both books err. The Red-Hill Lake is in fact the original location of the Garden of Delicate Brilliance, belonging to a Ming imperial relative. It is also the site of the present Garden of Uninhibited Spring. In front of the garden, there is an expanse of running water, popularly called the Bubbles of Water Caltrops, which I suspect belongs to the Red-Hill Lake. The water in fact flows from the south to the north. Because the Ba Ditch is south of the Bubbles, if the water flows from the Ba Ditch to the Sorghum Bridge as the books say, how could the water flow against the current into the Sorghum Bridge, which is further south? The water of Sorghum originates from the Jade-Spring Hill, converges into the Kunming Lake, flows out as the Clear River, passes by the Sorghum Bridge, and becomes the River of Reaching Benefits. All such details have been in my record of the Bridge of the Wheat Village and will not be discussed again here.

The name of the Ba-Ditch Bridge still exists today. To the south of the bridge, there are actually the Big-Sand Spring and the Small-Sand Spring. There are innumerable springs gurgling out from stalactite caves and flowing along the ground. This matches the records of the two books that the waters of Dongzhi and West Ditch flow underground. But the fact is that all the waters here flow to the north, with little to the south. This is different from the records in the books. As everybody knows, the nature of water is to flow to a lower place. The location of the Village of Ten Thousand Springs is higher than the Ba Ditch, which in turn is higher than the Red-Hill Lake. That the water flows to the north instead of the south should not be investigated by candlelight.

But the mistake was still made. My blaming the authors of the two books Yizun Zhu and Chengze Sun for depending upon hearsay rather than personal testimony is not such a harsh criticism. Furthermore, the two authors lived only over one hundred years ago and what they recorded does not trace earlier than the Ming dynasty, but the repeated influence of their mistakes has been quite serious. When going further in history, do we have to investigate by candlelight in order to find mistakes in records? Are those mistakes just like these ones about the Red-Hill Lake and the Village of Ten Thousand Springs?

Since everybody knows that here is the Village of Ten Thousand Springs and the origin of springs actually lies in here, the name has to be corrected and the facts have to be ascertained. I therefore ordered the relevant officials to build the Temple of the Spring Origin (Quanzong Si) here, while a stone tablet was respectively erected for recording the springs of Big Sand, and Small Sand, as well as Ba Ditch. Within the temple precinct, to the east and to the west, there are several pools, pavilions, and terraces. Each gurgling spring was also named and recorded, and there are in total twenty-eight stone tablets. Outside the temple, water gushes out from the rice fields and the willow banks. These springs look like nectar in a round jar or accumulated water in a horse-hoof print. It is impossible to record them all. The name of Ten Thousand Springs must belong to this place rather than anywhere else. I sum up the significance and erect a monument to demonstrate the above-mentioned mistakes in the two books.

Note: This translation is based on Qianlong's punctuated text, "Yuzhi Wangquanzhuang ji." The Village of Ten Thousand Springs was south of the Town of Shallow Lakes. The Lake of Red Hills was north of the Town of Shallow Lakes and was the site where the Yuanming Yuan and the Garden of Uninhibited Spring were located. The Sorghum Bridge was only half a mile west of the Xizhi Gate of Beijing. The bridge was a popular touring spot in the Ming dynasty (Y. Jiang 45; Liu and Yu 280-06). Located between the Fragrant Hill and the Longevity Hill, the Jade-Spring Hill was the site where the Garden of Tranquil Brightness (Jingming Yuan) was located. The hill was named Jade Spring for its superb spring water (Y. Jiang 47). The phrase "investigate by candlelight" means to work hard to understand. The phrase "not be investigated by candlelight" means to understand without effort. The two metaphoric phrases, "nectar in a round jar" and "accumulated water in a horse-hoof print," describe the small size of the springs.

5

Qianlong's record of Kunming Lake by Longevity Hill

In the year of *jisi* (1749), I examined the origin of the River of Reaching Benefits and inscribed a stele at the Wheat Village Bridge. Records of the Yuan dynasty state that the springs at Baifu and Urn Hill led into the river, but details about this past fact are difficult to find after such a long time. Rivers and canals are a crucial affair for a country. They can be used for transporting grains, crossing by ferry, and irrigating fields, and can also be useful for preventing flood and drought, because they disperse superfluous water and save water in case of shortage. But it is not good for us to let water flood out without an effective control.

I therefore made a decision to cut reeds and weeds in front of the Urn Hill, dredge the watercourse and include the West Lake to form a large area of water. At the beginning, the officials in charge of the project thought the volume of the new lake was twice as big as the old one and worried about a possible shortage of water. When the lake was made and water came in, its surface appeared vast and boundless and seemed several times larger than the original one. The officials then began to worry about floods in the summer and autumn and difficulties for distributing water.

How difficult it is to finish an undertaking. Maybe happy and successful persons always adopt the strategy of imitating and following precedents. It is normal that ancient emperors followed an old idea to benefit the people and did not want to inquire into further innovation. Today I make floodgates, dikes, and tunnels. Isn't it to prevent floods? Isn't it to support agricultural fields? Isn't it to control the upper reach in order to smooth the southeastern canal for transporting grains and traveling the river? The water level of the canal within the city was less than one foot in the past, but it is three feet in the present. There was no watered agricultural field in the town of Shallow Lakes in the past, but now new watered fields are opened every day. Therefore I do not overestimate its power, nor exaggerate my apprehension. It might be that national affairs must be consistently contemplated and assiduously thought over by one person, who personally attends to each affair in every detail without eschewing responsibility and who faces popular opinions without worrying about losing face. In doing so, even if he is lucky enough in some achievements, his gains are invariably less than his losses. This is why I sigh that it is so difficult to fulfill an undertaking.

After the lake was made, I named it the Kunming Lake of the Longevity Hill to express deference towards the achievements of emperor Yao and allude to the significance of martial exercises. The spring originates from the Urn Hill, and the reason that I rename the hill Longevity is because this year (1750) is the celebration of my respected mother's sixtieth birthday. I built a temple called Promising Longevity on the southern hillside and therefore gave the hill the name of Longevity. A record has been made for the temple. I especially write this record about the construction of the lake to conform to the Yuan records about the origin and vicissitude of the history of the springs in this area.

Note: This translation is based on Qianlong's punctuated text, "Yuzhi Wangshoushan Kunminghu ji." The River of Reaching Benefits was a canal whose construction was supervised by the scientist Shoujing Guo of the Yuan dynasty. In order to solve the problem of transporting grains to the capital, Guo was committed by the emperor to leading the water of the Spring of Baifu, at the southeast of Changping County, through the West Mountain and the Lake of the Urn Hill and into the Sorghum River. The Urn Hill was called Golden Hill in the Jin dynasty. Because a stone urn was found on the hill in the Yuan dynasty, the hill was called Urn Hill (Y. Jiang 73). The lake at the feet of Urn Hill was called West Lake during the Ming dynasty. Another major reason for Qianlong to construct the lake, which was not mentioned in his record, was the shortage of water due to the spreading of nearby imperial gardens. Legendary emperor Yao was said to paddle on the water that he harnessed. Emperor Wudi of Han trained his navy on the Kunming Lake in the capital Chang'an. Imitating these historical models, Qianlong ordered the royal battalion to do martial exercises on his own Lake of Kunming.

6

Qianlong's record of the Garden of Clear Ripples on Longevity Hill

My record of Kunming Lake by Longevity Hill was written in the year of *xinwei* (1751). It talks about the reasons for controlling the water and changing the name of the hill, as well as about the process of constructing a lake. The Garden of Clear Ripples (Qingyi Yuan) on Longevity Hill was built in the year of *xinsi* (1761). The reason the record is not written until now is because the name tablet was inscribed a bit late and I had some difficulties in wording the record. Since the garden has been built and the name tablet has been inscribed, why is there any difficulty with the wording? It is because something has happened against my original will and I thus have a guilty conscience. What I need to say is like a recitation of my fault, and I, at the end, must speak of it. It is the so-called fault of a gentleman. If I do not talk about it, will I be able to avoid the whole country's speaking of it?

The reason for constructing the lake was to control the water, and the hill is renamed accordingly since it is overlooking the lake. Since the lake and the hill already imparted beauty to the place, was it possible that no pavilions and terraces would embellish them? Any event has its cause and effects. Friends can be made by exchanging writings, because both sides correspond to each other. Moreover, the construction was funded by the imperial treasury; the laborers were paid; the principle of thrift was abided by and sumptuous decorations were avoided. All these follow the former model of the Yuanming Yuan without ever surpassing it. Although in my record of the Yuanming Yuan, I said that I would not use so much labor again to build a new garden, is not the present Garden of Clear Ripples such a case of making a new garden? Did I not break my promise? Since it overlooked the lake, the hill was renamed. Since there was a hill, a garden was created. If I say controlling the water is my original motive, who will believe me?

However, the Garden of Uninhibited Spring is my mother's residence. The Yuanming Yuan is constantly used for audiences. Connected by the same watercourse, the Garden of Clear Ripples and the Garden of Tranquil Brightness (Jingming Yuan) are places for quiet leisure, ease of the mind and tranquility. He Xiao's refusal that later generations should not add anything to the emperor Gaozu of Han's gardens is exactly what I intend for myself. This is really my intention. Although it is so, I suddenly feel lost when recalling Guang Sima's words.

After the garden was built, I usually go there in the early morning and return at noon, and never stay there overnight. This itinerary fits my original will, and people might thus forgive me.

Note: This translation is based on Qianlong's punctuated text, "Yuzhi Wangshoushan Qingyiyuan ji." This record was written around 1764. The mud dug from the construction of the lake was piled up onto the hill to adjust its contour. The Garden of Tranquil Brightness was on Jade-Spring Hill, located between the Garden of Tranquil Pleasure (Jingyi Yuan) on Fragrant Hill in the west and the Garden of Clear Ripples by Longevity Hill in the east. He Xiao was the prime minister of emperor Gaozu of Western Han. Xiao built such beautiful palaces and gardens in the capital Chang'an for the emperor that later emperors did not build any more for decades. Guang Sima was a scholar of the Northern Song dynasty. After a disappointment in politics, he retired to Luoyang and built a simple garden called Garden of Solitary Joy (Dule Yuan). In contrast to Sima's simple garden for high spiritual enjoyment, Qianlong felt ashamed for the extravagance of his garden.

7

Qianlong's record of the Best Spring of China on Jade-Spring Hill

The virtue of water lies in maintaining human life. Its taste is valued for sweetness; its quality, lightness. These three aspects support each other: when water is light, its taste must be sweet; drinking it will cure all sorts of diseases and will extend your life. Therefore, a water expert always differentiates spring waters according to their lightness or heaviness.

A silver ladle was thus made to weigh water. The spring water of the Jade-Spring Hill in the northwestern suburb of the capital weighs one *liang*; the water of Yixun River north of the capital weighs one *liang* as well, the water of the Pearl Spring in Ji'nan in Shandong weighs one *liang* and two *li*; the spring water of the Golden Hill of Yangzi (today's Zhenjiang) weighs one *liang* and three *li*, and is two or three *li* heavier than the spring water of the Jade-Spring Hill. As for the Hui Mountain in Wuxi and the Hupao Spring in Hangzhou, each of them is four *li* heavier than that of the Jade-Spring Hill; the water of the Ping Mountain in Yangzhou, six *li* heavier; the water of the Qingliang Mountain in Nanjing, Baisha (i.e., West Lake) in Hangzhou, the Tiger Hill in Suzhou and the Blue Cloud Temple on West Mountain in Beijing, each of them one *li* heavier. I have visited these places myself, and their waters were accurately weighed by my household servants. But is there any water lighter than the Jade Spring's? The answer is yes. Then, from which spring? It is not spring but rather snow water. I used to gather and warm up snow, and then find it is three *li* lighter than the water of the Jade Spring. Snow water is not always available, and no cold water that seeps out at the foot of a hill can surpass the Jade Spring in the suburb of the capital.

In the past, there was a debate between Yu Lu and Bochu Liu about which water was the best in China. The latter regarded the "valley curtain" of the Lu Mountain in Jiangxi as the best; the former took the water of the Golden Mountain in Yangzi as the best and that of the Hui Mountain as the second. Although southerners used to appreciate a trifle as a treasure, when comparing the weights of the water, the water of the Hui Mountain certainly takes the second place to that of the Golden Hill in Yangzi. It is clear that the ancients did not make things up, but it is a pity that not only did they not reach the Yixun River north of the capital, but also they even did not reach the capital. Had they been here, they would certainly have thought the Jade Spring was the best in China.

In the last few years, the West Lake [in the northwestern suburb of the capital] was expanded as the Kunming Lake. All around Longevity Hill, there have always been some famous springs. When tracing these springs to their sources, it appears clear that the Jade Spring is actually the origin of the divine vein and the hub of virtuous water. It is very light and has a sweet taste. Though I have not been to Lu Mountain yet, I believe the Jade Spring is better than the Golden Hill in Yangzi. I therefore name the Jade Spring "The Best Spring of China," and order the construction department to build a sublime and brilliant temple to secure the benefits of the spring and also order to inscribe my record on a stele.

The Jade Spring, in fact, jumps from and gushes out at the bottom of the hill and ripples into a lake. The poets mistakenly compared this scene to a "hanging rainbow" of a high waterfall. When I wrote a poem for the "eight scenes of the Yan Mountains" not long ago, was I not echoing what those poets said? This fully shows that truth exists in the human world; so does fallacy. Especially when a text has been made, the fallacy that it creates cannot be changed easily by later generations. A spring always brings some goods and no ills to human beings. Even so, it still cannot escape being misjudged. Therefore, a ruler, who brings goods and ills to human beings, might feel afraid of being misjudged. This is not something to be necessarily afraid of (because even a perfectly good spring can be misjudged).

Note: This translation is based on Qianlong's punctuated text, "Yuzhi Yuquanshan tianxia diyi quan ji." Located between Fragrant Hill in the west and Longevity Hill in the east, Jade-Spring Hill was the place where the imperial Garden of Tranquil Brightness was located. There were totally three springs on Jade-Spring Hill and the one at the root of the hill was the so-called Jade Spring. The weights given in the record correspond to the weight of a ladle full of water from each water source. With nine turns in total, Yixun River originates from the imperial hunting field Mulan, north of the Mountain Hamlet for Summer Coolness garden in Chengde. In Hui Mountain, there is the Spring of Luzi, which was applauded as the "second best spring water" in China. Luzi (namely, Yu Lu) in the Tang dynasty was famous for tasting the quality of tea. He was acclaimed as the Sage of Tea. The water of Jade Spring flowed east into Kunming Lake of the Longevity Hill and was the major source for all the watercourses of the imperial gardens in the northwestern suburb. The temple built near Jade Spring was called Temple of the Dragon King. According to an ancient legend, Dragon King lives in East Sea as the god of water. A temple is usually built near a water source for securing benefits of water for human life. Two steles were erected beside Jade Spring: one with the name inscription of "Jade Spring," another with Qianlong's record.

The scene of Jade Spring used to be called Hanging Rainbow of the Jade Spring (Yuquan Chuihong). Qianlong mentions here those poems of the Ming dynasty about this scene. The Hanging Rainbow of Jade Spring was one of the Eight Scenes of Beijing (Yanjing Bajing). These eight scenes had been known since the reign of emperor Zhangzong of the Jin dynasty. Qianlong poetized twice the Eight Scenes of Beijing. In the first time, following the Ming poems, he described the scene, Hanging Rainbow of the Jade Spring, as "The rapids fall a thousand *zhang* onto a hanging rainbow," which indicated the existence of a waterfall. But at the second time (1751), he rectified his mistake and changed the scene name of "Hang Rainbow of the Jade Spring" to "The Jumping and Gushing Jade Spring" (Yuquan Baotu) (M. Yu 1: 117-18).

8

Qianlong's record of the Garden of Tranquil Pleasure

In the seventh month in the autumn of the year of *yichou* (1745), the expansion of the outer city of Fragrant Hill began. Brambles and overgrowing weeds were eliminated, and waste tiles and broken stones were taken away. On the remains of an old camp palace, new buildings and a wall were built. Buddhist temples and jade palaces interlock and look out over each other. At each peak or valley which provides beautiful landscape settings and extraordinary views was erected a pavilion, a gallery, a thatched cottage, a pavilion leaning against a cliff, a painted boathouse, or a humble room. A building can be as small as one bay or as big as several bays. Certain groups of buildings were clustered. In the third moon in the spring of the year of *bingyin* (1746), the garden was made. It is not a completely new creation since it depends on its conforming to the landscape.

My grandfather, emperor Kangxi, visited extensively the scenic spots and ancient Buddhist temples in West Mountain. When his mood was high, he would chant poems to express his intentions. Grass and trees were thus brightened, and to peaks and valleys were thus added luster. In apprehension of overworking the retinues of laborers and officials, he decided to build up several camp palaces beside the

Buddhist temples. There were no colorful decorations. He went there at dawn and returned after two nights. He was not tired by the riding trip. Such was also the situation of the camp palaces at Xiuyun, Huanggu, and Fragrant Hill, but only Fragrant Hill, the closest, was ten miles away from the Yuanming Yuan.

In the year of *guihai* (1743), I began to visit this camp palace and felt delighted. Since then, whenever I can break away from public affairs, I will travel there. The happiness derived from mountains and waters cannot be forgotten, but my retinues' sweating in rain and struggling with wind and dusts should also be appreciated. On the site of my grandfather's camp palace, I did some small repairs and constructions, making a hall here and a small room there. Simplicity and thrift are cherished and the expression of this will takes precedent. Every action and every restraint from action derive from self-control and afford an experience of intelligence and humanity.

The name, Tranquil Pleasure (Jingyi), evolves from Zhouzi's idea and perhaps matches the origin of the world. The audience hall is called Diligent Administration, where I go day and night to consult with my officials for relieving common people's hardship, as I do in the Yuanming Yuan. Relaxation yields a sense of happiness. My catering to public affairs in the gardens saves the pains of a long trip to the Forbidden City and this shows my sympathy for servants. From my hillside residence, I can look over the distant villages and open fields. People engaged in ploughing, weeding, sending food, harvesting, and gleaning wheat come clearly into my view. Apricot blooms and herbs by the water can tell the season and help the understanding of agricultural books. The oddity and singularity of rocky hills and the resplendence and moistness of woods and grass are completely natural, showing no sign of human labor. Now I believe that the divine mystery of the creation of the world depends upon a serene spectator who can obtain his self.

[In the garden] there are total twenty-eight spot scenes, each of which is recorded and paired with a poem.

Note: This translation is based on Qianlong's punctuated text, "Yuzhi Jingyiyuan ji." The garden is located on Fragrant Hill in the northwestern suburb of Beijing. Fragrant Hill belongs to the West Mountain range. The old camp palace was established by Kangxi in 1677. Qianlong added an outer wall to define the border of the Garden of Tranquil Pleasure. The painted boathouse was called Green Clouds. Because the water in the garden was not deep enough for carrying boats, the Boat House of Green Clouds was built to imitate the Boat House of Clouds and Sailing Moon in the Mountain Hamlet for Summer Coolness garden in Chengde. The landscape scenes of Fragrant Hill were first identified by the emperors Shizong and Zhangzong of the Jin dynasty. The main Buddhist temples in the garden were, respectively, founded in the Jin, Yuan, and Qing dynasties. Zhouzi, namely, Dunyi Zhou, was a neo-Confucianist philosopher of the Northern Song dynasty. He created the circular diagram of *taiji*. His thoughts focused on the dialectic relationship between motion and stillness, between *yang* and *yin*. In his book *Zhouzi tongshu*, using the metaphor of a clear spring, he expressed his preference for tranquility that could bring to light the Dao of the world (D. Zhou 48). This relationship between tranquility and a clear spring was a direct source for Qianlong to name his gardens in the northwestern suburb. The concept of "obtain his self" originated from Mencius's statement that "A gentleman gets a deep understanding through Dao and obtains it by his own endeavor" (H. Liu 270).

Index

Adam, 105, 111, 125, 126
Alberti, 82, 83, 84, 117, 124
Aleni (Ai, Rulue 艾儒略), 92
allusive *jing*, 72, 74
Angelo, 122
appropriate (*yi* 宜), 27, 33, 43, 48, 55, 62
Aristotle, 82
artificial hill (*jiashan* 假山), 36, 59, 132, 134
Attiret (Wang, Zhicheng 王致诚), 13, 73, 74, 88, 108
A Wonderland in a Square Pot, 107

Bacon, 82
Bai, Juyi (白居易), 61
Benoist (Jiang, Youren 蒋友仁), 126
Ben-zhong-feng (本中峰), 32
Best Spring of China, 158
Bibiena, 109
bifocal perspective, 83
Big Water Method, 116, 126, 127, 128, 129, 130, 132
bizhen (逼真), 79, 95
Böckler, 123, 131
borrowed view (*jiejing* 借景), 21, 36
Bridge of Line Method, 10, 101
Brunelleschi, 83
building painting (*jiehua* 界画), 63, 68, 79, 81
Bureau of Imperial Households, 23, 24, 125

Cages for Raising Birds, 10
camp-palace garden, 11
Cao, Xueqin (曹雪芹), 59
Castiglione, 60, 86, 87, 89, 96, 100, 101, 103, 105, 109, 118, 125, 127
Chambers, 73
Chang'an, 4, 5, 148, 149, 156, 157

Chang, Lin (长麟), 127
Chan (禅), 47, 58
Chao, Fu (巢父), 44
Chengde, 7, 89, 150, 158, 160
Cheng, Hao (程颢), 50
Cheng, Yi (程颐), 34
chiaroscuro, 95, 100
Clavius, 92
clockmakers, 12
clocks, 121
close in on the real (*bizhen* 逼真), 79
Colonna, 87
comparative cultural studies, 17, 18
complete *jing* (*quanjing* 全景), 68
condensation of the mind (*ningshen* 凝神), 25, 99, 138
Confucius, 24, 25, 42, 44, 46, 47, 48, 149, 150
covered walkway (*lang* 廊), 111
cultural differences, 18
cultural fusion, 13
Cusa, 79

Damascenus (An, Deyi 安德意), 89
Dao, 24, 25, 26, 33, 37, 39, 41, 42, 43, 47, 51, 161
Daoguang (道光), 7, 114
Daoism, 44, 94
deep and distant virtue (*xuande* 玄德), 50
Deep and Remote Dwelling, 10, 39, 75, 136, 138
deep distance (*shenyuan* 深远), 36, 77
deliberate things to gain knowledge (*ge wu zhi zhi* 格物致知), 34
Deng, Yuhan (邓玉涵), 120
depth of the *jing* (*jingshen* 景深), 55, 63, 64, 68
Derrida, 85
Descartes, 91, 97

De Ursis (Xiong, Sanba 熊三拔), 120
De Vries, 131
dialectic materialism, 14
diffusion, 13
d'Incarville (Tang, Zhizhong 汤治中), 134
Ding, Gao (丁皋), 67
disegno, 95
distance-point method, 83, 85
Dong, Yuan (董源), 64
Dubreuil, 83, 84, 136
Du, Fu (杜甫), 152
Dunhuang, 77, 78
Du, Qiong (杜琼), 30, 32
Durchsehung, 87, 95
Dürer, 83, 84, 87, 95

Eastern Gate of the Hill of Line Method, 111, 134
Eastern Hall (Dong Tang 东堂), 86, 103
Eight Jing of Xiaoxiang (Xiaoxiang Bajing 潇湘八景), 62
eight trigrams (bagua 八卦), 5, 138
embodiment (tixian 体现), 48, 69, 104, 111
emotion (qing 情), 13, 14, 45, 52, 53, 58, 64, 65, 66, 93
Emperor Huang (黄帝), 113
Emperor Jianwen (简文帝), 5, 41
emperor's garden (yuyuan 御园), 6, 20, 40, 69
Emperor Yao (尧帝), 44, 156
English garden, 75
Euclid, 92, 94
expansive distance (kuoyuan 阔远), 78

fa, 95, 96, 97
face the jing, 57
Falda, 122, 131, 132
Fangzhang (方丈), 4, 5
Félibien, 84
fengshui, 5, 38, 40, 107, 121
five lakes and four seas (wuhu sihai 五湖四海), 5
Fontainebleau, 136
Fontana, 131
Forbidden City, 21, 26, 43, 160
force of the eye (muli 目力), 96, 102
Fortunate Sea, 28, 49, 71
Forty Scenes, 10, 16, 26, 29, 39, 43, 49, 51, 68, 69, 70, 74, 76, 81, 100, 103, 114, 130
Fragrant Hill, 7, 11, 38, 59, 154, 157, 158, 159, 160
framed jing, 63, 66, 112
frontal face (zhengmian 正面), 88, 89, 102, 134, 136
frontal jing, 59, 71
frontal view (zhengshi 正视), 128, 136

Gaozu of Han (汉高祖), 157
garden jing (yuanjing 园景), 59, 65, 72
Garden of an Unsuccessful Politician, 57, 65, 80
Garden of Clear Ripples, 11, 156, 157
Garden of Delicate Brilliance, 23, 148, 153
Garden of Eternal Spring, 7, 10, 26, 28, 29, 30, 31, 38, 40, 41, 105, 106, 109, 110, 116, 120, 124, 126, 127, 128, 131
Garden of Gorgeous Spring, 7, 10
Garden of Little Heaven, 10, 40, 41, 42
Garden of Solitary Joy, 58, 121, 157
Garden of Ten Thousand Springs, 7
Garden of Tranquil Brightness, 11, 154, 156, 157, 158
Garden of Tranquil Pleasure, 11, 157, 159, 160
Garden of Uninhibited Spring, 7, 11, 20, 23, 27, 29, 145, 148, 153, 154, 156
gardens within a garden (yuanzhongyuan 园中园), 5
Gate of Bright Spring, 106
Genyue (艮岳), 38, 56
gen (艮), 5, 138
Gherardini, 86
giardino segreto, 132
globalization, 17, 18
Gong, Xian (龚贤), 82, 100
Grand View (daguan 大观), 59
ground look (diyang 地样), 104
Guan, Tong (关仝), 30, 64
Guanzi (管子), 37
Gu, Kaizhi (顾恺之), 61
Guo, Ruoxu (郭若虚), 79
Guo, Shoujing (郭守敬), 155
Guo, Shuxian (郭恕先), 81
Guo, Xi (郭熙), 62, 77, 87
Guo, Zhongshu (郭忠恕), 79

Index

Hall of Diligent Administration, 21, 43, 114
Hall of Peaceful Sea, 10, 106, 114, 115, 126, 129, 130
Hall of Wet Orchids, 10, 116, 126, 127
Han, Chunquan (韩纯全), 78, 79
Han, Qi (韩琦), 79
harmony, 146
Harmony, Wonder, and Delight, 10, 105, 123, 131
head-on *jing* (*duijing* 对景), 57, 77, 135
head point (*toudian* 头点), 98, 100
heart (*xin* 心), 34
Heidegger, 13, 17, 104
Hill of Line Method, 10, 101, 105, 106, 110, 132, 134, 135
Hölderlin, 17
Hongyan (弘瞻), 89
Hongzhou (弘昼), 151
house phenomenon, 53
Huang, Gongwang (黄公望), 63
Huang, Yingzu (黄应祖), 65
Huizong (宋徽宗), 5, 56
Husserl, 53

illusionary *jing*, 138
imperial face (*yurong* 御容), 88, 89, 102, 116
imperial garden, 4, 11, 31, 114, 135, 148
inherent character (*xing* 性), 33, 34
intention (*yi* 意), 24, 30, 31
internationalism, 17, 18

Jade-Spring Hill, 6, 7, 11, 23, 38, 153, 154, 157, 158
Jesuit perspective of art, 82, 85, 89, 90, 92, 98, 101, 103, 119, 135
Jiangnan, 7, 10, 29, 30, 31, 33, 40, 41, 44, 65, 94, 120, 121, 125, 148, 150
Jiang, Shaoshu (姜绍书), 95
Jiankang, 5, 41
Jianzhang Palace, 4
Jiao, Bingzhen (焦秉真), 101
Jiao-Leng Style, 101
Jiaqing, 7, 20, 42, 72, 115, 116, 117, 124, 125, 127
Ji, Cheng (计成), 58, 110, 111
Jing, Hao (荆浩), 30
jing of a painting, 117
jing of the face, 67

jing phenomenon, 53
Ju, Ran (巨然), 64

Kangxi, 2, 6, 7, 10, 11, 20, 21, 23, 24, 26, 29, 44, 73, 86, 89, 90, 101, 145, 148, 150, 152, 159, 160
King Wen (周文王), 3
Kip, 85
Kircher, 90
Kunlun Mountain, 76
Kunming Lake, 11, 153, 154, 155, 156, 158, 159

labyrinths, 103
Lake of Collected Water, 6
Lake of Primary Liquid, 4, 6
Lake of Urn Hill, 6
landscape gardens (*shanshui yuan* 山水园), 11
landscape painting, 60, 66, 76, 81, 95, 101, 109, 131
Lang, Shining (郎世宁), 60, 86, 96, 105, 125, 127
Laozi, 2, 3, 18, 26, 27, 50, 98, 104
Leibniz, 90, 91, 93, 95, 97
leisure emotion (*xianqing* 闲情), 45, 72
leisure (*xian* 闲), 44, 45
Leng, Mei (冷枚), 101
Le Rouge, 74
level distance (*pingyuan* 平远), 77
Li, Bai (李白), 43
Li, Cheng (李成), 78
Li, Deyu (李德裕), 41
Li, Dou (李斗), 67, 121
Li, Gefei (李格非), 108
Li, Hengliang (李衡良), 121
Li, Jie (李诫), 113
Li, Madou (利玛窦), 91, 94, 95
linear perspective, 57, 73, 76, 81, 83, 84, 86, 95, 100
line-method (*xianfa* 线法), 76, 77, 95, 96, 97
Lion Grove, 10, 30, 31, 32
Li, Shanlan (李善兰), 92
Li, Song (李嵩), 81
literati gardens, 3, 5, 29, 38, 40
Liu, Bochu (刘伯刍), 158
Liu, Zongyuan (柳宗元), 53, 108
Li, Wei (李伟), 145
Li, Yu (李渔), 66

li (理), 33, 91, 94, 97, 98
Lodge As-One-Wishes, 105
Longevity Hill, 11, 36, 154, 155, 156, 157, 158, 159
Longobardi, 90, 91
looking-through painting (*touhua* 透画), 87
Lu, Hong (卢宏), 77
Luoyang, 5, 20, 41, 56, 157
Lu, Shen (陆深), 32
lute method, 83
Lu, Yu (陆羽), 158, 159

Macartney, 69
Ma, Yuan (马远), 63
Mei, Yufeng (梅玉凤), 152
Meng, Haoran (孟浩然), 53
Mengzi, Mencious (孟子), 3
Merleau-Ponty, 13
metaphysical brightness, 138
Mid-Autumn Festival, 2
Mi, Wanzhong (米万中), 38
Model Lei (Lei, Yangshi 样式雷), 110, 114, 124, 126, 135, 136
modern architecture, 17
Moggi (Li, Boming 李波明), 103
Moist, 94
Moist canon, 51
Mountain Hamlet for Summer Coolness, 7, 30, 69, 81, 89, 149, 150, 151, 152, 158, 160
mountains and waters of a fan-face (*bianmian shanshui* 便面山水), 66
mountains and waters (*shanshui* 山水), 63, 66, 80, 103, 123, 138, 160
moving-through-*jing* painting (*tongjing hua* 通景画), 87, 105
moving-through *jing* (*tongjing* 通景), 68
Mozi (墨子), 94
Mulan, 151, 158
multistoried building (*lou* 楼), 12, 60, 99, 108, 116, 118, 119, 128

Needham, 94
Neo-Confucianism, 34
Neo-Confucianist, 91, 160
Nian, Xiyao (年希尧), 96
Nine States, 35, 39
Ni, Yunlin (倪云林), 31, 32
Ni, Zan (倪瓒), 30, 31, 32, 72

non-polarity (*wuji* 无极), 33
northeastern corner, 5, 30
Northern Hall (Bei Tang 北堂), 86

obtain oneself (*zide* 自得), 23
one point (*yidian* 一点), 97
one pool and three island hills (*yichi sanshan* 一池三山), 4, 6
Ouyang, Xiu (欧阳修), 55

painter's intention (*huayi* 画意), 64, 65
Paintings of Line Method, 10, 106, 135, 136
Palace of Prince Yong, 44, 45
Panzi (Pan, Tingzhang 潘亭璋), 118
Penglai (蓬莱), 4, 5, 39
Peony Terrace, 20
perspectiva artificialis, 82, 95
perspectiva naturalis, 82
phenomenology, 17
picture-like (*ruhua* 如画), 80, 84
plainness (*pu* 朴), 26, 148
plane drawing, 104, 107
poetical, 41
portrait (*xiezhen* 写真), 61, 68, 88, 89, 95
Pozzo, 84, 85, 86, 96, 99, 100, 109, 135, 136
Pozzo style, 103
Proclus, 99
propensity (*shi* 势), 56, 63, 67, 79, 81, 111

qi, 35, 37, 38, 40, 46, 47, 51, 61, 62, 64, 66, 70, 91, 98, 146, 149
Qian, Gong (钱贡), 65
Qian, Weicheng (钱维城), 152
quadratura, 84, 87, 119, 136
Qu, Shigu (瞿式谷), 92
Qu, Yuan (屈原), 3

rambling within a mirror (*jingyou* 镜游), 65, 135
Ramelli, 120
real (*zhen* 真), 97
reason, 27, 32, 34, 97, 156
regional culture, 17
Rehe, 150
representations, 135
resemblance, 64, 67
Ricci, 90, 91, 92, 93, 94, 95

Index

Ricoeur, 17
Ripa (Ma, Guoxian 马国贤), 89, 122, 152
rivers and mountains are picture-like (*jiangshan ruhua* 江山如画), 80
roaming, 152
round brightness (*yuanming* 圆明), 2, 13, 22, 25, 33, 35, 103
round *jing* (*yuanjing* 圆景), 13, 52, 63
Ruhai (如海), 32
ruins, 143

Sartre, 25
secluded distance (*youyuan* 幽远), 78
seclusion (*you* 幽), 26, 78
sense of history (*lishi gan* 历史感), 13
Serlio, 82
Shallow Lakes, 37, 145, 148, 154, 155
Shanglin Park, 4, 146
shanshui (山水), 63, 103, 116
Shen, Kuo (沈括), 78, 96
Shen, Yuan (沈源), 16, 69, 75, 81
Shen, Zhou (沈周), 64
Shi Huangdi (秦始皇帝), 4
Shixue, 96, 99, 136
Shizong (金世宗), 160
shuifa (水法), 10, 113
Shunzhi (顺治), 6
Sichelbarth (Ai, Qimeng 艾启蒙), 89
Silvestre, 85, 89
Sima, Guang (司马光), 56, 58, 121, 157
Sima, Xiangru (司马相如), 4
sit in the north and face to the south (*zuo bei chao nan* 坐北朝南), 114
six *qi* (*liuqi* 六气), 149
Song, Yu (宋玉), 3
Southern Hall (Nan Tang 南堂), 86
spectacular views (*qiguan* 奇观), 29
Spinoza, 91
spiritual stroll (*shenyou* 神游), 99
spring terrace (*chuntai* 春台), 3
Square River, 10, 110, 135, 136, 138
standing look (*liyang* 立样), 104
Staunton, 70, 82, 88
still water (*zhishui* 止水), 24
Stöer, 83
Sun, Chengze (孙承泽), 154
Sun, Haoran (孙浩然), 80
Su, Shi (苏轼), 55, 79
Suzhou, 30, 31, 32, 65, 72, 80, 94, 106, 157
symbolic, 56, 134

taiji (太极), 33, 91, 160
Tang, Dai (唐岱), 68, 70, 100
Tang, Xianzu (汤显祖), 59
Tang, Yin (唐寅), 81
Tao, Yuanming (陶渊明), 30, 52, 72
ten-degree image (*shifen xiang* 十分象), 88
Terrenz (Deng, Yuhan 邓玉涵), 94, 120
theater, 137
Thébaud (Yang, Zixin 杨自新), 110
thematicizing *jing* (*tijing* 题景), 69
The View beyond the World, 10, 115, 117
thirty-six scenes, 7
three distances (*sanyuan* 三远), 77
Three Hills and Five Gardens (Sanshan Wuyuan 三山五园), 11
timely middle (*shizhong* 时中), 47, 48
Tin Sea, 130
Tötösy de Zepetnek, 18
trompe-l'oeil, 84
True Origin of All Things (Wanyou Zhenyuan 万有真原), 90

ultimate polarity (*taiji* 太极), 33, 34
ultimate sincerity (*zhicheng* 至诚), 33, 35, 48
unintentional painting (*wuxin hua* 无心画), 66

vast as such (*kuangru* 旷如), 116
Versailles, 122, 126, 128
view (*guan* 观), 115
Viewing the Water Method, 128, 129
View of Distant Sea, 10, 113, 114, 116, 118, 126, 127, 128, 129
Vignola, 83, 84, 85
Village of Ten Thousand Springs, 7, 11, 41, 145, 148, 153, 154
Villa Medici, 132
virtue of Round Brightness, 50
virtuous man (*junzi* 君子), 42
Walls of Line Method, 101, 110, 135, 136
Wang, Mian (王冕), 57
Wang, Shiyuan (王士元), 79
Wang, Tingne (王庭讷), 65

Wang, Wei (王维), 69, 76
Wang, Xizhi (王羲之), 25
Wang, Yuanqi (王原祁), 66
Wang, Zheng (王征), 120
water mouth (*shuikou* 水口), 30, 38
Water Storage Multistoried Building (Xushui Lou 蓄水楼), 10, 125, 129
Weize (维则), 32
Wen, Zhengming (文征明), 57, 80
Wenzi (文子), 28
Western Hall (Xi Tang 西堂), 14
Western-like and garden-like (*xiyangshi huayuanshi* 西洋式花园式), 105
Western method (*xiyang fa* 西洋法), 79, 97, 99
Western paintings (*xiyang hua* 西洋画), 80, 105
Western walls (*xiyang qiang* 西洋墙), 113
West Lake, 6, 7, 40, 136, 156, 157, 158
West Mountain, 7, 11, 43, 71, 156, 157, 159, 160
window of painting (*chifu chuang* 尺幅窗), 66
window theory, 95
winds of eight directions (*bafeng* 八风), 149
Wudi (汉武帝), 113, 156
Wylie, 92

xianfa (线法), 76, 97
Xianfeng (咸丰), 7, 20, 126
Xiao, He (萧何), 157
Xie, Lingyun (谢灵运), 52
xiyang lou (西洋楼), 119
Xiyang Lou (西洋楼), 10
xiyang yuan (西洋园), 105
Xu, Ben (徐贲), 32
Xu, Xiake (徐霞客), 58
Xu, You (许由), 44
Xu, Youwen (徐友文), 32

Yao, Guangxiao (姚广孝), 32
Yao, Yuanzhi (姚元之), 86
Ye, Tao (叶洮), 148
Yi, Lantai (伊兰泰), 16, 101, 102, 118, 137
Yingzao fashi (营造法式), 113
Yingzhou (瀛洲), 4, 5
Yinzhen (胤祯), 20

Yongjia (永嘉), 47
Yongle (永乐), 38
Yuan, Jiang (袁江), 100
Yuan, Mei (袁枚), 59
Yuan ye, 13, 38, 58, 104, 111, 113, 116, 121, 132, 134

Zeng, Jing (曾鲸), 95
Zhang, Hong (张宏), 100
Zhang, Lao (张老), 28
Zhang, Meng (张孟), 28
Zhang, Ran (张然), 148
Zhangzong (金章宗), 160
Zhao, Boju (赵伯驹), 81
Zhao, Ji (赵佶), 5
Zhao, Shanchang (赵善长), 30, 31
Zhao, Wu (赵武), 28
Zhou, Dunyi (周敦颐), 49, 160
Zhouzi (周子), 160
Zhuangzi, 2, 5, 22, 23, 24, 25, 27, 46, 99, 130, 138
Zhu, Gui (朱圭), 127, 152
Zhu, Yijun (朱翊钧), 148
Zong, Bing (宗炳), 76

www.ingramcontent.com/pod-product-compliance
Lightning Source LLC
Chambersburg PA
CBHW052045300426
44117CB00012B/1983